DEER FARMING

A practical guide to German techniques

DEER FARMING

A practical guide to German techniques

Prof. Dr Günter Reinken
Prof. Dr Wilhelm Hartfiel
Dr Eckhart Körner

FARMING PRESS

Acknowledgements

The publishers acknowledge with thanks the assistance given by the following in the preparation of the English-language edition:

Translation: H. Patricia Meadowcroft
Copy-editing: Kay Edge
Technical editing: Mike Cornwell-Smith
Advice: Sam Meadowcroft and Bill Hamilton

English-language edition first published 1990

Tranlated from the German *Damtierhaltung*, 2nd edition 1987
(Eugen Ulmer GmbH & Co., Stuttgart)

English-language copyright © Farming Press Books, 1990

British Library Cataloguing in Publication Data

Reinken, Günter
  Deer farming : a practical guide to German techniques.
  1. Livestock : Deer. Management
  I. Title II. Hartfiel, Wilhelm III. Körner, Eckhart
  IV. [Damtierhaltung. *English*]
  636.294

ISBN 0-85236-206-4

Published by Farming Press Books
4 Friars Courtyard, 30–32 Princes Street
Ipswich IP1 1RJ, United Kingdom

Distributed in North America
by Diamond Farm Enterprises
Box 537, Alexandria Bay, NY 13607, USA

Typeset by Galleon Photosetting, Ipswich
Printed and bound in Great Britain by
Biddles Ltd, Guildford and King's Lynn

Contents

Preface to the English-Language Edition

Günter Reinken and his colleagues have written a very full and comprehensive book on fallow deer farming under German conditions and regulations.

Their compilation of the trials carried out over the past years in Germany plus the use of information from other sources has given the book a wealth of information on all aspects of farming fallow deer, composition of venison and an insight into the marketing of farmed venison and its influence on German eating habits, and finally what the future of deer farming is likely to be in Germany.

In Great Britain, New Zealand and Australia, red deer are the major type of deer being farmed, larger in size than fallow, producing heavier carcasses more suited to the butchery styles of the countries concerned. In addition, in New Zealand and Australia, the heavier weight of antler on a red deer is an important fact when considering the market for antler velvet in the Far East. The taking of the antler velvet is prohibited in Great Britain.

Fallow deer do, however, have a place in deer farming and this book fulfils a need for an in-depth study of the farming possibilities of this type of deer.

The marketing of venison in the EEC is at this time under discussion due to the harmonisation of meat hygiene and other regulations and laws throughout the community; this will lead to changes in the marketing pattern due to compulsory meat inspection, rules on the transportation of carcasses and the classification of certain grades of venison into the 'red meat' category.

Whilst all the proposals outlined in this book may not be applicable to farmers in all countries, it does cover the basic needs for farming fallow deer and describes the German methods and regulations very well.

M. J. CORNWELL-SMITH
Deer Adviser ADAS Bristol
May 1990

Publisher's Note
In the English-language text sterling equivalents of German deutschmark values have been added at an exchange rate of 2.66 DM to £1.

Preface to 2nd German Edition

It is a great pleasure that a second edition has been demanded, six years after the appearance of the first, and twelve years after the start of the first experiments. Deer farming has started to develop in the way we hoped. There are now about two thousand herds in West Germany, while the advantages of fallow deer as compared with red deer are being recognised in Great Britain, Sweden, New Zealand and Australia. In Austria, Switzerland, Italy and Spain pilot schemes and experimental herds have been started, partly helped by the state.

Trials and research have led to the clarification of many questions, although there are obviously still more problems to solve. It is a welcome fact, therefore, that more courses on deer farming have been started at colleges and at Teaching and Research Centres in West Germany. The advisory offices of the Agricultural Departments and of the federal states have also shown themselves to be aware of deer farming, with few exceptions.

The development of a new production enterprise is achieved in several stages. In the first *Handbook on Deer Farming* in 1977 I quoted from Schopenhauer: 'Every new idea goes through three stages of development: in the first it is ridiculed, in the second it is opposed, in the third it is obvious.'

It would seem that there are now only a few people who are still in the first stage. In the second stage there are still some officials in the nature conservancy, countryside and hunting groups but, on the other hand, there are many in the third stage. Some legal measures and judgements have led to a clarification of disputed areas and a few authorities have shown that in a law-abiding country, only valid arguments carry weight. The debate about the descriptions of 'wild deer' or 'farmed deer', even within these groups, has not encouraged the use of the species *Dama dama* as an agricultural animal among those who are opposed to any form of progress. The vague distinction between the wild animal and the farmed one adds to controversy. We must hope that this question will soon be settled too. It would then be possible to do away with the regulations, which were undoubtedly wise and correct in the transitional stage. After the testing and research stage, the farmed deer deserves equal treatment with cattle, horses and sheep.

The precarious situation in the European Community milk and beef market provides a good opportunity for seeking alternative uses for grassland. Deer farming is one alternative which stands a good chance of future success. High-quality products meet a demand in the market place and, as has been proved, are very acceptable to the customer. Therefore deer farming needs more support than has been the case up to now, such as inclusion in the support for backward regions, resources for research and development, opening up market possibilities and the building up of sales organisations. The responsible authorities at national and regional level would be well advised to apply themselves supportively to this cause.

In the revision of the first edition my two colleages Professor Dr Hartfiel and Dr Körner have again helped with two important chapters, and I am grateful to them for this further fruitful and happy collaboration.

Thanks are due to all colleagues at the Agricultural Department of the Rhineland, who have served in various areas of deer farming over the years, especially the Teaching and Research Centre for Animal Husbandry at Riswick House, and its Director, Dr Coenen.

Working with the publisher, Roland Ulmer, has again been a pleasure. His concern for deer farming has been further demonstrated by his introduction of a magazine on the subject.

The authors hope that this edition will provide the necessary information for all those who may be interested in deer farming – the enlightened, the curious and the hesitant – but also for those who have until now been its opponents.

G. REINKEN
Bonn
Autumn 1987

1 Introduction

Ideas about land use are almost as ancient as the history of mankind but, with the increase in world population and rising industrialisation, problems are growing. The intensification of land use to a level such as there is in West Germany or the Netherlands leads eventually to the interests of agriculture conflicting with those of ecology and economics.

The natural landscape is under increasing pressure. Critics blame their forefathers, as for example in the deforestation of Scotland, England, Italy and Spain in the Middle Ages, the impoverishment of species of flora and fauna and finally the imbalance between intensively farmed areas and the wild landscape. Recently the contamination of surface water by nitrogenous fertilisers and effluent discharge has become an important point of discussion. The maximum level of nitrate in drinking water has now been set at 50 mg per litre throughout the EEC.

1.1 Markets and Prices

Conflicts such as these are exacerbated by the market situation for agricultural products. Technological changes have led to a steady increase in production in the EEC countries, and also in Austria and Switzerland. Thus between 1969–70 and 1983–4, the levels of self-sufficiency rose from 85 per cent to 105 per cent in cereals, from 87 per cent to 118 per cent in sugar, from 89 per cent to 145 per cent in butter, from 94 per cent to 105 per cent in beef and from 99 per cent to 103 per cent in pork. As Table 1.1 shows, self-sufficiency varies among

Table 1.1 Self-sufficiency in selected agricultural products in member states of the EEC, 1983–4 (in %)

Product	West Germany	France	Italy	Netherlands	Belgium/ Luxembourg	UK	Ireland	Denmark	Greece	EEC
Cereals	89	180	79	29	50	109	88	96	97	105
Sugar	120	197	83	132	222	47	139	178	104	118
Beef and veal	114	113	63	172	114	86	535	417	40	105
Pork	87	82	75	252	149	70	123	401	73	103
Butter	157	130	61	638	126	77	385	257	44	145
Skimmed milk powder	273	135	–	56	112	229	671	224	–	129

Source: Eurostat.

1

the member states, with high levels of over-production, notably Ireland and Denmark for meat and dairy products, West Germany and the UK for skimmed milk powder and the Netherlands for butter. The constant increase in productivity is all the more noteworthy as price levels for agricultural produce have risen much less sharply since 1970 than have wages and the purchase prices of agricultural supplies and trade products.

Consumption of foods such as meat, cheese and yoghurt has risen considerably at times over the last thirty years, because of improved animal husbandry, but milk consumption has dropped by a significant amount (see Table 1.2). At the same time consumer spending on food has fallen. In 1970 in a middle-income, four-person household 27 per cent of income was spent on food (13 per cent on meat and milk products), but in 1983 the figure was only 18.7 per cent (8.4 per cent on meat and milk products). In higher-income groups, over the same period, the share of consumer spending on food dropped from 18.8 per cent to 14.6 per cent.

Table 1.2 Per capita consumption of the more important foods in West Germany (in kg)

Product	1950–1	1960–1	1970–1	1982–3	1985–6
Total meat	39.0	59.6	79.0	87.9	100.5
Beef	11.7	17.7	22.2	19.4	21.4
Veal	1.8	1.8	2.1	1.5	1.7
Pork	19.9	30.2	40.2	49.6	60.1
Poultry	1.2	4.4	8.6	9.6	9.7
Milk	137.2	103.2	92.5	86.2	88.0
Yoghurt	—	—	4.1	7.6	7.9
Cream	0.9	2.2	3.5	5.3	5.9
Cheese	5.4	7.5	10.2	14.4	15.8
Butter	6.4	8.5	8.2	6.8	7.6

Source: Statistical Yearbook on Nutrition, Agriculture and Forestry.

Meat consumption per head in West Germany is biased in favour of pork, compared with other countries, a trend which is liable to increase. In the world table of per capita meat consumption the Federal Republic lies in fourteenth place, with 100.5 kg, while in the USA, 108 kg of meat is eaten per head per annum, in Australia 114 kg, and in New Zealand as much as 140 kg. Germany is the third largest meat importer in the world, behind Italy and the USA, with about 1.2 million tonnes of meat imports per annum.

The Marketing Regulations laid down by the EEC guarantee a variable subsidy up to a minimum price level for many agricultural products and provide for a certain guaranteed income. But they also place a financial burden by penalising the over-production of a product. Thus by June 1984 stocks of butter in the EEC had risen to 1.1 million tonnes, with 1 million tonnes of skimmed milk powder and 360,000 tonnes of beef. The surplus, including cereals and wine, was worth 17 billion DM (£625 million). Exports to the Third World were only possible with heavy financial support, e.g. 5 DM (£1.83) per kg on butter and 2 DM (73p) per kg on milk powder.

1.2 Land Use

Marginal land can pose problems for the farmer. There may be areas which are difficult to cultivate or only suitable for grassland or woodland, either because of soil conditions, the water table, rainfall, steepness or altitude. Table 1.3 shows land use in the various EEC countries. It shows clearly that in West Germany the proportion of permanent grassland and fallow land is relatively low. In comparison with the last EEC enquiry, in 1976, the areas of fallow land and of crops for green manuring have been halved, and the acreage of permanent grassland has declined slightly. The proportion of the land areas which have gone out of use is very significant.

Table 1.3 Land use in EEC countries, 1984 (in '000 ha)

	Germany	France	Italy	Nether-lands	Belgium	Luxembourg	Great Britain	Ireland	Denmark	Greece
Total area farmed	24,869	54,909	30,128	3,729	3,052	259	24,411	7,028	4,308	13,196
Permanent grass	4,607	12,385	4,965	1,141	679	70	11,670	4,562	233	5,271
Fallow and green manure	7	159	399	4	8	—	42	—	3	—
Other areas not otherwise named	5,067	8,155	5,748	1,074	962	47	3,138	914	872	1,388

Source: Eurostat.

1.3 Problem Areas

There has been no lack of initiative in finding uses for uncultivated and problem areas in recent years, or of state help in the public interest. The Italian government passed a bill in 1978 on the recultivation of fallow land. The main condition was that those areas (about 2.2 million ha) which had fallen out of cultivation because of the great exodus from the land over the last decade (10 per cent of the total area in agricultural use) should be brought back into cultivation. The aim was to avoid the dangers of erosion which arise with lack of cultivation, and also to create more jobs in these areas.

There are many alternatives available for utilising uncultivated ground or rough grassland. For some areas, such as those on the edge of heaths, moors and woodland, dry areas, and areas by river banks and coasts, a gradual change back to their original state can be an advantage – and not only for agriculture, as many authors have recently pointed out. But with increasing housing needs and the accompanying loss of agricultural land in favour of building or road construction, a compromise must be reached.

Plate 1.1   Rough grassland is heavily poached in some areas.

Wet or damp areas can be flooded to give constantly available water, which can then be used for water sports or fish farming. What is needed initially is detailed clarification of local requirements to suit water and fish specialists. The market for freshwater fish should be an expanding one in the future.

Afforestation is an answer in all areas which are adjacent to woodland, but it should be realised that the costs of planting one hectare of woodland, including care in the first year, come to about £940 for conifers and up to £3,760 for deciduous trees. Account must also be taken of the possible need for machinery, so the likely income from afforested areas might be seriously reduced.

A difficult, if not impossible task is the afforestation of remote stretches of open countryside and in valleys or residual areas in regions where 70 per cent of the area is already under woodland because the character and recreational value of the landscape might be seriously endangered.

1.4   Using Land for Livestock

Dairying is one way of making intensive use of agricultural land. It requires approximately 40,000 MJ ME (Megajoules Metabolisable Energy) of fodder per cow per year and, according to soil fertility, from 1.3 to 2 dairy cows can be kept to the hectare. The advantage of dairying lies in the relatively high income to be obtained per land unit and per animal – but set against this there are the disadvantages of increasing over-production, high building costs per animal and constant and intensive labour requirements. Twice-daily milking and feeding mean work at weekends and in holiday periods. Also, in order to maintain a reasonable income, high overhead costs demand heavy stocking of the farm, in spite of constant increases in production from the animals. One also has to cope with stagnating, even falling, milk prices.

The EEC's Milk Quantity Guarantee Regulations of 1 April 1984 laid down cuts in milk production for all member states. In the Federal Republic this cut was to be 7.7 per cent compared with 1983. The guaranteed quantity for the individual concern was based on levels at that time. Over-production was to be penalised by a reduction of 52.35 PF (19p). The cost of marketing the surplus milk would be deducted from this. In addition, a compensation scheme for those giving up milk production was decided upon. Farmers going out of milk production would get compensation for ten years of 100 DM (£37.60) per year per 1,000 kg quota, with a top limit of 15,000 DM (£5,640) per farm per year. We have the situation, therefore, whereby a rise in income to offset the ever increasing overhead costs of milk production is now possible only by keeping down direct costs. There is an exception in the case of the sale of milk quotas, however.

One alternative farming method is the suckler herd – where the cow suckles its own calf. The calf is either sold off to another farmer at eight or ten months for finishing or retained on the same farm until finished at fifteen to twenty months. Suckler herds are usually beef/dairy cow crosses, mated to another beef breed to produce its suckled calf. Terminal sires are usually Charolais, Aberdeen Angus or Limousin. Good quality keep, best meat quality, high fertility and good mothering are needed.

Plate 1.2 A suckler herd is one possibility for grassland.

In most circumstances buildings will be required, but obviously of simpler construction than those for dairy cattle. The advantages lie in the low labour requirements and building costs – about 3,000 DM (£1,100) per ha lower than for dairying. Disadvantages are the lower income per animal or per land unit and also high demand for grass keep. If a new building has to be put up, there is then no profitability in this type of enterprise. There could also be poaching damage on sloping land.

A similar way of utilising grassland is by finishing barren cows, but these are of low agricultural value.

Sheep rearing, using a number of breeds, enjoys increasing popularity on pasture or common land and is a means by which land can be extensively farmed. The highest sheep population in Germany is to be found in the Mittelgeburg area. Extensively grazed flocks are decreasing, however, and intensive, paddock-grazed sheep has risen to 26 per cent of the total stock. The development of quality breeds and the crossing of these with native breeds has led to an improvement in both numbers and meat quality. Lamb is in low demand on the German market and is favoured for exporting to EEC countries.

Plate 1.3   Grazing sheep in paddocks is on the increase.

The disadvantages of sheep production include the need for sheltered, intensive care during lambing, and high fencing costs. There is less risk of poaching than with cattle, but selective grazing can damage pasture that is in constant use. Coarse growth and thistles are not eaten, so topping of these will be necessary.

There are opportunities for some farmers near to their markets to specialise in the production of goat's and sheep's milk and, particularly, their products.

Specialist knowledge is needed for keeping horses and developing a riding school. If farms are close to towns, and therefore customers, though, renting out land for horse grazing can be a successful enterprise. The production of horse flesh is not so popular in Britain or Germany as it is in Belgium and France, because of the lack of opportunities to market it there.

1.5 Using Land without Stock

Finally, there are ways of using land for agriculture without stock, although land clearance must be tackled first.

Mulching (leaving the cuttings on the land) may be fraught with cost problems in the long term, while burning off or spraying the growth can be objected to on the grounds of conservation. The farmer must make his own decisions about this.

Selling forage, such as hay or silage, or grass keep, entails low costs and capital expenditure, which may lead to net profit margins similar to those of a sheep or beef suckler enterprise.

The fallowing of larger areas is increasingly being considered, with the object of deferring production until better opportunities for profit arise in the future. Part of the land (for example, any wet areas) might revert to its original state, or part could be afforested. The problems of bigger areas of rough land remain largely unsolved, but a clear distinction must be made between land in the neighbourhood of conurbations, those areas away from towns and water-gathering areas.

Deer, needing little permanent shelter and no arrangements for manure disposal, are a possibility for the extensive farming of areas of pasture land.

1.6 The Need for Alternatives

Cattle or sheep have generally been considered the only animals suitable for pasture or fallow land. In 1971 we began our search for an alternative livestock enterprise, and we came to realise that what was needed was an animal better fitted for extreme conditions — even one which had not previously been domesticated. The following criteria were of prime importance:

- Longevity.
- Resistance to disease.
- Winter hardiness, i.e. the ability to live outdoors throughout the year.
- Temperament.
- Good feed conversion efficiency.
- Low feeding needs, especially in winter.
- Early maturity.
- High fertility.
- Ease of calving.
- Good carcass quality.
- High percentage of saleable meat.
- Excellent meat quality.

After a thorough examination of experimental results and observations in the wild, we found these qualities in a number of animals and, after further critical consideration, we finally picked out: wild boar, roe deer, reindeer, elk, antelope, wapiti, red deer and fallow deer.

1.7   The End of Domestication?

In studying the history of domestication, sheep were domesticated in Asia Minor about 9000 BC, goats a little later. Domestic pigs were to be found by around 6500 BC. The earliest domestic cattle were seen from about 7500 BC in Greece. But it was only in about 3500 BC that the horse seems to have been domesticated: man's need for meat was, of course, a prime motive for domesticating animals (Röhrs).

Domestic mammals, according to Zeuner, can be divided into categories like the dog, reindeer, goat and sheep, which were domesticated before man began to till the fields, and those animals whose domestication coincided with the beginning of agriculture, like cattle, buffalo, yak and pigs. The elephant, horse, camel, mule and ass were primarily domesticated for use as work animals, while cats, ferrets and mongooses were used for keeping down vermin. Other mammals like rabbits and dormice were also kept, as were birds such as hens, peacocks, guinea fowl, quail, pheasants, turkeys, doves, geese, ducks, pelicans, cormorants, cranes, canaries and ostriches, and silkworms and honey bees. The following animals have been experimentally or occasionally domesticated: leopards, hyenas, foxes, elk, wild deer, gazelle, antelope and ibex.

From this it can be seen that the idea of taking wild animals into the domestic sphere is thousands of years old and very widespread. The possibilities for domestication are still not exhausted, although the incentives for doing so are diminishing due to man's more settled lifestyle and to the increasing satisfaction of his needs.

The development of domestication, according to Zeuner, is as follows:

- Freer contact between man and animal. Breeding is more successful in a free environment.
- Lessening of freedom, and breeding in captivity.
- Planned breeding with definite breeding aims and occasional back-crossing.
- Rearing of certain breeds for agricultural purposes.
- Hunting and killing of wild animals.

Fox sees four distinct stages in the development of the relationship between man and animal: wild animal, animal in the process of being tamed, tamed animal and domestic animal. This scheme, in a fuller form, embraces captivity, adaptation with a little more liberty, taming, training to be calm in man's presence, the intermediate process of domestication and finally domestication itself, while the undomesticated species remain to be hunted for sport.

According to Hemmer, several basic conditions must exist for a wild animal to be a potential domestic animal. It must be easy to tame and to master, it must be able to be kept in groups, and it must breed successfully. The only way to acclimatise an animal to the new circumstances of its captivity is by constant contact with man. The behaviour of domestic animals is instinctively subdued compared with that of wild animals. Their natural way of living has changed, and their freedom of movement reduced. There is a levelling-out of regular activity, a loosening of social ties, but also a one-sided intensification of sexual activity. Hemmer's interpretation is that red and fallow deer are more suitable for domestication, in contrast to elk, roe deer, sambar and white-tailed deer. The development from wild animal into the wild animal–domestic animal transition stage has been helped by the centuries-old tradition of keeping deer on estates. Variations within breeds such as distinctive markings have even developed on certain estates.

In Hemmer's view, the skin colour of a mammal is linked to the level of its activity, to the intensity of its reactions and to its powers of observation. It might be possible, by the selection of certain skin colouring, to breed a calmer captive animal and make it more tractable. In trials Hemmer was able to show that hinds with pale or dappled skin were significantly heavier than dark-skinned animals. A few animals in his herds showed clear tendencies to domestication.

1.8 Advantages and Disadvantages of 'Alternative' Animals

Wild pigs are not suitable for grassland, according to our research, and only with qualifications on dry and rough pasture. They can change the land they are kept on from dense forage to a completely bare or poached state. Keeping them might just be possible in fairly large areas of woodland where there is a natural supply of acorns or beech mast (Trauttmannsdorff). If the boars are not

Plate 1.4 Wild pigs root up the soil and destroy grass growth.

kept separate from the sows there are problems with piglets being eaten, and in wet years, where it has not been possible to let the sow farrow down in dry conditions, there are signs of greater losses of piglets after birth. Susceptibility to disease is relatively high. If feed is not of good quality there is a danger of the pig running to fat too early. Trials crossing wild pigs with domestic pigs have brought no significant increase in farrowing rates. The price of the meat compared with that from farmed pigs is not so attractive as to outweigh these disadvantages.

Keeping roe deer in enclosures can also be problematical, for several reasons. Roe deer like a very varied diet; and, owing to their small size and low grazing requirements, it would be necessary to keep a number in the same enclosure, to keep the forage at a high quality level. As roe deer maintain small family groups rather than herds this is not possible.

Reindeer can serve as a domestic animal, in contrast to caribou, although it is migratory. It is usually a question of man following it on its journeys to different feeding grounds. The chief areas of reindeer distribution are in the Soviet Union, Norway and Finland; altogether there are about three million of them. Main food sources are young green plant growth in the summer and lichens in the winter. In spring and autumn they feed on a mixture of these. The meat is of medium quality with little fat sold either fresh or smoked. Reindeer are very hardy and able to tolerate bad weather, but are not suitable for western European conditions due to their grazing requirements.

Elk are widespread in Norway, Sweden, Poland, the Soviet Union and China. They were also to be found in Germany in the Middle Ages and there were attempts to settle them there before the last war.

There were successful attempts to tame them: as beasts of burden, draught animals and for riding, even in town traffic (Sambraus). They do not need shelter, even in the Siberian winter, and can lie out in the snow. Milk yields of 6 litres per day and 400 litres per year have been known. The animals are ready for slaughter at two–three years old: the meat has a distinctive flavour with little fat. An experimental elk farm has been set up in the Petschora-Ilytsch Nature Reserve, in the Soviet Union, to look into the possibilities of meat and milk production. There are many problems with keeping elk on western European farms, however, because the animals obviously need a feed rich in crude fibre and cellulose (willow, alder and birch twigs).

Wapiti (*Cervus canadensis*) is one of the largest species of deer and widespread in North America. Up to now it has been difficult to keep in Europe: the calving index has been low and the males are usually aggressive at rutting time. Lately wapitis have been used in New Zealand for crossing with red deer, to obtain animals with a larger frame and stronger antlers for the production of antler velvet pantocrin.

In New Zealand, Australia, China and Russia there is a growing interest in sika deer (*Cervus nippon*), Père David deer (*Cervus davidionis*) and sambar (*Cervus timorensis*) for meat and antler production, in addition to red deer (*Cervus elephus*) and fallow deer (*Dama dama*).

Some varieties of antelope are very hardy, easy-calving and good-tempered animals with a low food intake. The Egyptians are doing many experiments in order to domesticate them. In the nineteenth century eland (*Taurotragus oryx*) were kept in the USSR. Recent trials show that these largest of antelopes, somewhere between antelopes and cattle in size, are suitable for milk and meat production.

The advantages of using wild animals – antelopes and gazelles – in Africa, as opposed to domestic animals, are shown in various ways: optimum and economical use of the different species of vegetation; resistance to endemic diseases; no need for dependency on watering places; production of valuable fat-free albumen; high reproduction performance; and good weight gain. Antelopes and gazelles do not have such a constant body temperature as domestic cattle. Variations of more than 3°C are quite normal, whereas in cattle the fluctuation is between 1.5°C and 1.8°C. The capacity for protein storage is also higher than with cattle (Huber).

The killing-out percentage of gazelles, according to trials by Ledger, is between 58 and 60.5 per cent, while that of oryx and eland was 57–59 per cent. Fat content was: gazelles 1.8–2.8 per cent, oryx 2.9 per cent and eland 4.2 per cent, while zebu showed a fat content of 13.7–28.6 per cent. The protein content of the meat was generally higher than with cattle. The hind quarters of the carcass were about 50 per cent of the slaughter weight, the muscle percentage 75–82 per cent (Ledger). It is not surprising, therefore, that, especially in central African countries and South Africa, the keeping of springbok, kudu, oryx-antelopes, eland and impala is widely practised and they are kept and 'harvested' on so-called 'game farms' (Hänel and Skinner).

In Texas trials are being carried out with impala, eland, kudus and other antelopes, and also with fallow and sika deer for the utilisation of rough grazing (Teer), while in West Germany there are now several holdings specialising in the keeping of dwarf zebu and bison.

We have been acquainted with the trials of the Rowett Research Institute in Aberdeen, Scotland, on the use of rough grazing for red deer since the start of our own experiments. For hundreds of years these animals were widespread in Great Britain, but are now restricted to Scotland and specific parts of England and Wales where a suitable habitat survives, or in the parks of stately homes. In Scotland they live under poor weather conditions, on land bare of trees and densely covered with heather (*Calluna vulgaris*) (Mitchell, Staines and Welch). The local ecological circumstances and the difficulties of keeping cattle and sheep there were the origins of the search for economic alternatives (Bannermann and Blaxter).

In 1970, the first red deer were raised at Glensaugh Experimental Farm, the aim being to stock 115 hinds on 212 ha, since when further trials have led to a much heavier stocking. The Rowett Institute has carried out trials into the physiological and veterinary problems of the red deer, studying breeding ratios, feeding techniques, the artificial rearing of calves and castration, along with fencing and health precautions (Blaxter and others). As a result of these trials a larger experimental farm was set up in the Scottish highlands in 1978.

There are now several farms in different parts of Britain where red deer are kept. The British government has promised to support the keeping of deer for meat production as distinct from hunting purposes. In Scotland an adviser has been appointed to oversee farms with red deer herds. The profitability calculations show that, in today's conditions, farming red deer can be an alternative to sheep farming in certain parts of Great Britain.

In our own assessments, red and fallow deer ran neck and neck. After close observation of wild herds it was established that both types of deer were very suitable for keeping on rough and upland pastures. However, in critical comparisons, we established that the meat quality of fallow deer was better. Fallow deer can also be kept within a lower fence and, according to the literature, have a higher rate of twin births than red deer. The fallow deer is a modern newcomer to Europe, but was herded for meat needs in olden times and during the Middle Ages. The colour variations shown today were already in evidence at the start of domestication (Herre, Hemmer).

The attitude of German red deer hunters to their trophies appeared an especially important consideration to us. There has been a centuries-old tradition that the red deer's antlers have a special, almost mythical significance for many of them – and considerable sums of money have been paid by German hunters for top-quality red deer heads. Fallow deer heads are not as highly prized as those from red deer stags. In the Federal Republic during the 1983–4 season, 29,576 head of red deer and 11,458 head of wild fallow deer were killed.

It was because of the above considerations that we decided, in 1973, to set up trials with twenty-eight fallow deer does and one buck on an area of 4.4 ha at the Education and Research Centre for Stock Farming, Riswick House, Cleves, in the Rhineland Department of Agriculture. The area lies 15 m above sea level, and has an average yearly temperature of 10°C and 784 mm of rainfall. In autumn 1974 a further trial was started on a farm at Marienheide near Gummersbach. Thirty-three females and three males were kept at a height of 380 m above sea level, with 1,194 mm average rainfall and an average temperature of 10°C. The farm was on sloping land with adjacent woodland. The soil at Riswick House is very fertile (Grade 2), while that at Marienheide is only moderately fertile (Grade 3–4).

Good results from these two trials led to the setting-up of forty-six experimental herds in different areas of North Rhine Westphalia in 1976–9. The total number of adult animals was about 800; the largest enterprise had an area of 7 ha and a stock of 105 adults. In this way it was possible to gather several years' experience of practical deer farming under varied geographical and climatic conditions – from the Lower Rhine to the Saar uplands – and with different farmers. At the same time many individual enterprises were set up, in different areas of West Germany, until a shortage of animals hindered the wider spread of deer farming, a natural limit being set by the breeding capacity of existing animals (see Table 1.4).

There are also experimental and research stations in Great Britain, Sweden, Austria and Switzerland as well as in Australia and New Zealand, some with state support. The position by 1985 was that there were about 400 farms in Austria with fallow deer; in Sweden, particularly in the southern part, 141 farms with about 4,000 deer; in Switzerland 76 farms with about 2,000 deer; in Australia about 400 farms with 15,000 deer; and in New Zealand about 2,000 farms with 40,000 fallow and 240,000 red deer.

In Great Britain there were at this time about 150 deer farms carrying 6,000 red deer hinds, with some fallow deer as well.

Table 1.4 Deer farming in West Germany in 1985

State	Number of enterprises	Number of animals
Schleswig-Holstein	75	1,000
Lower Saxony	77	1,075
North Rhine Westphalia	715	14,162
Hessen	71	2,200
Rhineland-Palatinate	167	4,019
Saarland	200	2,500
Baden-Würtemberg	145	1,650
Bavaria	600	11,000
Federal Republic	c. 2,050	c. 37,606

2   Fallow Deer (*Dama dama* Linné 1758)*

The deer family (*Cervidae*) has a sub-species of true deer (*Cervinae*) to which the four genera fallow deer, red deer, roe deer and Père David's deer belong, together with thirteen species and sixty-two sub-species. The fallow deer (*Dama*) species has two sub-species, namely the European fallow deer (*Dama dama dama*) and the Persian fallow deer (*Dama dama mesopotamica*). They are differentiated from other deer by a many-branched set of palmate antlers, and are medium to long legged, compact, mostly dappled, with a thickset neck with prominent larynx, a fairly short head and large eyes with well-developed lachrymal glands. The upper canines are lacking. The European deer differs from the Persian in the more palmate spread of the antlers, somewhat longer tail and usually less dappling.

Gestation time is seven to eight months and, usually, only a single calf is born. A deer's lifespan is about twenty to thirty years, but animals can still conceive when aged twenty or more.

The axis deer and several types of hog deer belong to the sub-species of the true deer. The noble deer family includes the sub-species sika deer, red deer, mule deer, branched deer and white-tailed deer. From their first known appearance the axis, sika and fallow deer were shown to be separate types, existing side by side.

2.1   Origins

Relatives of today's fallow deer appeared two million years ago in the late lower Pleistocene era, as finds in Val d'Arno, Olivola and Erpfingen have shown. These were of *Dama nestii major*. In the following, middle Pleistocene era (about 230,000 BC), *Dama clactoniana falconer* appeared in the so-called Holstein-Interglacial, as shown by finds in Edesheim (Norheim region), in Swanscombe (Kent), Riano (Rome), Menchecourt (Abbeville), Clacton and Grays Thurrock (Essex). This type of deer was about 20 per cent larger than those living today (Leonardi and Petronio, Kurten, Sickenberg).

The *Dama dama* species developed during the middle Pleistocene era, and was recognisable as such from about 100,000 BC. The oldest remains were found in many caves in England, Germany, France, Poland, Spain and Italy. It is probably a case of gradual development from *Dama clactoniana* to *Dama dama*. In the last Ice Age, between 10,000 and 30,000 BC, *Dama dama* was still only found in the southern regions of Mesopotamia and Asia Minor.

* I am grateful to Professor Dr M. Röhrs of Hanover for his information.

2.2   Development

Fallow deer have been living in the Near East and North Africa since the Ice Ages, according to present knowledge. Wilkinson's research has shown that deer were kept in Egypt in about 4,000 BC in the ancient kingdoms, as were antelopes and gazelles. Recent finds in eastern Macedonia in Greece (Bökönyi) point to the presence of fallow deer in the eastern Mediterranean in about 4,000 BC. The European fallow deer was well known to the Phoenicians, Hittites, Assyrians, Babylonians and Sumerians, who kept them as sacrificial animals, probably in a partly domesticated state. Exports of fallow deer for a cult also seem to have been made to Carthage. One of the Hittite goddesses was often portrayed standing on a deer.

There are many representations of deer from the second to third centuries BC in Mesopotamia and Egypt. In later times Syrian and Assyrian art depicts the keeping of deer. In the Fifth Book of Moses (Deuteronomy), Chapter 14, we read: 'But these are the beasts which ye shall eat: the ox, the sheep and the goat, the hart and the roebuck, and the fallow deer, and the wild goat, steinbock, the wild ox and chamois. Every animal that parteth the hoof and cleaveth the cleft into two claws and cheweth the cud among the beasts, that ye shall eat' (Mücke). (It must be mentioned, though, that according to present-day knowledge, the Books of Moses were not written by him, but in about 400 BC.)

The harbour at Rhodes displays two bronze deer to remind us that these animals are said to have freed the island from poisonous snakes in pre-Christian times. The fallow deer was sacred to the goddess Artemis of Ephesus. Coins from Eritrea, 369–336 BC, depict a deer which has been attacked by a lion, and pictures of it also appear on wall paintings in Pompeii and other places, and occasionally on Roman coins too. Emperor Aurelius is supposed to have been pulled by a span of deer in a triumphal procession in AD 274; he sacrificed them to Jupiter afterwards (Paul). It is not clear whether these were red or fallow deer.

In Celtic areas the deer played a not unimportant role: there was a god which was occasionally depicted with antlers or deer's hooves. An early Celtic decorated snaffle for deer was found in 1966, in the eastern Alp region, and in the Marne Department a deer was excavated which had been buried with headgear.

In the first century AD the Roman author Columella wrote a students' handbook of collected field and animal husbandry, *About Agriculture*. In the Ninth Book there is a lengthy chapter about the keeping of wild animals: 'I come now to the keeping of wild animals, because this also I would rightly count among the occupations which make up good husbandry; there used to be need for hares, deer and wild boar near to the villa, mostly below lords' chambers, and to place herds so that the enclosed game would please the eye of the owner looking on them, and one could take them as needed for meals, as if from a larder.' He goes on to say that, if there is a wooded area near the villa, one should not delay in earmarking it for animals. 'It is good if the master always has it in sight.' There follow details about management and feeding: 'So a knowledgeable landowner will not leave the ground itself to be sufficient fodder, but in the seasons when there is no food to be found in the woods, he will supplement it with stored grain from the granary, and give out barley, corn or beans, together also with grape skins and finally everything which really costs little. In order that the animals know when they are to be fed, it is useful to keep one or two tamed ones, which will roam through the whole herd and bring them without delay to the feeding places.'

Schmid informs us about fallow deer in Augst – Augusta Raurica – in Switzerland, pointing to the fact that, through the worship of Diana, Athena and Astarte by the Roman legions, fallow deer were spread to Gaul (Germany, France, Belgium, Netherlands), Switzerland, Iberia and England. A fallow deer antler from late Roman times was found in Trier.

In the Middle Ages the fallow deer is named as a provider of meat, together with other animals, in the game parks of the Frankish kings and in about AD 1000 in the 'Capitulare de villis' by Ekkehardt IV at the monastery of St Gallen. In his works he describes how: 'The common fallow deer . . . is hunted in many other places, and in the woods of Switzerland such as those near Lucerne many are often caught, usually they are called "little deer or little stag, preferably fallow deer". '

Petrum de Crescentiis writes in 1583: 'The common fallow deer, often called Platyceros by the Greeks because of its antlers, is hunted in many other places, also in the woods of Switzerland such as those near Lucerne, and is often caught and in great quantities. They are usually called "little deer or little stag, preferably fallow deer". The fallow deer by the nature and quality of its flesh is not unlike the chamois for it is of very good taste.'

Sources show that there were fallow deer in England, Denmark and Hungary from the eleventh and twelfth centuries, and in Alsace in the sixteenth century. Baron von Hoberg in his *Georgia curiosa or the Adelich land and field life*, which appeared in 1682, mentions fallow deer as being kept in Mediterranean countries in large game parks and town moats, and being quite tolerant of dry conditions. They were often caught in the woods of Switzerland and France, for their venison was milder and better to eat than that from other deer. Fallow deer were also kept in Austrian animal parks, and the baron describes in detail the layout of the estates, storage of winter fodder, feeding, watering and finally the management of the venison. In the eighteenth and nineteenth centuries we hear at last of great progress in France, Sardinia, Greece, Spain, Algeria and Tunisia.

In Germany, according to Niethammer, deer were introduced at the Sababurg by Count William IV of the Electorate of Hessen in 1577; he had received them from the Danish king. In Saxony deer were already known before the time of the Great Elector (1640–88) and, during his reign, they also reached Brandenburg, Mecklenburg, Pomerania, Bavaria, Würtemberg and Schleswig. They were killed in large numbers in Saxony, not only in enclosures but also in open hunting grounds, but generally, by that time, the deer was an animal of the estates, enclosures and animal parks. Deer were mainly intended to provide meat for the lord's table – and, as they were fenced in, meat was constantly available.

In *The Book of Nature* of Konrad von Megenberg, 'Of the use, characteristics, wondrous powers and needs of all creatures, elements and "creacurn" ' of

1544, fallow deer are not mentioned, only 'red deer and roebuck'. In the 1861 edition the expression 'of deer' is used. According to the author these animals were to be found in England. A similar statement appears in the 1897 edition of this work.

Kopstadt reports in 1822: 'The remaining pleasant juxtaposition of nature and art in the animal park, that pleasure ground of Cleves, has undergone a big change since the French occupation of Cleves; the many noble fallow deer, which grazed there happily together with the cows and horses, unfortunately are no longer there since the famous annexation year of 1794, but all went into the loins and stomachs of our very needy new brothers.'

In the comprehensive *Handbook of the Science of Hunting* by Bechstein (1806), we read: 'In the ranking of our hunted animals the fallow deer takes second place on account of its appearance and usefulness.' He gives four names for the males, including stag and buck, and three for the females, including hind and doe. He says that there are white, cream and black deer, less often brown and white or black and white dappled and also grey, brown and tawny. They spread at that time over Italy, France, Spain, Palestine, Persia, China and Sweden.

In the nineteenth century fallow deer were to be found in East Prussia and Schleswig-Holstein. According to Ueckerman, in the hunting season of 1885–6, 883 head of fallow deer were killed in the Plön region alone. In Schleswig-Holstein conditions favoured fallow deer rather than red deer, owing to the lack of forest. The large landowners and the links with Denmark helped the spread of deer.

Hansen and von Bülow-Lotze reported in 1937 that there were 11,000 head of fallow deer in the area now covered by West Germany. Over half of these were in Schleswig-Holstein, followed by Hessen, Lower Saxony and North Rhine Westphalia. Hunting accounted for 3,360 deer in 1937, of which 2,400 were in Schleswig-Holstein. In the Schleswig area, fallow deer were enclosed in 1937 and increased rapidly in comparison with the roe deer (Heidemann). Even on the island of Nordeney the fallow deer population grew quite well on the southern shores of the dunes, where there was no tree growth.

2.3 Distribution

In West Germany fallow deer are found mostly in the northern states, less in the south, as can be seen in Table 2.1. In 1958–9 the number of fallow deer

Table 2.1 Cull of wild fallow deer in West Germany

State	1958–9	1977–8	1983–4
Schleswig-Holstein	1,833	4,140	4,285
Lower Saxony	674	4,169	3,773
North Rhine Westphalia	309	1,355	1,494
Hessen	249	1,120	1,002
Rhineland-Palatinate	9	65	104
Baden-Würtemberg	124	293	454
Bavaria	105	313	333

killed was 3,310, while in 1983–4 the cull had more than trebled, to 11,458.
There was an especially large increase in Lower Saxony, where the cull had
increased almost sixfold in the same period.

To enable a comparison to be made with other game, the cull of red deer
in 1983–4 (1958–9) was 29,576 (20,336), 2,739 (1,382) chamois and 686,714
(432,448) roe deer. All these figures show considerable increases.

To arrive at a figure for live animals, we should quadruple the numbers
killed by hunting, so the population of live fallow deer stood at around
35,000–45,000 in 1983–4. Added to this there were also about 160 deer parks
in West Germany, with a total of about 6,000 head of deer.

In East Germany fallow deer are spread round Rostock, Schwerin, Neubran-
denburg, Potsdam, Magdeburg, Halle, Cottbus and Erfurt. The cull in 1977 was
5,201 head, in 1983 11,081; thus the total population was about 30,000 head.
If we compare the cull per hectare in East Germany with that of the separate
states of West Germany, we see that the overall area has a deer population a
little higher than that of North Rhine Westphalia.

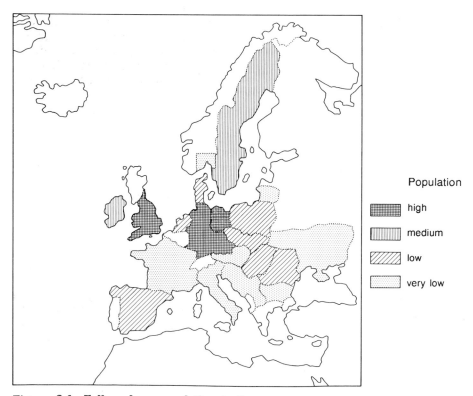

Figure 2.1   Fallow deer population in Europe.

The spread of fallow deer in the rest of Europe is very variable. In Great Britain there are about 50,000 head, mostly in open countryside (Gibbs, Herniman, Lawman and Sellers, Chapman). The largest population is in England and Wales, in the southern part of the country. There are only a few fallow deer in Scotland, although they have reached some of the islands off the west coast. As a general rule fallow deer do not co-exist with red deer, which are dominant in Scotland, or with roe deer, which are to be found more in the northern parts of Great Britain. According to research by Chapman there are nearly one hundred estates with fallow deer herds in England, and five in Wales and Scotland, with about 8,500 animals altogether. Feral fallow deer do not only originate from animals which escaped from parks; more often they have been in the countryside for many hundreds of years. The distribution of deer in the British Isles is not static but constantly changing, due to road building, forestry, the building of new towns and changes in land use.

In Ireland there are about 10,000 fallow deer with the yearly cull standing at about 2,000. Unlike the red and sika deer, they are found over the whole island, with the heaviest concentration at present south of the line from Dublin to Galway. The main deer population is in Waterford and Tipperary. Apart from this there are eleven park herds.

In Iceland there are no fallow deer. In Norway only a small number of fallow deer are to be found, in the south-east, in a park. The population in Sweden consists of 15,000 head, evenly spread over the country south of Dalälven; only a few are found to the north of this. The yearly cull is 3,000. Finland has a feral fallow deer population of about 50, which have escaped from captivity. A few small estates in the south coast region of Finland and west of Helsinki keep fallow deer. In Denmark fallow deer are spread throughout the country, with a total population of 3,900, the cull being about 2,000.

In the Netherlands deer are kept mainly as a hobby by landowners. There are about 400 game parks holding approximately 2,500 females. There are practically no feral fallow deer: in the Netherlands deer kept in parks are not wild in the meaning of the game laws.

In Belgium there are about 700 registered head, while Luxembourg has 40 head of fallow deer in the Ardennes, and 190 animals in eleven herds. France has, according to an estimate from 1976, 900 fallow deer, with a yearly cull of 272. The number of herds is very small, and the main population is to be found in the departments of Upper and Lower Rhine and Moselle; there are others in Calvados and Tarn.

There are no fallow deer in the wild in Switzerland, although occasionally they wander over the border from Germany. Fallow deer are kept in twenty game parks, along with other sorts of animals. In Austria fallow deer are of little importance in comparison with other wild species. There are about 400 animals kept in approximately twenty herds; the yearly cull is 148 head.*

Italy has a larger population of fallow deer, in Circio National Park and

---

* I am grateful to the district offices for these figures.

in twelve state farms, mostly in the central and southern part of the country. Altogether the number of animals is about 1,920. The only hunting is on estates for tourists, and the cull is very small.

In Spain there are about 3,600 head of fallow deer spread over the whole country on twenty-six state farms and reservations and there are also about 4,000 head in privately owned herds and free-range areas.

The fallow deer population in Hungary is about 4,450, 80 per cent of it in the communes of Tolna, Pest and Békés. The cull is about 2,100. Czechoslovakia has about 5,000 head, Poland approximately 3,275 (cull in 1977–8, 322). There are smaller numbers in Bulgaria and Yugoslavia, while in Rumania about 3,500 animals are kept in state-run herds. In Greece there are about 150–200 head of fallow deer on the island of Rhodes.

In the Soviet Union there are fallow deer in the Ukraine (595 head), Lithuania (170 head) and in smaller numbers in White Russia, Moldavia and other regions, partly in state-run reservations. The total population in 1977 was about 800, the cull 6 head.

In other parts of the world the fallow deer population is very small. In Israel, Algeria and Tunisia there are no fallow deer at all. In South Africa there are about 50 head. In Australia fallow deer were introduced in 1840, by settlers. The herds have grown considerably and today there are about 7–8,000 head. In New Zealand introductions started in the mid-1800s, mainly in the South Island. They increased swiftly, to be declared a 'pest' in the 1930s, being hunted extensively until deer farming started in the 1970s.

There is no wild population in North America, but in the United States fallow deer were introduced at about the turn of the century, into Kentucky. The population was about 200. Up to 1930 there were enclosures in Colorado, California and Maryland, and in later years in Alabama, Massachusetts, Nebraska and Texas. In comparison with the native breeds of deer – white-tailed deer and mule deer – today's fallow deer population is very small, and most are to be found in parks and zoos. In Texas there are about 6,000–7,000 head on private hunting estates; 600–700 deer are sold annually to about 50 hunting enterprises. There has been little increase in enclosed animals on a larger scale.

In South America fallow deer have been introduced to Argentina, Chile (17 groups with about 500 animals) and Peru, without much expansion.

To sum up it can be stated that fallow deer, judging from the number of attempts to enclose them, have an important economic role in the world. Their great adaptability is demonstrated by their survival under a wide variety of environmental and climatic conditions.

2.4 Appearance

Fallow deer – it was also given other names in the past – is a medium-sized deer which appears to have a stockier conformation than red or roe deer. The adult female also has a sharper curve to the stomach area. Shoulder height is 75–105 cm in the adult, and body length 130–175 cm. Yearling calves have a body length of 110 cm. The body width goes up to 15–20 cm. Body weights are shown in Table 2.2.

Table 2.2   Live weight of wild fallow deer in kg (range)

	Sex	
Age	Female	Male
12 months	22 (7–31)	20 (5–25)
1–2 years	31 (18–47)	43 (16–57)
2–3 years	38 (23–54)	50 (28–78)
Over 5 years		70 (43–103)

The normal body shape of the female is narrow at the hind quarters (Haltenorth, Heidemann), the pelvis being higher by 3–6 cm. In males the withers and hind quarters are the same height. The head is quite short.

None of our native wild animals shows as many colour variations as the fallow deer. The normal colour of the wild species is rusty brown on the upper parts in summer, with lighter, cream-coloured spots and a light streak on the flanks. There is a darker, brownish streak over the back. The belly is pale cream, while the back of the upper part of the thigh is white, with dark surrounds on both sides. The short tail is white underneath, black on top and stands out sharply from the light coloured rump patch. The winter coat is dark grey-brown on the upper parts, the spots are lost and the light belly areas become grey-brown.

Dark coloured animals, which can total as much as 30 per cent of a herd, have dark upper parts with paler, sometimes hardly distinguishable grey-

Plate 2.1   Adult fallow deer.

brown spots, while the belly is mousy-grey ranging to dark brown, like the rump patch. The winter coat is darker. These animals can be picked out from the normal coloured ones by the lack of colour contrast between the rump patch and the tail. According to research by Hemmer, a specific allelomorph is responsible for a softening of the colour contrast: it is a recessive trait in fallow deer, i.e. inter-breeding of black animals can result in natural coloured calves. Also dark-coloured young can come from the natural coloured animals.

The calves of pale coloured animals are born beige with paler spots. During the first year these lighten to creamy-grey in the winter. The creamy-white colour of the adult appears in the second year, but the forehead is more strongly pigmented and so appears darker. The winter coat may be lightish brown on the neck. This pale coloured allelomorph is also recessive, and pale animals have it doubled: that is, white as well as natural coloured parents can later produce pale coloured calves. A pairing of white animals, however, can never produce natural coloured offspring.

The so-called porcelain colour often occurs. With this bright colour the summer coat is light rust, as is the streak, while the belly, up to the flanks, and the spots are pure white. The top of the tail is rust-brown. The contrast and dappling also remain in winter. The genetic reasons for this colouring are still largely unknown.

Just occasionally one comes across a deer with colouring showing grey-brown top and mousy-grey belly or brown top combined with light brown lower parts.

Plate 2.2 A white male deer. This colouring occurs occasionally.

In Germany, the spring moult starts about the beginning of May. By mid-June, depending on location and weather conditions, the summer coat has appeared. The moult is fairly slow and the animals often look unsightly during this time. The autumn change of coat begins at the start of September, lasting until the end of October with females and the beginning of November for males. This coat consists of soft whiskery and woolly hairs, the latter being the shortest. Fallow deer hides are particularly valued because of their flexibility and softness.

Plate 2.3   Moulting – fallow deer.

Plate 2.4   Tail and rump patch.

A conspicuous body marking is the nose patch on the upper lip between the nostrils. The skin pattern is individual and is unalterable from birth onwards, like human fingerprints.

The skeleton of fallow deer is largely similar to that of red and roe deer, with prominent and strong neck vertebrae and elongated metatarsal bones.

Plate 2.5   Skeleton of a fallow deer stag.

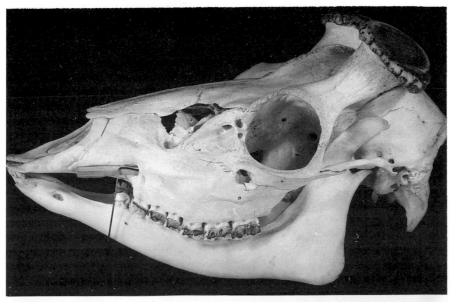

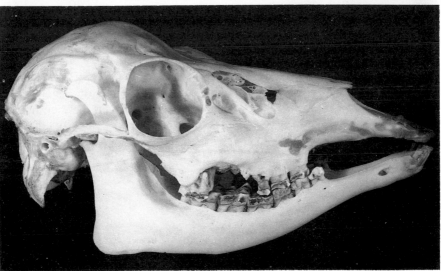

Plate 2.6   Skull, side view: *top*: 7-year-old male; *bottom*: 16-year-old female.

The skull and its construction are shown in Plates 2.6 and 2.7, from the side and from above. On the forehead bone in males is the pedicle with the coronet.

At birth the jaw consists of the six lower incisors and two canines, which are completely formed, and three premolars in the process of being formed. Other molars develop in the first year of life, with the cutting teeth of the

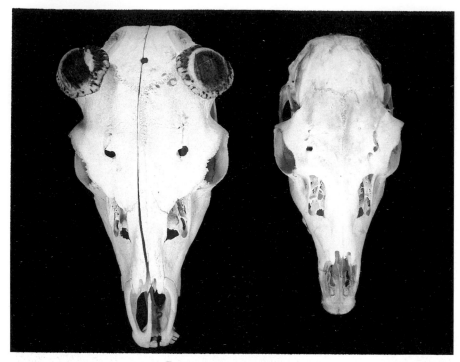

Plate 2.7 Skull, top view: *left*: male; *right*: female.

milk set completed by the last incisors. In the second year the second set are complete, and consist of thirty-two teeth altogether. There are neither incisors nor canine teeth in the upper gum, just three premolars and three molars. The lower gum has three incisors and one canine plus three premolars and three molars making twelve grinding teeth on each side of the jaw.

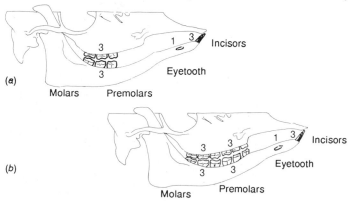

Figure 2.2 Number of teeth: (*a*) Milk teeth (at birth); (*b*) Second teeth (two-year-old).

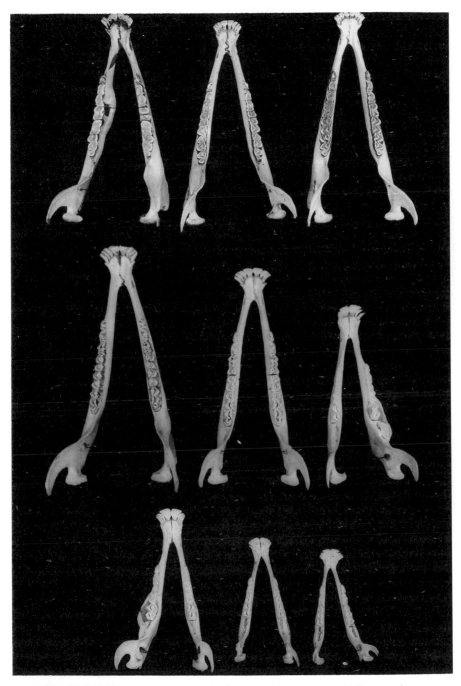

Plate 2.8   Dentition: *top row*: 3 weeks; 8 weeks; 8 months; *middle row*: 1 year; 2 years; 3 years; *bottom row*: 8 years; 10 years; 16 years.

Plate 2.9 Adult stag with antlers.

Up to this age it is possible to use the teeth as a definite age check. From the third year onwards one can only go by the wear of the molars, so estimates can only be approximate. One factor which can help fix the age is the length of the lower jaw which grows up to the age of about six years and shows a clear change in the head shape (von Braunschweig).

Plate 2.10 Rutting fight – the antlers have been removed.

Research by Fischer and his co-workers has shown that we must differentiate between two separate phases of antler formation in fallow deer: the formation of the pedicle, which remains throughout the lifetime of the animal, and the development of the antlers through the annual change. The annual phase of antler-growth lasts four to four-and-a-half months, with the end of the rubbing-off period occurring at about the end of August in young and adult deer. The start of antler growth is not determined by exogenous factors, but by changes in hormone levels. Antler growth takes place during a cessation of testicle growth, lowered testosterone level and 'Kreatining' content of the blood serum, rising cholesterol level and alkaline phosphates. No yearly rhythm was found in the potassium, calcium, sodium or triglyceride levels.

In adult males the antlers grow up to 75 cm long, a spread which is strongly palmate with increasing years, the central width is up to 60 cm, and the weight up to 4 kg. The antlers consist of a fibrous bone as outer covering, with a darker area of lamella bone going through it. The inside is formed from spongy bone, producing a network of fine bone tissue.

According to research by Ueckermann, Heidemann and Knief the average constituents of the antler are: 10 per cent water, 50 per cent inorganic substances (including 20 per cent calcium, 10 per cent phosphoric acid, 7 per cent nitrogen and 6 per cent magnesium) and about 40 per cent organic matter. An antler's stability is considerable, with no weak points in its structure, yet the central growth region, according to Heidemann and Knief's research, is a 'pre-formed breaking point', which can stop damage to the skull at maximum load. Under very high stress this area is broken before other parts of the antler's branches.

Removal of the pedicle before formation of the coronet permanently prevents growth of both coronet and antlers. Transplant experiments have shown that the formation of coronet and antlers can be stimulated in other areas of the skull. Through trials with human hormones Jaczewski and Mischalokowa found that they could influence antler growth in deer. Goss showed that with sika deer testosterone and oestradiol could encourage the casting off of antlers and the start of new growth.

The antlers during growth are covered with velvet, which is thick, deeply pigmented, and has many sebaceous and scent glands and numerous arteries running through it. A fallow buck's head, like that of red and roe stags, has a comprehensive artery system, with the blood supply of the coronet and buds being fed by the coronary arteries. The arteries of the knobs are unlike the rest of the body's arteries: they are formed from flexible muscle cells and can contract immediately when necessary. There are numerous nerve systems in the knobs, more than in other animal organs.

The central stimulus for bud growth is the hypothalamus part of the brain, which regulates the pituitary, thyroid and para-thyroid glands, kidneys and testicles. The effects of the separate glands are still largely unknown, but it has been proved in several experiments that light plays a large part in the growth and shedding of antlers. By changing the light researchers have succeeded in creating three cycles of antlers over one or two years with fallow, sika and red deer, and two cycles per year with roe deer.

In calves as young as four months a club-like thickening develops in the skull, from which the so-called 'spikes' (first year's antlers) grow from February to August. In older deer the old hard antler is shed in April, new antler grows from then on with cleaning occurring between the end of August and the beginning of September. From Lau's observations of fallow deer, the average length of time between cleaning and shedding of the hard antler is 8.3 months, which is longer than with most other species of deer.

2.5 Characteristics

From their distribution (see Figure 2.1), it can be seen that fallow deer thrive everywhere, with the exception of high mountains, although they prefer a park-like landscape with small woodlands. Gentle valleys and shallow slopes, groves, thickets and deciduous woods, with short grass, are specially suited to fallow deer (Pechuel-Loesche). Long, snowy winters do not suit fallow deer but, at the same time, they are hardy and resistant to cold: no fallow deer died in the harsh winter of 1939–40 in Rominten-East Prussia, but red and roe deer suffered losses. From his research in Ostholzheim, Heidemann comes to the conclusion that the appearance of the fallow deer is similar to that of animals dwelling in areas of dense growth, although it also shows features of animals from open areas because it finds its way mainly by sight, rather than by scent and hearing, as with exclusively woodland dwellers. There are also behaviour patterns similar to those of animals which inhabit country devoid of cover.

Social grouping is largely similar to that of many animals which live in herds in open country. There is much flexibility in the formation of groups,

Plate 2.11 Formation of groups.

Plate 2.12 Eyesight is particularly good.

so fallow deer can thrive in constantly changing surroundings. According to preferences, and varying with the season, they seek out completely open fields or thick cover. Lastly, the fallow deer may be said to be something of a 'slippery character' in its reaction to its enemies.

As regards perceptive senses, the good eyesight of the fallow deer is especially important. In contrast to most species of deer it can recognise a motionless person: it has been shown that wild deer shied when 700 m away from a man moving in open country. According to Heidemann, deer will only take flight when it has established visual contact with the approaching man and would stop when this contact was broken. Its sight in twilight and at night is similar to that of humans.

A fallow deer's sense of smell is poorer than that of red deer and reindeer. It can smell man from about 200 m, while red deer, depending on humidity, react at up to 1,200 m. Occasionally partners find each other by scent; during the rut, bucks seek out females with their noses lowered and the smell of urine has a clearly sexual connotation. From Heidemann's observations, however, the sense of smell is not used in the initial approach, prior to pairing-off for mating. He is also of the opinion that, compared with optical signals, warnings of enemies through scent have little importance. As a rule, after picking up a scent, fallow deer try to find their enemy with the aid of eyes and ears and, if they cannot do this, then further restlessness is a normal reaction after a certain time. The distance at which fallow deer show a reaction when picking up a scent is less than if they become aware of an enemy by sight. Also, scent alone plays less part in picking up man's presence than does sight.

The hearing of strange sounds provokes a reaction too, but even sounds occurring naturally in woodland, like the rustle of leaves or moving twigs, can cause restlessness. Generally, though, sounds bring about flight relatively slowly. An exception is when other adult deer cross their path. Then audible stimuli, in combination with visual or olfactory awareness, leads relatively quickly to flight.

Fallow deer have several ways of expressing mood such as calling, posture and position, and movement of the tail. From Gilbert's researches the calls are divided into: lowing, bleating, mewing, wailing, screeching and the rutting bellow.

Bleating is similar to the sound made by sheep, and is only emitted by females with calves. Gilbert describes it primarily as a warning cry, whereas Heidemann thinks it is more of an identity call to strengthen the bond between female and young calf. According to Meier the mothers bleat to call their young to suckle and to keep contact when on the move. The young are alone in making a short piping or peep-peep noise. This is a sound which shows awareness, but also creates a bond between mother and calf. It can be heard throughout the year.

Mewing, a more choked 'mi-mi-mi', is heard from both sexes and all ages. Gilbert notes that it is always linked with a soothing gesture.

Wailing is a long-drawn-out, high-pitched bleating and is heard from calves in need, when they are in bodily pain and sometimes as a death cry.

The 'screech' is a short bellow, mostly a single cry, sometimes repeated, and is made when danger threatens or sudden disturbances occur. According

Plate 2.13   Position of tail expresses mood.

to Heidemann the screeching stops when the danger has been recognised. It is also a sound made when danger is first suspected.

The rutting call of the fallow deer is a belching noise similar to snoring, made with the mouth partly open and head slightly raised. Short bursts follow in quick succession. This call is mainly used to attract females. Some observers have come across several males giving the rutting call at the same time in a small area. (Fallow deer differ completely from red deer, not only in their rutting call but also in the behaviour of the females.)

The tail of the fallow deer stands out clearly, with its dark, often black colour, against the white background of the anal region, the 'rump patch'. Its skin is rich in glands. According to research by Alvarez, Braza and Norzagaray the tail shows the mood of the animal. In undisturbed animals it normally hangs down loosely and is occasionally waved from side to side, which also serves to keep away annoying insects. This tail position is also held when on the move or feeding. When enemies are suspected, and when defending, the tail is held stiffly away from the body, on a level with the whole body posture. When jumping up and in flight it is upright. It lies directly on the back when calves suckle or in female sexual foreplay, a position which also occurs in the sexual arousal of the male.

Body posture and gait are also dependent on the mood of the deer. Normal movement is at a walk, singly or in groups, with the body easy and relaxed. The alarm position sees the body taut, head and neck held high, front legs close together and ears pricked. When mildly excited, movement is at the trot: the legs are extended in a regular rhythm and the tail is raised in the horizontal

Plate 2.14 At the trot.

Plate 2.15 Flight at the gallop.

Plate 2.16 Deer can leap very high.

position. If the excitement rises, the fallow deer executes its typical spring, taking 2–3 m leaps, with front and hind legs close together, tail raised and ears pricked. This movement is a means of conveying messages to other members of the group. Finally the quickest motion is a gallop-like step, with long strides each covering several metres.

2.6   Behaviour of Fallow Deer

The social behaviour of the fallow deer sees them tending to form groups almost all year round.

A female group may range from two to several hundred animals. The larger groups are mainly found in winter, and the smaller ones in summer. The composition of the female group is also variable. After mating, female groups are formed: adult does and calves born during the summer, also unmated yearling does. (The mother has a close relationship with her young. Calves and yearlings keep close to the mother when there is any disturbance.) According to Heidemann, the reason for this is the greater need for security when young calves are around. At the rut the groups split up, with bucks collecting a 'harem' of fertile does. After mating larger groups are formed again, which stay together till the early spring according to feed availability and weather conditions.

Researches by van Acken into the daily rhythm of adult fallow deer show that the first feeding period starts at dawn and finishes about two to

Plate 2.17 Fallow deer feeding.

two-and-a-half hours later. There is then a ruminating period of about two hours, in which there are periods of sleep of about twenty minutes. During the summer, up to the start of the rut, five to six grazing periods alternate with periods of ruminating. During the rut there is an irregular daily rhythm, while in the winter there may be only two grazing and ruminating periods.

With young animals there is a much more regular daily rhythm. Making observations during daylight from mid-May to the end of September Puttick found that adults grazed for 27.5 per cent of the time; 7.2 per cent was taken up in lying down ruminating, 5.3 per cent in resting without ruminating, 14.4 per cent in moving and standing and 2.2 per cent in other activities.

Male groups are largely similar to the female ones in size and seasonal changes. The rutting period in autumn brings about a break-up of grouping. The younger animals go about singly or in small groups between mating, or they stay close to the females. The older males find their own rutting area and follow the females singly. The splitting up of the large winter groups usually occurs at the time of antler-shed, that is in April. The variations in group size are more clearly pronounced with males than with females (Heidemann). Intentional bodily contact between males is rare, with the exception of 'pecking order' fights.

The daily rhythm of male deer is not so clearly organised as with the females. The end of the first grazing period shows a link with the time of sunrise. Feeding and ruminating times alternate in summer, up to ten times per day, with each phase seldom lasting longer than two hours. Ruminating/sleeping pauses of fifteen to twenty-five minutes occur. During the rutting period the younger stags only spend a short time feeding. After mating there are, especially during the winter months, periods of separation from the group, which can last from a few minutes to an hour. Grazing and ruminating periods are cut down to about two per day. During the summer older males have only four to five periods of grazing and ruminating, and their feeding time is shorter than that of the other animals.

Mixed groupings are to be observed in fallow deer from October to April, while from May to September, that is for about five months, the sexes stay separate. The young males must be considered as a separate entity. Calves and yearlings of both sexes come together at times in groups of young animals. During the rutting period especially a complete separation of the calves from the females can be noticed. The next time of isolation comes before the birth of the new calves.

The calves' play behaviour often consists of chasing with sideways pushing, head-to-head pushing and riding, the younger females already showing greater alertness than the males. With the latter, those individuals which are physically stronger are already taking the lead.

A solitary animal which is noticed in summer will often be a female before giving birth, or a young male, or from September to November an adult stag. Overall, there will be more solitary males than females.

Fallow deer have been observed living with other species in the wild, like roe deer, red deer and sheep. According to Carne's observations fallow deer will push roe deer aside. For choice of habitat, fallow deer prefer less dense woodland with larger trees than red and roe deer (Batcheler).

Group leadership is undertaken by an adult female with most species of deer, but with fallow deer the leader can be an adult female, or male, or even, in moments of danger, the nearest available animal. In groups of females

Plate 2.18   Group of calves.

Plate 2.19 Mixed group.

and in mixed groups the leading position is usually taken by an adult female. She is particularly alert, gives warning of danger and indicates the possible route of flight. Within groups of males one of the elders always takes the lead. At the time of antler-shedding his leadership is retained, even if other stags still have their antlers.

Fallow deer usually live in a closely bounded area. The choice is dependent on the time of year and differs according to sex. Thus in Schleswig-Holstein it was noticed that in the average year females spent almost half the time in the open and up to about a third of the year in cover (Heidemann). During March and April they were almost always to be seen in the open, from September to October mainly in woodland. Males in the average year were mostly observed in cover, only up to about a third of the time being spent in the open. The longest stay in the open was in March and April, the shortest in July and August, that is during the rut, a time which is linked to the lowest feed intake. When it comes to moving, important considerations are gentle slopes, paths and the tracks of other animals, together with existing routes in the terrain – ditches, springs, brooks and the edges of woodland.

The fallow deer is not very choosy in its choice of position for resting. Only areas with no growth or very damp places are avoided, the preference being for a sheltered spot. The resting place is usually scraped with the forelegs, so that the greater part of the body can lie on the cleared area. The chosen resting places of the males are larger than those of the females. Even during rest periods the animals often stand up to change position or to groom themselves. The look-out is undertaken in turn by the animals.

Before lying down deer drop their head and neck, bend the forelegs and shake and turn the body. The most common resting position is the ruminating

Plate 2.20   Resting.

Plate 2.21   Adult lying down.

one, with forelegs drawn up underneath the body. The neck is usually held vertically but sometimes it is laid down on the ground. In the lying position the head leans against or is supported on the flanks. When the sun is shining fallow deer often take up a position on their side, with fore- and hind legs stretched out from the body. When getting up the head and neck are lifted, and first the forelegs and then the back legs are raised.

Signs of contentment include scratching with the hind leg, rubbing, grooming with the mouth, snorting, stretching, yawning, shaking and tail-swishing.

While eating, fallow deer take short, quick bites of plants, which are bitten off or ripped out by closing the incisors on to the gums. The lips are not often a part of the movement. Rest periods between bites are not regular. Deer can take leaves or fruit from trees by rearing up on their hind legs, to reach about 2 m high. Plastic bags and short twigs may be ruminated and swallowed. In winter, snow is scraped away with the forelegs and pushed aside with the snout and forehead so that food can be reached.

Unlike the red and roe deer fallow deer prefer soft grazing. Matzner stated, after examining the rumen of fifty animals of varying sexes and ages killed in November–December, that meadow grasses formed the greater part of the feed intake of fallow deer. Among these grasses cocksfoot was clearly preferred, followed by white bent, annual meadow grass and red fescue. The other meadow grasses, two varieties of sedges and meadow fescue were also present in noticeable quantities. In spite of its hairs fallow deer like eating Yorkshire fog, which is only taken in its young state by horses and cattle. Coarse hair-grass was also found in the rumen. The proportion of young shoots, leaves, skins and the fruits of deciduous trees was relatively low.

Plate 2.22 Adults feeding.

Matzner thinks that, from a comparison of the feeding range of the fallow and red deer, there is little competition for feed and also that fallow deer are not as selective as roe deer. They graze on the plants most commonly found on site and are indifferent to variety of feed plants. Stubbe puts the favourite grasses of fallow deer as heath hair-grass, red and sheep's fescue, bent and Yorkshire fog. They also like to eat bilberries, raspberries and blackberries, heather, chestnuts, acorns and beech mast, rowan berries and other fruits.

From trials in Nebraska, USA, it was reported that in adult animals slaughtered in May, 48 per cent of the rumen contents were grasses and 32 per cent other forage followed by sedges, weeds, etc. (Uloth). Elliott and Barrett also noted that feed in California consisted mainly of grasses. In Great Britain, Jackson undertook trials of three years' duration with 325 animals and found that from March to September grasses made up the main feed, together with smaller quantities of weeds and foliage. From September to late December acorns and beech mast were the usual feed. During the winter the diet was mainly blackberries, bilberries, grasses, heathers, holly, ivy and pine needles. Depending on time of year and food available there were also many variations. Even in winter, however, the proportion of grasses was over 20 per cent of the total intake and it rose to 57–67 per cent from March to September. In some animals insect larvae, pieces of material, paper, plastic bags, bones and crumbs were found. Observations of many wild herds determine that fallow deer are very varied feeders: normal feed intake is best described as 'pasture'.

Jackson undertook research in the New Forest in England, with a population of 1,551 deer, on the feed intake of 416 dead animals, some of which had been slaughtered and some accidentally killed. He found that it was mainly grasses that had been eaten, providing 57–75 per cent of the intake from May to September. During the winter months grasses still accounted for more than 10 per cent of the diet, with acorns, blackberries, rosehips, conifer twigs and heathers (*Calluna vulgaris*) making it up and in January and February holly (*Ilex aquifolium*).

Entzeroth studied wild herds at nine different sites in the Rhineland, notably in the Eifel mountains, and found the commonest *uneaten* plants to be the following: stinging nettle (*Urtica dioica*), thistle (*Carduus aranthuides*), sedges (*Carex*), chickweed (*Stellaria media*), white clover (*Trifolium repens*), bracken (*Pteridium aquilinum*), narrow-leaved plantain (*Plantago lanceolatha*), wood groundsel (*Senecio sulfaticus*) and red foxglove (*Digitalis purpurea*). The possible causes of these being avoided, according to the author, were: with nettles, thistles and rushes the physical unpalatability; with bracken the combination of poisonous contents and physical components; and with white clover and chickweed the high regrowth potential after the constant trampling down of large areas. With more wild thickets per hectare the average number of uneaten plants was somewhat less.

Ruminating takes place mainly when deer are lying in the resting place, only occasionally when standing. There are on average about forty grinding movements per bolus, with each grinding lasting about 0.7 seconds.

A fallow deer's drinking needs are low, due to the moisture content of the feed. After scraping with the forelegs, the head is lowered and dipped into water to drink.

Both sexes remain standing while urinating. The male fallow deer generally retains his usual body posture or spreads out his hind legs. The female's position is with hind legs spread or a slight bending down of the body. Defecating can also take place while moving and walking. Body posture is unchanged, with the tail being held upwards or to the side.

Apart from rutting periods, defecating and urinating do not take place at a regular spot. Before and during the rut, urine, with its distinctive sharp smell, is used by the males to mark the rutting area boundaries, and they also spray their flanks and belly. Females, when urinating close to males, make a nose-wrinkling gesture.

Plate 2.23 Defecating.

2.7 Reproduction

The breeding season for fallow deer is longer than the rut. This latter is a characteristically short period for many species of deer but with fallow deer it lasts from October to March. The greatest number of conceptions takes place during the main rutting period, in October, but they may occur up till March, in a secondary rut.

2.7.1 Males

The male reproductive organs consist of a scrotum with testicles and side-testicles. A canal links these to each other and to glands in the pelvis. The penis is surrounded by skin and joined to the skin of the belly along its whole length. Tufts of hair mark its position. Sperm is produced in the testicles and the male hormone or androgen in the Leydigs cells in the interstitial tissue. The main hormone is testosterone, which stimulates sperm growth and the auxiliary glands, instigates the rutting scent and behaviour; and plays an important role in the formation of antlers. The side-testicles function as stores for the sperm, where it becomes fertile.

In calves the reproductive organs are small, and remain inactive until the age of seven months. There is then a large weight gain and the first appearance of sperm; antler growth starts at the same time. At one year old, from July until shortly before the rut, there is a big increase in the weight of the testicles, until about ten times the size of a new-born calf. Sperm is present. The glands reach maximum weight just before the rut, then drop again during the winter; likewise the production of sperm. Young males reach puberty between seven and fourteen months; in spring and early summer there is minimal sexual activity. With female calves puberty is reached from sixteen months onwards. Thus it is possible for adult females to mate successfully with a yearling buck, at least in captivity. In the wild this is prevented by the social hierarchy of the bucks.

With adult stags sexual function begins in late summer. Glandular activity, size of glands and formation of sperm all reach maximum level in autumn, for the rut. In winter, they gradually decline: Chapman likens this period to a kind of annual puberty. The weight of the glands lessens to that of a yearling; this is also an annual cycle.

There is close correlation between the weight of the glands and total body weight, with weight increasing each year with the age of the stag. Not all males reach the same level of sexual activity at the same time. According to environmental conditions they are able to breed for the six months from September to March, i.e. the sperm are fertile even towards the end of the breeding season and can impregnate normally. In the southern hemisphere, for example in New Zealand and South America, the peak of the rut occurs in the latter half of April.

During the rut secondary sexual signs appear, such as the call, strong rut smell, increased growth of the neck, and also stretching and colour changes to the skin at the end of the penis. This skin becomes dark to almost black in colour, and marked papilli are formed which give out a strong rut scent (Hildemann). It is suggested that this change is a way of synchronising with the female's season. At one time stags were castrated in parks in Great Britain, often as calves, as a way of ensuring supplies of fresh untainted meat during the rut.

Researches by Field and others on several males before and after the rut showed that there was a significant change in the growth of the neck muscles. A clear correlation with the testosterone level was seen.

Sexual behaviour is marked by restlessness in the bucks at the start of the rut, when they make for the areas where the females gather. From the end of August to September, the young bucks starting earlier than the older ones, they wander among the females. The oldest stags remain in their own territory, which they defend against intruders, collecting a group of does. All these animals, who are normally very wary and keep to cover, now become bold and lose their fear of humans.

Many older stags return every year to the same rutting area, marking it by scraping holes in the ground with their antlers and hooves. These rutting scrapes are 30–300 cm across, width and depth varying according to the hardness of the ground, and they are often sprayed with sharp-smelling urine, the tufts of hair at the tip of the penis helping to scatter this. It is unknown for fallow deer stags to roll in their pits as red deer and wapitis do.

Marking of the area is done by the bucks rubbing and knocking against bushes and trees, using their antlers on the branches and trunks, often stripping off large areas of bark. Whole branches are often broken off and strewn about, and even large trees are not safe from antler attack. The start of antler-rubbing usually coincides with shedding the velvet and the start of the rut. As was mentioned earlier, there are about 8.3 months between the rubbing of the velvet off and the shedding of antlers in the spring by fallow deer.

During antler-rubbing the lachrymal glands excrete a fluid which marks tree trunks, and whose smell also marks the area. Rubbing at the start of the rut does not always coincide with the shedding of velvet, however. From Chapman's observations the earliest date for rubbing in England was 27 August and the latest mid-April. According to Cadman each buck has chosen his rutting site by about mid-October, an area of about 65 × 35 m or one-fifth ha. He observed that the closest distance between two rutting bucks was between 100 and 150 m. More widespread activity by the bucks is possible, with the peak of this activity coming between 5.30 and 8.00 hours and 16.30 and 18.00 hours (Espmark and Brunner).

Apart from blows with the antlers and scraping, digging and boundary marking during this period, Hassenberg noted further activities such as pushing, threatening, fighting and the rutting call.

When pushing, as an occasional precursor of threatening behaviour, the bucks walk in a peculiarly stilted way, stiff-legged and with the neck held horizontal. In doing this they turn mainly towards the females.

When threatening, the buck approaches his opponent with head slightly raised. He then drops his neck below the horizontal and lays his ears back, opens his mouth and steps towards his opponent. With further threatening the antlers are extended forward. A smaller buck will turn away. One of equal weight will face up to the stag threatening him and they will exchange blows with their antlers.

The period of fertility is from the beginning of September to the middle or end of April (Gosch and Fischer). Semen ejaculation can be induced by electro-ejaculation or with the aid of an artificial vagina and a teaser animal. This has been successful with white-tailed, red and fallow males (Bierschwal *et al.*, Bobeck, Gosch and Fischer).

According to Müller-Using and Schloeth the rutting display of the fallow buck is like a ritual fight which is perhaps evolving from a purely aggressive battle. The contest is nevertheless fought with great vigour throughout, and in a serious battle the unprotected parts of the opponent's body are attacked straight away. Deaths are not uncommon as a result: in deer parks, hunting areas and to some extent in the wild the annual death toll can reach about

Plate 2.24   Fighting with the antlers.

3–5 per cent. One-eyed or blind animals are sometimes seen, and with a higher concentration of older animals in a herd the loss of antlers during fights increases. From Chapman's observations of fallow deer in Epping Forest, losses during the rut are especially high during October. Fastenbeg noted that using the antlers with a feint of a secondary parry was employed by a third buck fighting against two, by young bucks against females or by a smaller buck against a wounded animal or one not in rut.

A high level of sexual activity – seeking out females on heat, testing readiness for mating and mating – together with a swollen testosterone spot can also lead to clashes with immature females (Cadman, Chaplin and White, Chapman, Gradl-Grams, Holdorf, Lau, Whitehead). During these clashes, too, considerable injury, even death, may be caused, especially by young bucks.

With fallow deer the function of the antlers as signalling devices is controversial (Bubenik). Antlers play an insignificant role as carriers of information, the surroundings being mainly discerned by scent (Müller). There is a correlation between antler development and body weight (Chaplin and White). From several trials with red deer, antlerless by heredity (so-called hummels) it was seen that they can dominate in a herd of normal red deer (Mitchell, Stonehouse). An antlerless Père David's stag was widely treated with respect as the head of the group by its lower-ranking social partners (Altmann). Bützler came to the conclusion that intensity of aggressive behaviour and size of forequarters are decisive as dominant characteristics, but not the size of the antlers. This is confirmed by Gossow and Lincoln.

During fighting, antlers clash and often become entangled with one another. After separating the stags will make another attack. In serious battles, which are always between older stags, the legs are outspread on the ground, the effectiveness of the antler thrust is strengthened by turning the head and attempting to knock the opponent off balance. The fights last from five to twelve minutes. The defeated animal usually takes flight but he is not generally followed, except for a few steps. Observations of younger bucks have shown shadow fighting, scraping with antlers and forelegs, bucking, striding around and marking trees and bushes.

The rutting call is not a bellowing, as with the red deer, but a snoring or belching sound. The head is raised, mouth opened, throat moved up and down over about 15 cm, the lachrymal ducts are open and the tail lifted. This rutting call lasts about one second. Gilbert noted that over four minutes up to about 134 calls may be made, with the gap between two calls no longer than four or five seconds. The buck usually walks about restlessly when calling, but he can also emit his call when lying down. A particular territorial position is not evident, as with the red deer stag. Sometimes rutting calls are also emitted after a successful fight with a rival.

Other sexual behaviour is shown in nose-wrinkling, salivating and spraying urine. With nose-wrinkling the head is raised, the nose goes up and down, the mouth is slightly opened, ears laid back and eyes half-closed. In strenuous nose-wrinkling the upper lip and nostril are gently pulled back. This is usually brought on when sniffing the ground where females have urinated, either on paths or at resting places. Especially strong nose-wrinkling occurs after sniffing the genital scent of a female, but even the sight of a female urinating can bring it on. The greatest nose-wrinkling and lachrymal gland activity is shown when the adult females are on heat.

When salivating there is an in-and-out movement of the tongue – the mouth meanwhile is almost closed – and drips of watery fluid come from mouth and nostrils. Finally urine-spraying is seen during threatening behaviour, and when smelling and licking the females' scent glands.

2.7.2 Females

Fischer established that among a group of young animals, the yearling females were capable of reproducing at seventeen to twenty months as a rule, with the exception of weaklings. The reproductive season began two-thirds of the way through November and lasted until around 20 February. Late breeders were mainly later maturing females requiring two additional cycles before conception. Unlike red deer, fallow deer which conceive late can successfully rear their calves. With a group of fallow deer, not mated until 25 January, the calving-down dates were from 13–29 September.

Fallow deer are polyoestric. The length of cycle is between twenty-four and twenty-six days. Ovulation is seen from September to January (Hamilton, Harrison and Young, Sterba and Klusák). As a rule the follicle appears in only one of the ovaries and an egg forms at this place. In 20 per cent of cases examined, Sterba and Klusák found a movement of the embryo to the opposite side of the uterus. The two ovaries functioned equally. In different places in England and Scotland Chapman found that in November 72 per cent of the females in the trials were carrying embryos, in December 86 per cent and in January 96 per cent. Asher researched thirty-four fallow deer and found 177

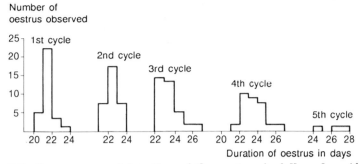

Figure 2.3 Frequency and duration of the oestrus in fallow deer (*Asher*).

ova. The length of cycle was 22.4 days (plus or minus 1.3). During the rut the length of cycle increased and was more variable (see Figure 2.3). This was not influenced by age or live weight, however. The first egg appeared within a period of twelve days. The length of the mating period and the number of cycles are linked with the age of the animal. Younger animals (sixteen months old) had fewer cycles than older ones. Ovulation occurred when the progesterone concentration was low; after that it increased and reached its maximum between the twelfth and sixteenth days. Young animals (sixteen months old) had an average 3.6 cycles, middle aged (eighteen months) 4.2, and adults (forty months) 5.4. With animals over two years old there was no longer a difference between the percentage of ovulation and the conception rate. The rate of conception, according to Chapman, lies between 91 and 94 per cent. According to Fizi and Monk it was 98 per cent, Baker 90 per cent and Armstrong 95 per cent. The first movement of the fertile egg, according to trials by Armstrong, Chaplin, Chapman and Smith, is earlier in free wild animals than in those kept in game parks.

The average sex ratio was judged by Chapman on adult animals with 145 foetuses. With newborn calves this was 1.2 males to 1 female, with older calves 1.6 males to 1 female; from research by Sterba and Klusák with embryos and foetuses the figure was 1.2 females to 1 male. According to Baker the fatality rate of male embryos and calves is higher than that of females.

The number of twin births is far less than was first thought. Chapman gives a twinning rate of 0.7 per cent, Hamilton 0.3 per cent. In Riswick it was only 0.5 per cent over eleven years.

The mammary glands undergo an annual cycle of growth and shrinkage. The lactation period lasts up to nine months. From research by Chapman the udder, which has four teats, weighs 400–800 g after calving and shrinks again from October to January.

Females may display rejection signals, by means of which they show their unwillingness to mate. These include lying down or chewing, with the head and neck stretched well forward. The ears lie close to the head, the eyes are open and the mouth closed. By chewing in quick bursts this unwillingness is given added emphasis. They may also make loud, deep peeping noises during

Plate 2.25 Stag following hind.

this time. Their behaviour is very similar when feeding newborn calves in their first days of life.

When urinating, mostly when standing, the female's tail is either slightly raised or hangs loosely. If she is willing to mate she stands with legs spread wide apart, pointing backwards. Urine runs down from the tail, which is pressed close to the genital regions. Later in this display, the scent of the urine is stronger. The body posture and position of the tail give a clue to the mood. Finally mating animals rub their lower jaws, flanks or cruppers or lick each other's flanks. This behaviour is noted particularly in the main rut and during the phase of mounting by the male.

2.7.3 Mating

Mating behaviour consists of courtship and mounting. The male attempts to arouse the female by touching her head and body with his mouth, licking her and finally rubbing his head on her flanks. This is usually followed by pushing, nose-wrinkling, smelling, then the rutting call and the mounting attempt. The male's head and neck are laid on the cruppers of the female, while several attempts at mounting are made. The female withdraws often, stepping forward or turning away. After renewed attempts there will be pauses, during which the female in her turn chases and tries to arouse the male. Any external distractions usually lead to an interruption of this lengthy foreplay.

The coupling is of short duration. The stag rises on his hind legs, his head and neck are pushed along the female's back and his forelegs hang down by the cruppers or belly of the female. She lowers her head and neck and, after mating, leaves the male at the rutting place.

2.7.4   Birth

According to several observers (Lau, Rieck, Meier), calving time in central Europe is from May to the end of August with the peak period in June. For several hours before giving birth female deer are very restless and take almost no food. They try to keep a distance of at least 50 m between themselves and the other members of their group. They prefer sites with long grass and tall weeds where they stride to and fro, head against flanks or cruppers. If disturbed, birth will often be delayed although severe disturbances caused, for example, by fire, low flying aircraft, etc., can lead to premature calving. The presence of the mate, on the other hand, can delay the birth.

The birth itself is usually in the lying position, with labour taking anywhere

Plate 2.26 Calf's resting place.

Plate 2.27 Suckling.

between 20 and 340 minutes. With breech presentation or with weak elderly females the birth can be even longer. Sounds of pain, such as moaning, piping, groaning and panting can be heard. During labour the female licks the vagina and protruding amniotic sac: this is constantly pulled at and the waters licked off. When the calf emerges the mother stands up, thereby severing the umbilical cord. Standing up also eases the calf's emergence; birth when standing has been observed.

The mother immediately begins to tend her calf, licking it, and removing and eating the birth sac. The calf's rear quarters are licked particularly well, apparently to remove dirt from the skin. A weakened mother will lick the calf while she is lying down. After about twenty minutes the afterbirth is passed and is almost always eaten by the mother. She will also eat up all traces of the birth, such as stained grass, earth and leaves from the site – this is important for the survival of the newborn calf in the wild. The calf begins its search for the udder after four to eleven minutes. Its initial attempts to stand are not successful, but it will be able to stand for the first time within thirty minutes. First attempts to suckle take place twenty-five minutes to an hour after birth, and suckling may be done either standing up or lying down.

After a few hours the mother and calf leave the birth site and look for a resting place with cover. Here the calf will lie low down on the ground between suckling periods. As it grows older it will increasingly follow its mother and other members of the herd.

The mother usually moves the calf from cover for suckling. The calf nuzzles up to the belly and flanks of its mother, suckling from the side or between the hind legs. The length of suckling on the first day is five to ten minutes, at intervals of two to three hours. After that the suckling time is shorter and the intervals longer.

The suckling behaviour of both male and female calves has been observed by Gauthier and Barrette. They found that calves from hinds calving for the first time had a significantly higher rate of suckling than those from older animals, i.e. 2.9 suckling times per hour in the first five days as against 1.24. If it was the doe which initiated the suckling in the first ten days, it lasted longer than if the initiative came from the calf. There was no difference in suckling behaviour between the sexes up to the age of eighty days.

The doe will move away, lie down or turn away from her calf after suckling. There is also some pushing away of the suckling calf. From observation of 83 deer in England, Jackson found 100 per cent of them suckling in June and October, an average of 75 per cent in November to January, and only 6 per cent in February. The calves will pull grass stalks and suck them as early as the third and fourth day, while the first eating of grass was noted from the tenth day on.

2.7.5 Mothering Behaviour

There is close rapport between mother and calf in the first days of life. Does usually keep an eye on the calf's resting place, calling the calf from its cover by bleating and piping. Smelling and touching are important factors in the mother–calf bond: they will lick each other on the head and neck while lying down side by side. Older calves give out piping and wickering noises.

Plate 2.28 Mother and calf.

During attacks and danger periods the mothers run at a gallop or trot, head erect, ears alert and tail raised. Later the neck is outstretched, the ears laid back and the mouth opened, snarling. Pawing with the front hooves may be noticed, and a blow might even be turned on the aggressor.

Play among calves consists of trotting and galloping close to the mother, bucking, chasing, kicking out with the hind legs, bounding, and rubbing and pushing with the head. As they grow older – at about four months – play lessens and feeding, ruminating and herd activities fill up the day.

If calves were brought up in isolation, Gilbert observed, they responded to situations in the same way as calves growing up with the herd. They were not accepted by the herd, however, and still formed an isolated group after three years. Social behaviour and ties with their fellows were therefore lacking.

2.7.6. Behaviour in Estate Herds

Gradl-Grams researched the behaviour of fallow deer on estates of between 1.4 and 29.8 ha, which gave each animal between 18 sq m and 70 sq m of living space. It was noticed from September to February that, away from the main visiting times, and especially in the early morning, the animals reacted much more sharply to stimuli and were more timid. Familiar noises, such as building work, children shouting, bicycle bells, coughing and sneezing were ignored or produced little reaction. Unusual noises caused the deer to seek safety, but hardly ever to huddle together. Visitors filing past in a group caused more attention than normal walking past. These trials confirm the observations that fallow deer living in the wild take little notice of commonly occurring noises in their surroundings.

On farms, too, the deer reacted most strongly to visual stimuli, which often caused them to take flight. Distance from the effective stimulus was greatest in the morning, went down during the day to 2–3 m and was greater during feeding. Males were calmer than females. Calves reacted much more readily to disturbances than did adults; as they grew older they became less timid.

Animals running free could be enticed by food, and would eventually feed out of the hand. Their preferred foods were maize, ground nuts, oats, apples and biscuits; bread was the least favoured. Thrown-away plastic bags were sometimes greedily picked up and swallowed. There were noticeable instances of begging behaviour during feeding – possible motives were hunger, preference for certain foods or the need for attention. However, the animals only begged when they had been alerted by stimuli such as smell, noise or a visual presence. When attracted the animals would even come at a run from a distance of 150 m.

Certain individuals even reacted to the names given to them by visitors. They came up at different paces – walk, trot or gallop – stretching their heads forwards, often into the feed container, and sometimes raising themselves up on their hind legs to reach food held up high. On occasions visitors were nudged lightly with the snout by female animals. Bucks threatened people by lowering their heads and even by pushing with their antlers. (We should note that man is likened to a member of the herd who is a possible rival. The

Plate 2.29 Begging for food.

highest-ranking buck is enforcing its position over the lower-ranking ones by threatening behaviour.) With older animals there was less tendency to take flight than with younger ones, which held their bodies tense. Defecating and urinating as signs of excitement were also encountered.

As for social behaviour, the following loose groups were to be found throughout the year: mother and family; group of young females; bucks; young animals; mixed groups; single ranging animals. Mixed groups would be formed before, during and after the rut, but the rest of the time male and female animals were separate. Isolated males were more common than females.

The rut was marked by a high level of sexual activity among the bucks, with aggressiveness increasing as the number in the herd grew. There were many instances of females being wounded, having been attacked by bucks which had disturbed resting females and been driven off. Particularly on small estates nearly all the females had bloody scars on neck, back and flanks, but Cadman and Chapman's researches found that in the open, too, females were gored to death. When this happened the rutting periods of their mates were shortened.

From her researches, Gradl-Grams comes to the conclusion that the fallow deer is a very suitable animal to be enclosed, on account of its lack of aggression towards humans, swift adaptation to its surroundings, ease of breeding and simple feeding. She recommends 600 sq m per beast as the smallest area for show enclosures which are busy with people visiting; also sight screens and protection against weather conditions. If the enclosures are small, males and females should not be kept together throughout the year, only during the pre- and main rut. It is sensible to have fewer males than females on the farm, because only the oldest stag would normally mate on account of his domination over younger bucks. No young bucks should be kept with an adult buck during the rut, as the yearling males can receive severe wounds from the dominant buck or inflict wounds on other bucks or the does. To reduce aggressive behaviour Gradl-Grams recommends that where males are kept without opponents to fight, they must have other opportunities to strike with their antlers throughout the year.

3 Wild Deer – Farmed Deer

The deer classified as fallow deer – *Dama dama* – is known in Dutch as *damhert*, in German as *Damhirsch* and in French as *daim*. The English names for the male – buck – and the female – doe – omit the adjective 'wild', as do the phrases 'captive deer', 'game farming' and 'deer farming'. In English-speaking countries, i.e. the USA, Great Britain, New Zealand and Australia, the adjective 'wild' is not used when describing the farming of red or fallow deer. This also applies in the Netherlands, where it is known as *herten teelt* and in Sweden, where deer farming is called *Hjortavel*.

In the choice of our term 'farmed deer' the decisive factor was that it was a case of the farming of mainly female animals, with a sex ratio of 1 male:20 females up to a ratio of 1:30, as opposed to the situation in the wild, where the ratio is about 1:1. It must also be made clear that it is a case of using for agricultural purposes an animal which at present is still in the eyes of German law a captive wild animal. The term fallow deer does not specify whether the farmed beasts are domestic or wild. The law might not take into account the fact that domestication was under way.

Heinen points out that Merkel-Gottlieb has advocated the interpretation: 'That the different terms "wild deer" and "fallow deer" would not be upheld in court, as "wild deer" kept on farms cannot yet be counted as domestic animals. In the related matter, of whether different terms should be used for the same animals depending on circumstances, it does not apply.' He is of the opinion that: 'They include those animals which go through and are used in the agricultural production process commonly known as "farm animals" and as with bees, for example, it is not a case of domestic animals.' A further reference occurs in his supplement: 'Fallow deer kept on agricultural holdings are to be regarded more as domestic animals in the meaning of the animal health laws.'

Recken points out that in Germany there are no clear, comprehensive definitions or systematisation of holdings. Included with wild deer reserves, therefore, are: game parks, hunting parks, hunting syndicates, wild parks, zoos, wild animal and fur farms, demonstration farms, special farms and winter parks, either directly or indirectly serving hunting purposes. On the other hand, there is certainly no hunting on agricultural deer farms.

The meat produced by deer farming is good enough to be compared with meat from other farm animals, and superior to meat from feral deer. As for the German legal aspect, Heinen states: 'In this respect it could be doubtful whether meat from a commercially farmed deer could be described as "wild venison". From this point of view I have no misgivings about using the description "venison".'

A decision of the European Community Court of 12 December 1973 is particularly important in this connection. In a case brought by a game importer against the main customs office in Hamburg the question was raised whether reindeer meat could be described as game. The law concluded that reindeer, unlike caribou, cannot be counted as wild animals. Rather they are domestic animals. The living style of the animals has to be considered: they are domesticated to the point where they can be kept in herds for agricultural purposes and can be slaughtered. (It should be noted here that reindeer are free-ranging animals; the keepers follow the herds. Breeding selection is carried out by castrating surplus male animals.) The court ruled that all animals are wild which exist in a natural free state, not under man's control. 'It would appear sensible also to remove from this the question of whether the meat from the wild animal was taken by hunting or not. With this criterion a clear distinction can be made between wild game and meat from a slaughtered animal.'

The abandonment of present prejudices and feelings is only possible if a distinction is made between the farmed animal and the wild deer. After almost fifteen years of experience we think that acceptable husbandry and management, careful siting of buildings, and responsible marketing and development policies must be taken into account.

4 Setting Up a Deer Farm

To avoid failure or the unexpected when starting a farm it is first important to take a critical look at the site and the farmer's suitability for the enterprise, and then study approved husbandry.

4.1 Site Requirements

The local climate must also be considered, along with the site. From our experience we know that deer can withstand an annual rainfall of up to 1,000 mm without the shelter of either a closed or an open shed. In places with over 1,000 mm of rainfall, particularly where it is concentrated in only a few months, it is advisable to erect a simple roofed shelter with a wall on the exposed side. (Building details are given on p. 84.) Trials to date have shown that deer are tolerant of cold and snow. Precipitation combined with strong winds, however, does cause distress because the sodden coat then provides little protection. Losses can occur with weak or poorly nourished animals. In places which are both exposed to the wind and lacking in natural shelter, protection in the form of evergreen hedges or a shed open on three sides should be provided. We are not aware that purely mountainous sites have been tried out for fallow deer, but in some coastal regions, e.g. on the island of Norderney in the North Sea, deer have flourished for many years.

Basically, almost all types of land are suitable for deer farming, with the exception of marshy and wet areas. Deer are susceptible to infection by liver fluke, the intermediate host of which is a water snail which lives in wet ground. Fears that the hooves grow too long when the deer are on soft ground have not been substantiated. It is unnecessary to provide areas such as hard pathways for wearing down the hooves, but rocky or stony slopes can be included in the enclosure. What is advisable, before starting a deer farm, is to carry out a detailed examination of several places on the prospective site, digging out samples to a depth of about 60 cm so that a chemical analysis of the soil can be made (see Figure 4.1).

The topography or slope of the ground is relatively unimportant. Hilly areas are just as suitable for deer as flat ones, since neither needs to be cultivated with machinery. As a deer's hooves are smaller than those of horses or cattle, year-long trampling leads to soil compaction and a measurable reduction in erosion. Hilly conditions also offer natural windbreaks for the animals, which may be absent in flat areas.

On sloping sites it is important to make sure that the feeding, drinking and handling facilities are centrally located, if possible, and that there is road access for vehicles. The whole of the prospective site should preferably be in one

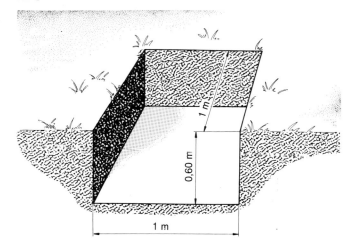

Figure 4.1 Sketch of block cut for soil analysis.

block. Roadways through the fields should have specially constructed gates for crossings (see p. 68). Areas near towns or busy roads should only be used when unavoidable, as they demand special provisions such as higher hedges or stronger fences.

The vegetation of the site should be thoroughly examined at the outset, although it is true to say that the majority of places are suitable for deer farming, even areas which have been completely neglected. The exceptions are marshy or wet areas, and those with only heather or bracken growth.

In West Germany the State Department of Ecology, Countryside Development and Forestry of North Rhine Westphalia in Cleves-Kellen undertook valuable long-term trials at the experimental plots in Riswick House, Cleves and Bommert-Marienheide. These had previously been used for the grazing of cattle. On the moderately damp pastureland of Riswick House (Lolio-Cynosuretum) it was shown that certain grasses – perennial rye-grass and annual meadow grass – increased slightly, while cocksfoot, meadow foxtail, and meadow fescue decreased (see Table 4.1). It is interesting to note that the number of varieties of grasses increased when deer were grazing throughout the year. The proportion of weeds declined and dandelions disappeared. On the mainly sloping site at Marienheide, a damp to medium damp pasture with an area of partially damp red meadow fescue, perennial rye-grass increased its share among the grasses; meadow fescue and meadow foxtail decreased (see Table 4.2). The variety of grasses increased, while clover species and weeds decreased. The density of sward was exceptionally good following year-round grazing. On other deer farms, too, there was a better effect on the sward composition than by grazing sheep, and much better than if the land had been grazed by cattle or horses.

Experiments by Schick on different paddocks at the trials centre at Romenthal near the Ammersee and in Losbergsgereuth in the northern Franconian Alps in 1976–80 showed no change in sward composition after three years

Table 4.1   Herbage analysis on the deer pastures at Riswick, 1974–85 (mean of three selected areas)

	1974–5	1976–7	1978–9	1980–1	1985
Number of varieties	20	18	13	12	13
Perennial rye grass	40	45	32	45	67
Cocksfoot	10	11	22	27	5
Meadow grass	6	8	5	4	1
Meadow fescue	3	1	1	+	+
'Liesch' grass	6	4	2	+	+
Yellow oat			+		
Good-quality grasses	65	69	62	76	73
Bent	3	3	3	6	7
Annual meadow grass	2	1	+	1	8
Common meadow grass	7	6	18	6	8
Couch-grass	8	10	10	6	1
Meadow foxtail	11	6	6	5	+
Red bent		1	+		
Medium-quality grasses	31	27	37	24	24
Soft brome grass	+	1	1		
Yorkshire fog	+	+			
Low-quality grasses	+	1	1		
White clover	+	+	+	+	+
Dandelion	3	2	+	+	
Chickweed	1	+	+	+	1
Creeping buttercup	+	+	+	+	
Fine-leaved buttercup	+	1	+		
Small stinging nettle				+	1
Other weeds – traces (+)	+	+			1
(18 varieties)					
Total grasses	96	97	100	100	97
Total clovers	+	+	+	+	+
Total weeds	4	3	+	+	3

Source: State Department of Ecology, Countryside Development and Forestry, North Rhine Westphalia.

grazing by deer, and only a small change after four years. The proportion of grasses was somewhat higher, while that of legumes and weeds was less. Similar results were obtained on sheep paddocks. The average proportion of grasses rose by about 4.5 per cent to 81–85 per cent, legumes fell by between 1.2 and 2.1 per cent. The average proportion of weeds fell by 5.8–6.3 per cent. English meadow grass and white clover spread and were useful forage

Table 4.2 Herbage analysis on the deer pastures at Marienheide, 1975–85 (average of 12 (1975) and 8 (1981) sample plots)

	1975–7	1979–81	1983–5
Number of varieties	*30*	*26*	*20*
Perennial rye grass	19	32	34
Cocksfoot	17	20	17
Meadow grass	8	3	4
'Liesch' grass	2	2	2
Meadow fescue	3	2	1
Good-quality grasses	49	59	58
Red bent	10	13	17
Red fescue	13	9	10
Common meadow grass	3	7	5
Meadow foxtail	3	2	1
'Comb' grass	2	2	2
Couch grass	3	2	+
Bent	+	1	1
Annual meadow grass	+	+	+
Medium-quality grasses	34	36	36
'Ruch' grass	3	2	2
Yorkshire fog	2	1	1
Meadow hair grass	+	+	1
Soft brome grass	1	+	
Low-quality grasses	6	3	4
White clover	2	2	2
Other clover species (6 types)	+	+	+
Yarrow	2	+	+
Dandelion	2	+	+
Field thistle	1	+	+
Buttercup	2	+	+
Creeping buttercup	1	+	+
Sorrel, dock	1	+	+
Other weeds – traces (+) (39 types)	+	+	+
Total grasses	89	98	98
Total clovers	2	2	2
Total weeds	9	+	+

Source: State Department of Ecology, Countryside Development and Forestry, North Rhine Westphalia.

Plate 4.1   Bark may be stripped.

species, as were varieties of sorrel. Schick, Bogner, Matzke, Braun, Burgstaller and Vollert concluded, from their research, that there had not been a change for the worse in the vegetation. Sward composition would be more affected by the intensity of stocking.

Before starting deer farming one should ascertain from the local agricultural advisory service the potential value of the pasture to be used.

Woodland should only be included in exceptional cases, when it is a matter of a small existing area where individual trees could be protected by wire netting. In our experience bark-stripping by deer is to be expected and may occur suddenly, especially in winter, when the trees can quickly become bare, stark stumps. The reason for this behaviour is still not fully understood. There are several theories, such as a lack of fibre, minerals or water in the diet, or just behavioural traits. However, it has so far proved impossible to prevent bark browsing.

If the inclusion of woodland is deemed necessary to provide protection against severe weather, it is advisable to discuss the scheme with local forestry authorities before including the woodland. Single trees should always be left in position on the proposed site, but protected by wire guards. Shrubs, bushes and low growing trees are also likely to be damaged by deer. Schick noted that all types of trees and bushes in the area with a circumference of up to 20 cm would be browsed in the first three years, and in later years even the roots and trunks of chestnuts, pines, sycamore, cherry and oak trees might be stripped.

Raspberries, brambles and briars are particularly liked by deer and, from several years' research at Riswick House, it was also found that the following ornamental varieties had been eaten: holly, *Berberis*, *Pyracantha* and *Prunus spinosa*.

Trials by Sullivan and Nordstrom with different repellents, such as the urine and dung of various animals, ammonia and human urine, showed that these had little effect on browsing by black-tailed deer. The most effective antidote was coyote urine. So the present position is that the most effective and lasting protection against browsing is strong wire or wood fencing around the trees.

Weedy areas, with a lot of dandelions, docks, nettles and thistles, can be greatly improved within a few years by deer grazing them.

Provision of water throughout the year is very important and it must be available in winter, even in freezing conditions. Springs, streams, a well or public piped water are all suitable sources, but it is important to be certain about the quality and year-long availability of the supply. Care must be taken to check water that has flowed underground or through industrial plants, to make sure that it has not become contaminated: test it and enquire through the local water authorities about its suitability for drinking purposes. If there are plans to sink a well on the site, check the depth, availability and quality of the water beforehand. Permission is required from the water authorities.

On sites which lie within conservation areas there are special regulations to adhere to. Deer farming may be suitable in such areas, if there is no need for new buildings, and the collection, storage and disposal of dung and liquid manure is no problem. Fencing stakes are also spaced further apart than is customary and necessary with other farmed animals, and so look less unsightly.

Obviously the conditions of the site must be assessed from all these points of view, and a decision made about its suitability for deer. If necessary, professional advice should be sought on the long-term planning of the site, on the installation of water and electricity, and on transport links.

4.2 The Farmer

It would be a fallacy to assume that anyone could become a deer farmer, especially someone with no experience of livestock. Deer are not just a substitute for the mowing machine, but an alternative to cattle, sheep and horses for grazing grassland. As a great deal of capital must be invested, much of it in livestock, the importance of consistently careful husbandry cannot be over-stressed. A lot of time must be spent daily on caring for the animals, especially during the calving period – from the beginning of June to mid-July – and during the main rut – from mid-October to the beginning of November. The behaviour, health and condition of the stock must also be checked constantly. It is true that care of the pasture, fences and drinking water supplies, feeding the adults and calves, marking, castrating male calves, weaning, slaughter and the sale of live beasts demand less time than with sheep or cattle but, all the same, the deer farmer must be available for these jobs, even with a small enterprise.

The farmer must have some knowledge of the habits of the animals, their feeding, behaviour when calving, worming, marking, catching and slaughter. If he has not had basic agricultural training, he must acquire this knowledge through special courses offered at agricultural colleges and by research centres. Most countries' agricultural advisory services and private consultants can offer specialist advice. Joining the appropriate Deer Farmers' Association will help the new farmer with contacts, friendly advice, help and outlets for stock sales. The address of the local association can be obtained from the agricultural advisory services.

The willingness of the farmer to accept advice cannot be emphasised too much. Lack of knowledge or a 'know-all' attitude to livestock husbandry can lead to harm being done to animal health, to the extreme of fatalities, and also to the total failure of the deer farm.

4.3   Regulations

The law in the Federal Republic of Germany recognises under Regulation/Section 960 BGB, only two types of animal: tame animals (pets, working animals, animals kept for slaughtering) and wild animals (those living free, captive wild animals and tamed wild animals). In court judgements it has been agreed that fallow deer kept for agricultural purposes should be regarded as captive wild animals, but the judges have taken into account the domestication process of farmed deer and are setting up regulations which will lead to their classification as domestic animals. Until complete legal equality with domestic animals has been established, though, each case must be looked at separately, and judgement made on whichever criteria apply to fallow deer. There are already proposals to make changes in the laws and regulations which are in force at present.

Licences may also be needed in certain cases under the Building or Planning Regulations, for example for fencing, or for the building of shelters, or a slaughter-house. This is important whether it is an agricultural enterprise with deer farming or stock farming with tenancy rights. In the Agricultural Statutes of the State Court at Cologne, for instance, it has been decided that deer keeping for breeding and meat production is agriculture. (For further details about German legislation see Appendix 1.)

The separate states of the German Federal Republic all have regulatory laws concerning nature conservancy. In Rhineland-Palatinate it is clearly laid down that wild animal and fur farms, exclusively for the production of meat and fur, are not stock farms in the meaning of the law, so they are not bound by the regulations. The states of Bavaria, Baden-Würtemberg, Hessen, Lower Saxony and Schleswig-Holstein have laid down rules in their administrative regulations on the requirements for deer and wild game farms respectively. In general authorisation comes from the nature conservancy offices, partly in co-operation with the agricultural offices and other existing departments such as forestry or veterinary offices, and the local authorities. In North Rhine Westphalia authorisation is via local groups after information has been gathered by the junior agricultural authorities such as the agricultural board.

In general the rules provide for a minimum space of one hectare, a certain stocking density and regulations about the height of fences, feeding and drinking arrangements, handling facilities and general guidelines concerning accounts, trademarks, herd books, meat inspection and humane killing. The Federal Government's Ministry of Food, Agriculture and Forestry has issued a set of general directions.

In Switzerland the regulations of the Confederation Veterinary Office on livestock farming, animal health, slaughtering and butchering must be adhered to. The rules on licensing procedure differ from canton to canton. Hunting administrators, agricultural directors, cantonal veterinary officers, forestry or finance controllers may be the authority (Hager and Zimmermann). In the case of research farms it is considered correct to operate deer farming according to licensing procedures so as to avoid serious errors and mistakes, a precaution which has proved wise over the years. The agricultural production regulations are well known to both advisers and local agricultural offices. There is also plenty of additional factual literature available.

The successful relaxation of regulations for deer farming in Rhineland-Palatinate has shown that equality with other farm and domestic animals will shortly be achieved. In any event, as the situation develops the authority of the local agricultural offices may well be questioned. This is the only way to avoid frequent miscarriages of justice, mistakes and vague orders from the agricultural and nature conservancy authorities, who are mostly lacking in factual evidence. Deer farming is a way of using pasture land for agricultural purposes, so it would seem sensible to talk about deer pastures and not deer herds.

The present regulations in North Rhine Westphalia are as follows, and provide a good guideline for all would-be deer farmers:

1. *Fencing*: overall height 1.50–1.70 m. Height of netting 1.40–1.50 m; on top of this one or two high-tensile wires. Posts 15–20 m apart, closer on undulating ground. Spacing of intermediates 5 m.
2. *Stock density*: ten to fifteen deer per ha (apart from calves), according to fertility of the land. One or two stags to thirty to forty hinds.
3. *Antler removal*: stag antlers to be removed by a vet.
4. *Marking*: identification by numbered ear tags or neck bands.
5. *Herd book*: a herd book is to be kept in which are entered details of purchase and sale, arrival and despatch of animals with date, origin, delivery address, etc.; also cause of death or other special circumstances.
6. *Slaughter*: to be carried out according to the rules for domestic animals. Killing with a humane pistol at point-blank range is allowed if permission is granted.
7. *Feeding*: a supply of water is to be provided throughout the year. In addition, covered racks should be erected for holding forage.
8. *Advice*: it is the farmer's duty to seek advice from the agricultural office and to follow their stipulations on animal welfare.

4.4   Layout and Fixed Equipment

Advice on the best form of animal park was given as long ago as the seventeenth century by von Hohberg: 'If one would be able and willing to set up an animal park, there should be either a fresh stream running through it or springs and ponds. The site must be surrounded and secured by a wall or a good high fence.'

A deer farm having the necessary facilities for handling and keeping the animals will consist of outer and inner fences with gates, handling, feeding and drinking arrangements and perhaps buildings for shelter.

4.4.1   Facilities

Right from the planning stage, the position of the handling layout should be decided upon; if possible, sited in the middle of the holding and combined with feeding and drinking facilities and with easy access for heavy transport carrying foodstuffs or animals. If there is already a suitable house or building (e.g. barn, shed) which is connected to the road, water and electricity networks, then the unit could be designed round it. Depending on the size of the overall area, the paddocks can be laid out from this centre. Depending on the fertility of the land and the proposed stocking density, the paddocks should be not less than 2–3 ha each. In West Germany the fertility of the land is measured in MJ ME per hectare and this varies, according to soil, climate and intensity of fertiliser use, from 40,000 to 90,000 MJ ME per ha.

The nutritional needs of an adult female fallow deer are approximately 4,800 MJ ME per year, those of a buck, according to age and weight, between 5,000 and 10,800 MJ ME. With a sex ratio of 1:20 to 1:30 this increased need can be disregarded, however.

The calves, sharing the same paddock as their mothers, need a nominal amount of fodder from the September after their birth, through to the September or October of the following year, when they will be sold or slaughtered. They require approximately 2,200 MJ ME and, if they are kept longer, an additional 140 MJ ME per month. The annual fodder requirement is thus about 7,500 MJ ME for one 'fallow deer unit' (i.e. doe, calf and yearling follower and the necessary additional proportion of stags).

To help decide the stocking density of the proposed area there are, depending on the soil fertility, the following recommended stocking rates per one fallow deer unit:

- low fertility (40,000 MJ ME): 5.3 deer units per ha or 16 on 3 ha.
- medium fertility (60,000 MJ ME): 8 deer units per ha or 24 on 3 ha.
- high fertility (80,000 MJ ME): 10.5 deer units per ha or 26 on 2.5 ha.

It is better to wean the calves before the rut, however, and provide a separate grazing paddock. The need then is to aim at a fodder production of 4,800 MJ ME per adult female, so one can have:

- low fertility (40,000 MJ ME): 25 hinds on 3 ha.
- medium fertility (60,000 MJ ME): 25 hinds on 2 ha.
- high fertility (80,000 MJ ME): 25 hinds on 1.5 ha.

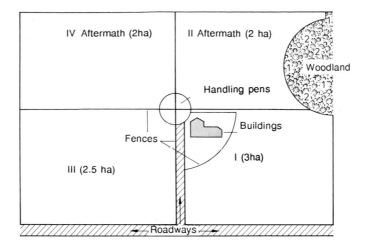

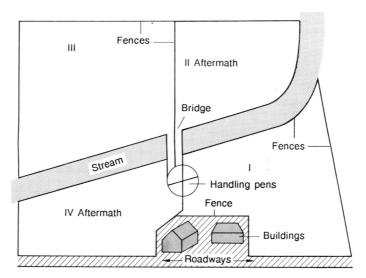

Figure 4.2 Dividing up a plot.

From our experience it is advisable to wean calves from their mothers in the autumn, before the rut starts, and to separate the young bucks at least for castration and eventual slaughter. For this, smaller 'follow-on' paddocks should be provided for the calves, from weaning in the autumn up to sale or slaughter the following autumn. With a breeding index of 95 per cent and a

Table 4.3   Area required for follow-on paddock

Quality	MJ ME/ha	Number of adult hinds	Area needed (ha)
Low	40,000	20	1.4
		30	2.1
		40	2.9
Medium	60,000	20	1.0
		30	1.4
		40	1.9
High	80,000	20	0.7
		30	1.1
		40	1.4

fodder need of approximately 4,000 MJ ME per calf, a follow-on paddock of the size shown in Table 4.3 will be needed.

If the fertility of the site is not known, stocking density should be such that can be carried, and built up as the fertility builds up or new more productive grazing becomes available. More paddocks can be fenced as the herd is built up, but it is important to ensure that the central buildings complex is accessible

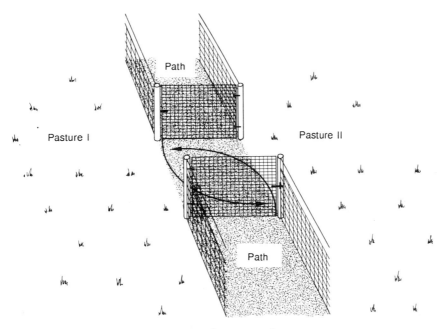

Figure 4.3   Construction of gates where a path crosses.

from all parts and that the beasts can be fed and watered there. Considerable savings can be made in this way. Small areas of woodland, wet or damp patches should be taken into consideration when dividing up the individual fields, so that fencing them off can be accomplished as economically as possible. In hilly or mountainous areas each paddock should contain an area sheltered from the wind, if possible, so that the deer have some protection from the weather. There should be gates across the paths between the paddocks, to enable the animals to be driven easily from one paddock to another. If the land is divided by public roads, on the other hand, each area may need its own handling, feeding and drinking arrangements.

4.4.2 Fencing and Gates

Spacing of the posts for the boundary fence should be 15–20 m, according to the contours of the land, and somewhat closer if the land is sloping, rocky or undulating. Posts should be 2.5–2.7 m high with a diameter of 8–10 cm, and at a depth of 60–100 cm in the ground. Wide spacing of the posts, which are expensive, not only cuts costs but also avoids injury to the beasts if they panic and run up against the fence. A fence with widely spaced posts will be flexible, whereas with closer spacing it will act like a wall and could cause injury to the animals. Power-driven tools will make fencing work much easier.

If possible use round, stripped but not split wooden posts, as these are

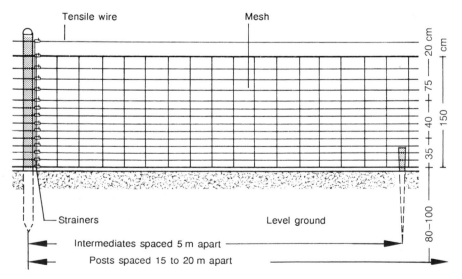

Figure 4.4 Outer fence.

stronger; tanalised posts made from guaranteed 6–8-month seasoned oak, acacia, larch, Douglas fir, fir or pine are particularly recommended. Many suppliers will give a twelve-month guarantee. Experience shows that it is better to choose good materials of guaranteed quality rather than cheap posts which will have to be replaced after only a few years. It is possible to test for impregnation of the wood to the core by making a sample cross-section cut.

Metal posts are not recommended as they are liable to rust, while concrete posts are expensive and spoil the look of the environment.

'Intermediate' posts should be driven into the ground between the main posts. These are 1.25 m long and 5–7 cm thick, and should be spaced about every 5 m. They keep the fence anchored to the ground which, in our experience, is particularly important otherwise the newborn calves tend to crawl underneath. Even older animals will try to creep under a fence rather than jump over it. The 'intermediates' should be somewhat closer together when the ground is undulating, and where there are dips in the ground the fence can be extended and fitted to the contours, without interrupting the desired line.

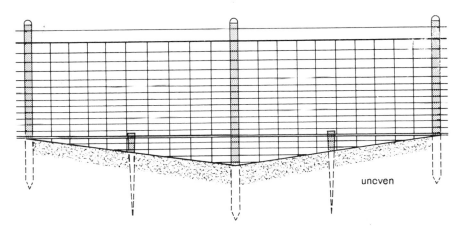

Figure 4.5 Fence construction on uneven ground.

As regards the distance of the fence from the boundary, one must always bear in mind any local 'rules' which are in force. Where there is a right of way, for example, a distance of 0.6 m from the boundary is advisable. In North Rhine Westphalia, for instance, the space between the boundary and a piece of ground which lies outside an existing built-up area and which is not designated as building land must be 0.5 m. There is an exception in the case of pieces of land which are to be cultivated in the same way as the fenced area or which do not come under the heading of agricultural use because of position, quality and size.

When it comes to the internal fencing a height of 1.4–1.5 m is sufficient,

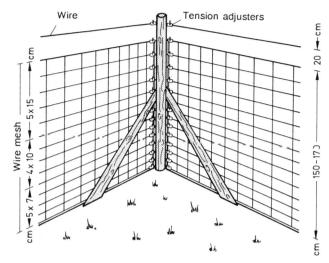

Figure 4.6 Strengthening the corner post.

with posts 2.1–2.2 m high, and with a diameter of 6–8 cm.

It is important to strengthen the corner posts. Each should have two angled supports, one in each direction of the wire, so the posts are not lifted out of the ground or become loose when the wires are tightened. Extra care should be taken when putting up the corner posts, which should be a larger diameter than the intermediate fencing posts, 12–15 cm across. Corners or sharp angles should be avoided if possible when erecting a fence. It is also important to fix the wire on to the *outside* of the corner posts. If there are no strainers on the corner posts the wire cannot be nailed to them, because the nails will be pulled out when the wire is stretched.

The wire mesh for the outer fence should be 1.4–1.5 m high, and a tensile wire should be stretched 20 cm above this. It is definitely not advisable to use barbed wire for this: persons trying to climb over could be hurt. Examine the quality of the material when choosing wire mesh: it should be galvanised to give better durability, if possible, and the top and bottom strands of the mesh should be thicker than the rest as they have to withstand more stress.

Up to a height of 30 cm the horizontal wires should have a gap between them of no more than 7.5 cm, to stop newborn calves crawling under and escaping or straying from one paddock to another. If the gap were wider the calves could get out but might not be able to get back and would perish. Towards the top of the fence the gap between the horizontal wires can increase to 15 cm. Vertical wires keep the spacing between the horizontals even, and so prevent the stock escaping or the entry of dogs or thieves from outside. The verticals should be spaced about 30 cm apart.

With animals born or raised on deer farms, which therefore have a certain tolerance of humans, the outer fence can be lowered to 1.5 m overall, and the inner fence to 1.2 m. In areas which are subject to deep-lying snow the fence

Plates 4.2 and 4.3   Tightening the screws is essential.

should be higher, however, so that animals cannot get out over it when the snow is packed hard on the ground. Up to now we have found that the above design has prevented animals jumping over the fence.

Tightening the wire is best done by tractor (see Figure 4.7). A solid iron bar is fixed to the end of the mesh. This is kept upright with wires or chains to the tractor. The post from which the wire is to be stretched must be strengthened and supported by a strainer post. The wire is then stretched by the tractor,

Mesh width: up to 40 cm high − 7.5 cm; over this height − 15 cm

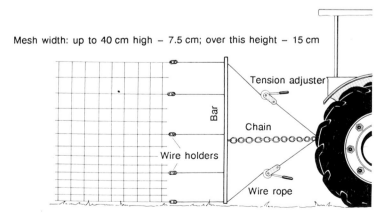

Figure 4.7   **Tightening mesh with a tractor.**

Plate 4.4 Outer fence on gently sloping land.

which has its lowest gear engaged. It is advisable to secure the top wire of the mesh to the posts. The desired tension can then be adjusted by the tractor driver and the mesh fixed to the next post.

Each horizontal wire should have a strainer attached at a maximum distance of 100 m. By tightening or loosening these strainers the mesh can be kept at a firm but not too tight tension throughout the year. (Remember that metal expands when hot and contracts when cold; also the material is likely to sag with age.) Care must therefore be taken to ensure that the strainers are easy to use and have large enough threads. With small strainers the wires could come loose.

The following types of fencing have not proved suitable in our trials over many years:

1. Strainer post spacing 50 m, intermediates at intervals of 5 m, 5 mm steel wire between the posts, and mesh 1.4 m high. This fence is relatively expensive and needs more upkeep than the normal type.
2. Post spacing 10 m, no intermediates. Instead of mesh, ordinary tensile wire is used with a spacing of 10–20 cm. With this fence, which was tried as an internal fence, there were many escapes by calves creeping into the next paddock. In addition, the continual need for the wires to be tightened was labour intensive.
3. An electric fence with three wires. This fence, which is used in cattle farming, is respected by the adult deer but not by the calves, which can get through the wire and out of the farm or on to neighbouring fields.

In special cases it might be advisable to use an electrified wire, for example when there are foxes about on the outside which might cause losses at calving time. An electric fence can also help to prevent wild deer from jumping over the fence into the farm or stop competitive battles between stags at the fence. An electrified wire is useful on the fences between adjacent paddocks, when the stags are antlered and there are several paddocks of females, to prevent fighting through the fence, with the consequence of antler and/or fence damage.

The price of materials, especially posts, obviously has an effect on total fencing costs, but the height of the mesh is also an important consideration. Labour can make up about half the overall cost of fencing, so considerable savings might be made by using any farm help that is available. It is recommended that materials are ordered in bulk and that, if the job is to be done by professionals, estimates and precise specifications are first obtained from several firms.

The farm and all the separate parts of it should be accessible to tractors and lorries, and good gates must be installed. Single, self-closing spring gates have been proved to be the most effective, and it is again important that the gate is close to the ground, to stop calves from creeping underneath. Obviously any gates in the outer fence must be properly secured. Rust-free (galvanised) materials are recommended.

The gate should be at least 2.5 m wide, if direct entry from the road is possible, and must certainly be wide enough for a tractor and trailer or a lorry

Plate 4.5 Main gate – metal construction.

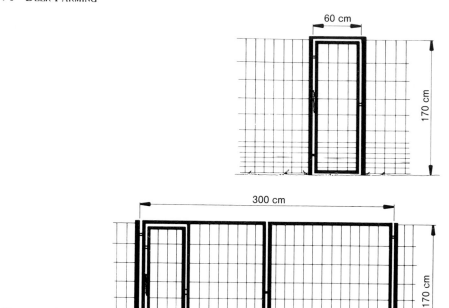

Figure 4.8 Diagrams of small handy gates.

Plate 4.6 Inner gate.

to get through without trouble. The gate posts should be strengthened with angled supports and should be concreted in.

Lighter-weight gates can be erected between fields, as these are used less often than the main gate. One possibility chosen by a deer farmer was a plastic curtain such as is used in industry, for example when fork-lift trucks are going in and out. This has the advantage of closing quickly behind the vehicle.

When animals escape from farms it is almost always because doors or gates have not been closed, so special care must be taken when selecting them and they must always be properly secured.

Use wire netting to protect single trees, fixing it firmly to posts so that the animals cannot tear it out. However, wire mesh cannot be used if there are stags with antlers in the herd, as one cannot exclude the possibility of their antlers becoming entangled. Tree trunks should then be protected with suitable wooden fencing.

4.4.3 Feeding and Watering

Roofed and portable wooden feeding racks have proved satisfactory, in our experience. Hay and straw can be eaten from the racks at the top, while underneath are two troughs for the feeding of compounds. As bulk fodder is only given in winter, the roof should be constructed so that the feed and the beasts stay dry. Racks with relatively steeply angled bars for hay feeding have the disadvantage that quite a lot of the hay falls to the ground (see Plate 4.7);

Plate 4.7   Movable feed racks.

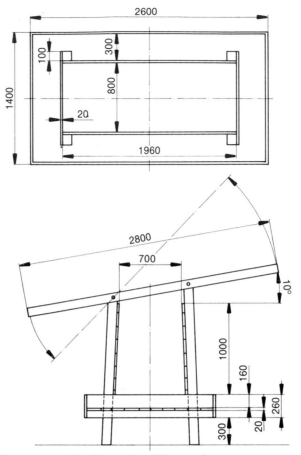

Figure 4.9 Diagrams of double racks (*Rüssman*).

a construction devised by Rüssmann (see Figure 4.9), where the hay bale is enclosed by the roof swinging over, is better. The concentrates are put in a surrounding trough into which the hay can also fall. Another advantage of this design is that the beasts are completely in the dry when it is raining. Care should be taken to make sure the racks are far enough from the ground to prevent the animals standing in them.

To ensure equal intake of feed, even by lower ranking animals, each animal should have about 30 cm frontage of rack.

Fodder racks can either be purchased from a specialised firm or made on the farm by craftsmen following suitable plans. DIY construction is also possible. If the hay rack is not adjacent to the handling area it is absolutely essential to concrete under the rack and for about 2 m round it, otherwise the ground will become very muddy in winter. With feed residues and manure this means a

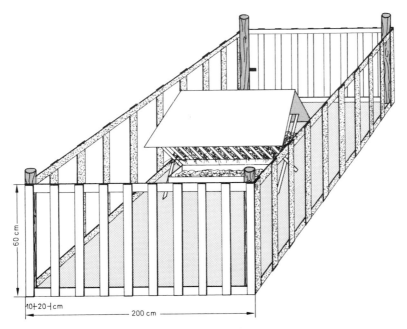

Figure 4.10 Calf feeding area.

considerable source of infection. Laying down coarse, ridged concrete makes it possible to remove fodder residue and manure frequently with a front-loader on the tractor, and the area should then be disinfected.

We have found, over the years, that it has proved beneficial to give additional feed to the calves as soon as possible: it can be started from July. It cannot be given in the feeding set-up arranged for the adult deer, as the calves are timid and would be pushed away. Calf feeding should therefore be carried out at a separate site, and arranged so that it is not accessible to other animals. The best site is the area where the mothers most frequently stand, because the calves must learn to find fresh food all the year round.

Clean water is essential throughout the year as, depending on the type of fodder available, the suckling hind will drink up to 2 litres per day. When dry fodder such as hay or straw is fed all animals may drink 1–2 litres of water per day.

As regards quality, the German regulations for drinking water should be followed. The maximum levels of salmonella bacteria and of streptococcus are set at 10 cells per ml. Permitted levels per litre are: sulphates 240 mg, nitrate 50 mg, zinc 2 mg, chromium, cyanide and fluoride 0.05 mg, arsenic and lead 0.04 mg, copper 0.02 mg, molybdenum 0.01 mg, selenium 0.008 mg, mercury 0.04 mg and cadmium 0.006 mg.

Because the animals are kept on the same site all year the water supply must be prevented from freezing. The easiest way is to have the supply near

Plate 4.8 Drinking arrangement.

to the buildings. Containers which can be heated are obtainable. Large bowls are more likely to become dirty and must be cleaned out more often. Smaller containers, such as those sold for pets, have been found efficient. Where the natural water supply is limited, self-drinkers can be put in, but care must be taken that the deer, like horses, cattle or sheep, do not start off a pumping mechanism by pushing against it. The water must also drain off readily or be pumped away. If springs or streams are used, access must be such that the water is not soiled by the deer poaching the adjacent ground. The access area should be hard but not slippery, and only a small area adjacent to the source should be utilised so that the animals do not tread in the water.

Silage is conserving surplus grass in summer. Silos are best sited in central areas, easily accessible to all the beasts, and should be built of 10-cm-thick concrete on a frost-resistant base (sand, lava, etc.). A silo floor area of about 1 sq m will be required for each animal. The width of base needed is governed by the number of animals in the herd. With about forty animals, it should be at least 1 m wide, so that there is not too much of the surface exposed in winter. To facilitate even fermentation of the silage, it must be tightly packed in strong plastic sheeting, which should then be buried about 20 cm deep in the ground and covered over with soil so that it will not come loose even in a strong wind.

A labour-saving self-feeding system can be set up by adding a wooden grid about 1 m high and with bars spaced 0.2 m apart, which fits on the shorter

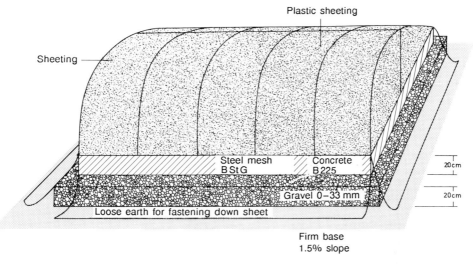

Figure 4.11 Silo.

side of the silo. The animals can push their heads through the bars to reach the fodder. Soiling and treading the feed is thus avoided. After several days the grid is moved back up to the silage face. Any fermenting effluent must be cleared off the ground frequently. It is also vital to ensure that the animals cannot reach the plastic covering, which they like to eat, because it can cause twisted bowels and often fatalities.

4.4.4 Handling Arrangements

A handling set-up makes it possible to catch, separate, treat (worm, castrate, vaccinate), gather for sale and slaughter the deer without immobilising them. At the same time it can serve as a feeding and watering place, and provide shade and shelter from the wind. On red deer farms in Great Britain and New Zealand quite complicated buildings have been put up. We are of the opinion, however, that handling facilities should be as simple and inexpensive as possible: they should fit into the landscape, not be enclosed like a stable, and each area should be suitable for its desired purpose.

The simplest set-up is a funnel-shaped race. Boards or planks are put up to make walls 2.5 m high, and there should be enough space for feed racks and water containers. Under no circumstances should any wire be used on the inside of the walls, as the deer might jump against it and injure themselves or break their necks.

It is important that the deer become accustomed to the race. This can be achieved by offering them concentrates or other tempting food there.

The deer enter the race through an opening under a sliding drop door, and go out again via a narrowing race. A carrying crate can be installed at this end. Remote control, whereby the drop door can be closed after enclosing

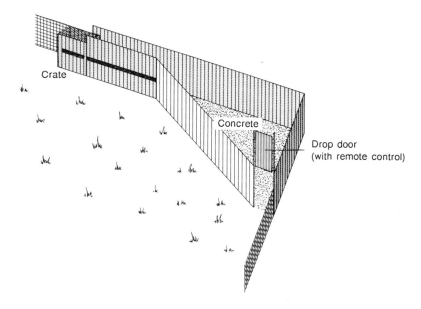

Figure 4.12 Handling unit – funnel.

Plate 4.9 Crate at end of funnel for catching and transporting.

the animals, is a very helpful device. The raceway has access slots at the side, through which one can reach to tend the deer. This is a suitable arrangement for small enterprises with only one or two paddocks, which can be connected to the race by gates.

For larger farms a handling ring is more advisable. One was tested at the teaching and research centre at Riswick House, Cleves, which was constructed in a similar way to sheep folds. The 2.5 m walls can be made from wood or the pre-fabricated metal sheeting used for silos. The animals can get into the handling ring from several directions at all times of the year, and food and water is always available there.

In the Bavarian State Centre for Animal Husbandry at Grub, a holding pen was set up, with radiating gangways (see Figure 4.13). It consisted of

Plate 4.10 Handling enclosure – external view.

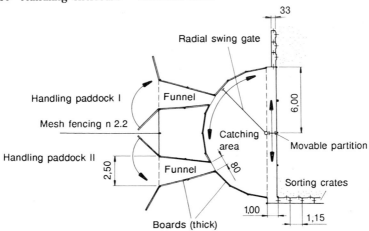

Figure 4.13 Catching area with radiating gate.

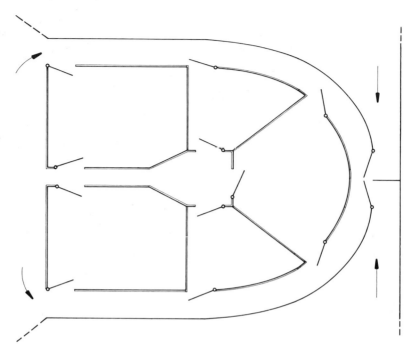

Figure 4.14 Central handling arrangement for the larger deer farm (*Drew and Kelly*).

large wooden barriers with a remote-controlled swing door and a movable inner wall.

In Australia and New Zealand even larger set-ups have been installed, mostly for the bigger enterprises (see Figure 4.14).

A useful combination of feeding, shelter and catching arrangements is possible by erecting a polythene sheeted building as installed at the Rüssmann farm (Plate 4.11). This transparent and relatively spacious building encourages the animals to become quickly settled, and they soon get used to being indoors if fed and watered there.

Of course similar arrangements can be made using existing barns, sheds and stables or in conjunction with these. It is important to make sure, by means of light slots, windows, etc., that the animals have daylight and do not have to enter a dark building.

There should be collecting areas for the animals between the paddocks and the handling area, surrounded by a heavier wire mesh fence, or preferably a wooden or plastic sheet fence. The smaller the area the animals have for movement, the more important it is to have clear space. Some animals may become distressed and try to escape by jumping through a fence or over a wall. A visible boundary is absolutely vital, but at the same time there should be a gradual transition from the pasture to the handling area.

As Rüssmann has been able to establish from a long period of research, deer

Plate 4.11 Plastic-covered, low-cost shed.

Plate 4.12 Barns or sheds should have openings or windows so that the animals have enough light.

Plate 4.13 Walls of black plastic or sheeting are very practicable.

seem to prefer black or dark walls of wood, plastic or rubber, and do not try
to jump against or over them, as they do with white walls or wire. For this
reason dark materials should always be chosen.

4.4.5 Shelter Construction

Where weather conditions are bad, for instance in windy locations with heavy
rainfall, it may be necessary to provide a shelter for the deer. This should be
made as simple as possible – and not merely on the grounds of cost. It is not in
the interests of the animals' health to take them away from their natural surroundings and weaken their resistance to disease and severe weather by housing them in a stable or similar building. Unfortunately, in recent years, such
considerations have been forgotten for both humans and domestic animals –
the health and longevity of domesticated animals have declined, not risen, with
new husbandry methods. One should not fall into the same trap with deer.

A shelter is for keeping the animal dry and protecting it from cold in severe
weather, when heavy showers are combined with winds. The structure must
have a roof and a wall on the windward side, therefore, but it should be open
on at least two sides. The roof construction, supports and spaces should be
such that one can get in with the front-loader on the tractor to clean out. The
floor can be concreted and a light covering of straw is practicable. Cleaning
out must be done frequently.

4.4.6 Stands

For many farmers, particularly those with only a small number of animals, killing with a pistol is best. From extensive trials which we have carried out with the German Research and Experimental Centre for Hunting and Sporting Guns in Altenbeeken, we have found that the best arrangement for human safety and for avoiding injury to the animals is to shoot them in the head from a stand with a platform 2.3 m above the ground.

The construction of the stand must comply with the German regulations on accident prevention. This applies particularly to ladders and rails and to the protection of body, knees and feet. The stand can be made of good quality treated timber or metal bars of simple building steel quality. All metal parts and weldings should be treated against corrosion. After climbing up, the platform must be made secure by means of a gate, bolt or chain.

Working with the Rhineland State Agricultural Training Board in Düsseldorf, building plans for stands on deer farms were developed, and copies may be obtained from there. Figure 4.14 shows a wooden shooting stand. A similar one in wood or metal could also be erected against the wall of an existing building. A portable construction to a similar design is also a possibility.

The side sections should be built first, placed in prepared holes and temporarily positioned, then the cross-pieces fixed. The holes are filled in and made firm. Then the stabilising boards, the platform floor, the rails and the roof can be put on. Lastly the ladder can be nailed or fixed on. A sloping, hinged ladder could also be used.

Plate 4.14 Shelter construction.

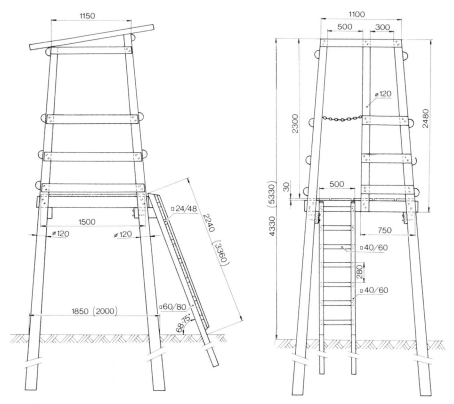

Figure 4.15 Diagram of DIY shooting stand and platform (*Rhineland Agricultural Training Group*).

4.4.7 Slaughter-house

Erecting one's own slaughter-house is only sensible if there is already space which can be used for it and if one intends to do one's own marketing.

First ascertain local slaughtering controls. A licence to erect the slaughter-house will mean high standards for buildings, equipment, water supply, removal and disposal of waste and condemned material, etc. (see p. 262). In Germany, there are particular laws concerning animal protection, slaughtering, meat quality, and food and hygiene regulations which have to be observed when erecting and operating a venison slaughter-house and preparation unit.

5 Purchase and Rearing of Deer

5.1 Obtaining the Animals

If possible one should first take a close look at the animals at the seller's premises. This is the only way to establish the size, colour and condition of the deer, their previous rearing, their tolerance of humans and the feeding methods used. All this is important when it comes to dealing with the animals later on.

It is also advisable, when starting up a new enterprise, to buy a few tame beasts as this will facilitate the taming process of the whole herd.

5.2 Timing

The best time for buying and transporting the deer is after the rut until March. If possible moving the deer in autumn, before the rut, should be avoided. The rut itself is a time of considerable stress for the deer; moving them to a new location, with changes in feed and management, could lead to a high barren rate or deaths. After the rut the animals are calmer; in colder weather it is natural for them to move about less and they are tamer than in the autumn as they are receiving supplementary food because of the lack of pasture. In April changing the environment of the heavily pregnant hinds is a problem, as is actually moving them. Over-energetic catching or careless handling during the move can lead to abortion, and later difficulties with calving.

Particular care should be taken when buying calves, and they should be moved as late as possible. Under no circumstances should calves be bought and transported before the rut, i.e. before mid-October, and in any case very special care is needed because of the greater vulnerability of the young animals to stress, weather conditions, changes in diet and parasitic infection. It is also advisable to keep them with some adult does.

5.3 Transport

Deer can be transported in groups in a suitable lorry or cattle truck. On longer journeys they must be supplied with water and, if possible, offered concentrates as well to start getting them used to handling. Timid deer can, if necessary, be carried in individual crates 1.5 m long, 1.3 m high and 0.4 m wide. They should also be given food and water on longer journeys. Males should first have their antlers removed under anaesthetic.

Plate 5.1 Carrying crate for hinds.

Plate 5.2 Large carrying crate for hinds or stags.

On arrival at the new location there should be a rest for about an hour to calm the animals down. Never put them straight out to pasture. There should be a good distance between the crate or truck and the nearest fence. If there is a funnel-shaped race, shed or handling set-up the animals should then be released into these. It is also a good idea to put down some hay or concentrates at a distance from the transport truck. Avoid shouting, and have as few helpers as possible to avoid panicking the deer. The deer are less restive in twilight or in the dark than during the day. They become more quickly used to their handler after being kept for about a week in the dark.

Deer imported into Germany must be in quarantine for the first two weeks so that veterinary checks can be carried out. Before turning deer out into the paddocks, they should be drenched against stomach, intestinal and lung worms as a precaution.

5.4 Marking

A good opportunity to mark the deer is when they are collected in a small area for transportation. In established enterprises marking of calves should be done during the first three days after birth: the calves will stay put, even if the mother jumps away. At calving time check the paddock for newborn calves at least once every day – they can be marked immediately with ear tags or neck bands and, at the same time, the sex noted to give a clear overall picture of the herd. Hinds seem to prefer to drop their calves among clumps

Plate 5.3 Notched ears.

of stinging nettles, so if there are any of them on the pasture the daily search is made easier.

We have tried various methods of marking deer over the years. The least acceptable to the animals is notching the ears, which is done on the top or bottom of the ear, at different distances from the head, by means of a clipping tool. With four possible positions on the ear and about five different gaps from the head there are many possibilities, but this method of marking has the disadvantage that one cannot immediately pick out the number of the animal.

Ear-marking with tags is a rather better method: the tags can be small, medium or large, and are metal or plastic with coloured numbers. Ear tags must be impervious to cold and sunlight, should not become jagged or break off, and should not be too heavy. The colours should be colourfast for at least a year. The disadvantage of ear tags is that they are easily torn off if the deer puts its head through the mesh of the fence when feeding and then pulls back. Also, the number can only be seen from a short distance away and when the tag is turned towards the handler. If tags are chosen in spite of these disadvantages, they should be fixed close to the head. The ear is pierced with a punch, and the tag placed over the hole and attached by a metal or plastic clip.

Collars are much better. They do not harm the animals, are quick to put on and to identify the individual deer clearly even from a distance. If a deer should happen to escape into the open, its ownership is clear and recapture is made easier. (We also tried plastic straps with numbers on coloured discs, but these were not suitable, as the deer nibbled them and tried to eat the strap.)

Plate 5.4   Ear tags.

Plate 5.5 Hind with collar.

Plate 5.6 Calves with collars.

As with ear tags, collars must last at least five years and not be too heavy. They should be of different colours, to show the animals' ages, and the colours should neither fade nor alter. The collar must fit close to the neck of an adult deer without rubbing. Letters or numbers should be on both left and right sides so that they can be seen and distinguished from as far away as possible. The marking of the hinds is particularly important for breeders.

We have had good results for several years with close-fitting, brightly coloured plastic collars, 2–3 cm wide, with a vertical diameter of 14 cm, horizontal diameter of 9 cm, narrowing at the bottom, and numbered on both sides. These collars can be fitted on newborn calves without any problem, provided that the ends of the collar are joined with a small clip: buckles on calf collars may rub when the calf is eating and can cause sores.

5.5 Buck: Doe Ratio

There has been much discussion about the appropriate ratio between the sexes in a herd. In the wild there are approximately equal numbers of males and females, because the almost equal ratio of births cancels out yearly variations. The law of survival of the fittest applies for the buck when it comes to mating. Bodily strength, aggression and skill determine which buck is head of the herd and how many females he collects round him. Rutting fights demand considerable strength, the bucks losing much weight, as they take little or no food during the rutting period, as they are active day and night covering the does and warding off competing bucks. For some of the defeated bucks the fights can be fatal, for rivals butt and strike a fallen opponent in the flanks with their antlers.

In our trials, therefore, we decided that when handling a domesticated herd a group should consist of does and one breeding buck. In this way the breeding buck could devote himself fully to the does. A ratio of 30–40 does:1 buck was found to be acceptable. As the main period of heat stretches over about three weeks, there is an excellent possibility of the buck covering all the does during this time. On the evidence of our experiments, over several years, adult does conceived almost without exception and young well-grown does in about 80 per cent of cases. In January and February the few non-pregnant females might have a second heat.

The ratio of the sexes should be considered on economic as well as on purely physiological grounds, however. With deer farming productivity is entirely dependent on the doe herd, so the ratio of females should be as high as possible. In several years' trials on different farms we found a ratio of 1:30–1:40 to be best. In twelve years' research this gave no reduction in fertility, no change in the ratio of the sexes at birth, and no significant delay in the date of summer fawning.

Occasionally there is the danger of infertility when using only one stag. Also, a low level of libido in an individual male would result in some hinds not being mated. In such cases it is recommended that a second, but certainly younger – possibly a yearling – buck be introduced. Under no circumstances should the two bucks be of the same age and strength because, when antlered, they very often fight to the death. From our experience we would also not recommend a lone yearling buck to be put with a large herd, as both fertility and the calving rate may be reduced.

5.6 Age

As far as possible the age of the animals should be taken into consideration when determining the composition of the herd. Up to three years the age can be judged according to the teeth (see p. 25), but after that a deer's age can only be estimated.

Important pointers include the size and shape of the deer's head. In a calf the head is short and squat with prominent cheeks; by the age of one year it has noticeably lengthened; and by the third year, given good nutrition, the skull has elongated: ears, eyes and snout have reached their full growth, and the cheeks are taut and well muscled. With good nutrition and health this facial configuration, with bright eyes and alert ears, continues up to about twelve to fifteen years. The bones around the eyes and cheeks then begin to stand out more, the skin becomes slacker, the ears droop and the eyes become duller. A similar development will be noticed throughout the body.

The best age for buying does is at the beginning of their first breeding season – with farmed animals in peak condition this is in November–March of their second year. With extensively reared animals of corresponding condition it is one year later. The advantages of buying these younger animals lie in their long useful life, their fitness and in the building up of a herd of balanced age-profile. The main disadvantage is their timidity. Fear of man is greatest with the young animal but reduces with age. From experience, it is lowest with does from deer farms, but it must be said that if purchased as older animals, they obviously have a shorter productive life than those bought in at a younger age. Consequently the establishment of a balanced age-profile herd should be embarked on early.

Special care must be taken when buying calves in the October after their birth. On top of the natural stress at weaning they have to undergo changes in environment and feeding, plus the upheaval of transportation. In our experience only completely sound animals in top condition come through this severe stress unaffected. In addition, considerable setbacks, even losses, are to be feared through stress, parasitic worms or disease. Young calves also need especially intensive care and better feeding through the winter. These disadvantages should be weighed seriously against the advantage of lower costs, before purchase is decided on.

The greatest care is advised with the purchase of bucks, and keen observation of the animal and a sound knowledge of market values cannot be over-stressed. With a male:female ratio of 1:30–1:40 the sire is of considerable importance in animal breeding. If a buck from the desired genetic line is not available, look for a healthy animal with a large frame, good conformation and colour, lively expression, and ease of handling. If you propose to sell the skins, animals with distinct markings are to be preferred. There is no correlation, from our observations and experience, between the colour of the hide – white,

Plates 5.7, 5.8 and 5.9 The determination of age from head shape: calf; adult; old deer.

spotted or dark – and the body weight. With all variants of colour there are light- and heavyweight animals. If possible, try to buy buck with burnt-off antlers as this will inhibit further antler growth and the yearly cost of antler-removal will be saved.

Sexual maturity comes at about sixteen months. It is not advisable, however, to start breeding with buck until they are fully grown, i.e. three to six years old. After a few years the buck should be changed to avoid in-breeding.

Records should be kept of the source of all the animals, including their date of purchase, number, age and special characteristics (colour, skin pattern, head details). This data is a necessary basis for the subsequent recording of the herd age-profile, the replacement of bucks and the breeding records.

Plate 5.10 Much depends on a good stag.

Plate 5.11 Pricket (16 months old).

Number of births

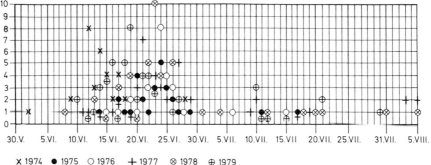

X 1974   ● 1975   ○ 1976   + 1977   ⊗ 1978   ⊕ 1979

Figure 5.1   Calving dates at the Teaching and Research Centre, Riswick House (number of births).

5.7   Growth

Our trials have shown that calving in the herds at the Teaching and Research Centre at Riswick House, Cleves, occurs mainly between 15 and 28 June. From Figure 5.1 it is clear that births in 1974 were generally earlier than in subsequent years. This was the year in which the herds, of middle-aged and older animals only, were first put out in the pastures in April. The deer had come from a wild herd. In the following years we see later calving dates, going into the summer months. Also, of course, the number of young animals, mated in their second year, was constantly rising. The calving percentage over the twelve years averaged 93 per cent, varying between 80 per cent and 100 per cent. The birth weights of male calves were on average 4.6 kg (between 4.2 and 5.1 kg), and of female calves 4.3 kg (between 3.6 and 4.9 kg). The percentage reared was 87 per cent. The male:female ratio over the twelve years averaged 1.2 males to 1 female, varying from 1.8:1 to 0.6:1 (see Table 5.1). Infertility was not observed.

Deer were delivered to the trials station at Bommert-Marienheide in October–November 1974, so the rut was still in progress when they arrived at their destination. They were mainly middle-aged animals. Most of the calves were born between 13 and 28 June, but a few does did not calve until the beginning of September. These were young deer, calving in their second year. The calving percentage averaged 85 per cent over four years. The proportion of female calves was 49 per cent, while the average for all our recorded herds was 47.6 per cent.

Births at both sites always took place without human assistance. There was one fatality, due to prolapse and torn skin, while the proportion of still births was 4.4 per cent. The average for all the recorded herds was 3.2 per cent.

In the early years of the trials we came across problems in the weeks immediately after calving when calves slipped out through gaps in the fencing, could not get back and died. One year there was heavy rainfall during the main calving period, and a few calves died of cold.

Marking the calves with ear tags during their first three days of life, and

Table 5.1 Birth weights, calving dates and sex ratio of calves at the Teaching and Research Centre, Riswick House, Cleves

| | Birth weight (kg) | | Date | M : F | Number |
	Male	Female			
1974	4.96	4.93	2.6–28.6	1.1 : 1	21
1975	4.34	3.58	14.6–17.7	1.8 : 1	26
1976	4.16	4.36	15.6–15.7	1.7 : 1	26
1977	4.20	4.26	11.6– 5.8	1.1 : 1	27
1978	4.22	4.30	8.6– 5.8	0.8 : 1	32
1979	4.40	4.33	10.6–30.8	1.7 : 1	41
1980	4.51	4.39	28.5– 9.7	0.8 : 1	41
1981	4.45	4.27	14.6–18.7	0.8 : 1	41
1982	4.74	4.39	2.6–23.8	1 : 1	44
1983	5.07	4.39	12.6–30.9	1.8 : 1	46
1984	5.01	4.56	16.6–18.7	1.1 : 1	64
1985	5.14	4.41	11.6– 8.9	0.6 : 1	46
Average	4.60	4.34	2.6–30.9	1.2 : 1	30

in later years with collars, was no problem. In spite of being disturbed by the keeper the calves were accepted again by the mother. At the trials centre at Romenthal, the Bavarian State Animal Husbandry Centre, the calving index

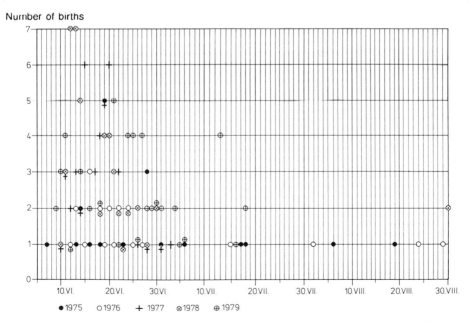

Figure 5.2 Calving dates at the Trials Station at Bommert (number of births).

was 78–100 per cent over the six years. The birth weight of male calves varied between 5.06 and 5.14 kg, with an average over the four years of 5.09 kg, while the average for females was 4.77 kg, varying between 4.56 and 4.96 kg.

Questionnaires returned by farmers in North Rhine Westphalia since 1978–80 show that there are only very small variations each year in the male:female ratio. The largest percentage variations so far have been 87 per cent male calves and 66 per cent female calves; these figures are from farms with over twenty hinds. As at trials centres, there were cases of calving as late as 20 September. The number of recorded twin births was very low.

The live weight graph is important, and is shown in Figure 5.3. The development of calves, yearlings and adults was recorded by frequent weighing, between 1974 and 1976. Female calves with normal feeding reached a weight of about 20 kg in the autumn, and male calves about 23 kg. From then to the end of the year there was an increase of about 7 kg, and during the winter months there was little further increase in spite of supplementary rations of concentrates being fed.

There was considerable weight gain with spring growth and the high availability of forage, especially among the males, and an average of 47 kg was reached in October. The yearlings in November (seventeen months old) weighed over 40 kg and most had reached puberty. From birth to the

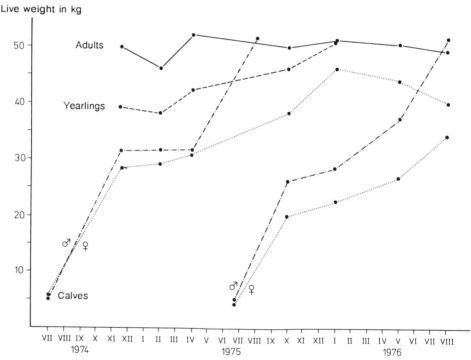

Live weight in kg

Figure 5.3 Live weight development at Riswick House (in kg): (a) adults; (b) yearlings; (c) calves.

beginning of October the average daily live weight gain was 152 g for females and 207 g for males. Up until slaughter – between the beginning of July and the end of September – the average daily live weight gain from birth was 94 g (mean of four years). Later slaughtering can lead to a fatty carcass. Fully grown females reach a weight of 50 kg, males 60–64 kg by the end of their second year and up to 127 kg in their fourth and fifth years.

From several years' weighing in October, at the trials centre at Romenthal, Schick recorded weights of between 19.3 kg and 20.3 kg for female calves, and between 22.2 kg and 23.2 kg for male calves. In April weights of between 26.4 and 28.3 kg were recorded for bucks, and 20.6 to 24.4 kg for yearling does. The highest daily live weight gain was shown in calves during their first year: males 156 g per day and females 154 g per day. By the summer the increase had already slowed by about a third: about 100 g per day for males and 70 g per day for females. The results from the trials centres are shown in Table 5.2.

Table 5.2 Live weight and daily gain at different ages

Age	Sex	Weight (kg)	Daily gain (g)	Source
Birth	f	4.5	—	Riswick House
	m	4.6	—	
	f	4.8	—	
	m	5.2	—	Schick
4 months (autumn)	f	20	152	Riswick House
	m	26	207	
	f	19.8	144	Schick
	m	22.7	156	
10 months (spring)	f	22–24	—	Riswick House
	m	26–34	94	
	f	24.0	—	Schick
	m	28.8	—	
2nd year 14 months (autumn)	f	32–38	—	Riswick House
	m	48.2 (44–54)	—	
16 months (autumn)	f	37.8	70	Schick
	m	47.0	100	
	f	39.0	—	Riswick House
3rd year (Spring)	f	47.1	45	Schick
(Autumn)	m	50.1	—	
(Autumn)	f	50.0	—	Riswick House
	m	70–127	—	

According to Mulley and English, castration leads to a setback in growth. Our research on the size of the animals showed the following figures:

Table 5.3

	Length *(shoulder to rump)*	*Height* *(at withers)*
Does	68–84 cm	76–83 cm
Yearlings	63–73 cm	68–79 cm
Calves	60–76 cm	62–76 cm

In contrast to animals in wild herds, farmed deer show a faster growth due to the constant availability of food. This is not only displayed in their higher body weight but also in their earlier maturity. On several farms it was noted that bought-in bucks with small antlers developed a much improved set within a year.

5.8   Behaviour

As early as 1809 Bechstein wrote in his *Handbook of Hunting Knowledge*: 'Of all German indigenous deer species, this is the only one suitable for a small park. This is because the fallow deer is more placid than other types of deer and seems not to suffer from lack of freedom.' He is also of the opinion that 'fallow deer are the most useful of all wild game for a small area'.

The following information is based on our own observations of different deer enterprises over several years, on accounts from the research station at Bommert, and on Pietrowski's two years of research at the Rhineland Agriculture Department's Teaching and Research Centre at Riswick House, Cleves. There were twenty-seven does and one buck on 1.9 ha here, while the other site studied was a deer enterprise of 2.4 ha in the Oberberg region, with thirty does and one buck. The deer at both research centres had come from wild herds, and had been set up according to the guidelines of the state of North Rhine Westphalia.

Pietrowski established that, averaged over the year, 42 per cent of the day was spent feeding, about 40 per cent resting, about 13 per cent ruminating and about 5 per cent grooming. In both herds, in each season, the number of animals lying down was lowest at sunrise and sunset. These were the times when movement was greatest.

Activity was governed by daylight, as it is with wild deer, and the daily routine of activity and rest periods also corresponded with that of deer living in the wild. The animals covered an average distance of 40 m per hour. There was a marked uniformity in the periods of time they spent moving.

The activity of the calves increased with age. Whereas at two days old they spent only about 9 per cent of their time standing or walking, at an average of twenty-nine days this was already about 40 per cent.

The herds spent the greatest part of their activity time feeding. The seasonal differences were quite small, and there were slight variations according to the area. On the observation site in the hilly area, for example, grazing activity was highest in August to October. The maximum grazing activity was in August, then it dropped considerably with the bucks, with a minimum during

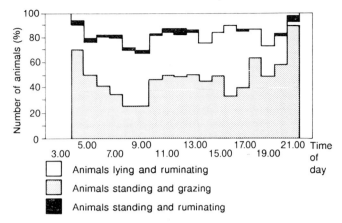

Figure 5.4 Daily periods of feeding and ruminating in June–July – average hours (*Pietrowski*).

the main rut from the middle of October to the beginning of November.

The daily periods of ruminating were especially high (16–17 per cent) in June and July. Ruminating always took place while deer were lying down, although in December and January there were rather more instances of it while standing up.

Clear daily patterns of behaviour were noticed in all the herds under observation. During the winter and through to spring the first period of eating was just before sunrise, and lasted until about 7 o'clock when the first period of ruminating would start. Figure 5.4 shows the daily times of feeding and ruminating during June and July, as recorded at Riswick House. They are largely similar to those recorded in April and May, and in August and September, and also to the behaviour of the animals at the other research site. A decreasing feed intake between 04.00 and 08.00 was noticed, with an increase in ruminating. Between 09.00 and 16.00 there followed a period of intensive feeding, with a ruminating phase of about two hours. After that came an eating period followed by ruminating for one to two hours. Then, before sunset, there was a further, particularly intensive time of feeding.

There were quite clear differences to be noticed at mating time. The typical day's pattern was changed, and there was less grazing activity in the morning. There was also some grazing at night, when there was a full moon. Sunrise and sunset had an important influence on the beginning of feeding times. Salt-lick blocks were not used by the animals being observed at Riswick House.

The calves, averaging thirty days old, spent 12.5 per cent of the day grazing, adult deer 53.2 per cent. The first rumination was observed, on average, at 19.6 days old and always, during the six weeks of the observations, took place while the calf was lying down. The average proportions of time spent grazing and ruminating were: with the does at calving time 1:0.38; with calves averaging eighteen days 1:0.11; and with calves averaging 23.3 days 1:0.31.

According to Pietrowski water was drunk an average of twice daily over the year, with the maximum from December to March (four to five times daily) and the minimum from June to September (0.4 times daily). The drinking troughs were used relatively infrequently during calving, at the beginning of lactation and during high summer. Greater water requirements resulted from the offering of supplementary feeds high in dry matter content. It was also observed that deer would eat snow.

The formation of close-knit mixed groups was noticed quite often: at Riswick House an average of 36 per cent of the times observed, while at the other site the average over the year was 31 per cent. Groups were seen mostly from December to March, and least often in the summer, from June to September. During the calving period there were less – 16–20 per cent – and during the winter months group formation was affected by the feeding of hay and silage. Single does, but in particular the buck, would isolate themselves from the rest of the herd. During the mating period the buck was seldom seen on his own. On the other hand, during the calving period the isolation of the solitary does was at its height. There were no particular times of day at which this occurred. It is interesting to note that those does which were heavier, of higher status and with a greater degree of tameness were often to be seen alone. The animals did not react when, as often happened on the hilly site, single wild fallow or roe deer appeared close to the fences.

Social grooming, i.e. licking, nuzzling and rubbing heads, was observed over 0.8 per cent of the year. Scratching and scrubbing each other did not take place. The main form of social grooming was the licking of another member of the group, most often observed in January, but none of this behaviour was seen in August and September. There was no noticeable correlation between

Plate 5.12 Grooming by licking.

the frequency of grooming of a fellow deer and its place in the 'pecking order'. We did observe deer nipping each other on the rump, mostly in the winter, when the animals were at the feeding racks; this also happened where water and supplementary feed was available. At calving time this aggressive behaviour increased, when other mothers, notably, were bitten to keep them away if there was a calf nearby.

As for the 'pecking order', at both observation sites the buck (whose antlers had been removed) was at the top of the ranking. The does would give way at his approach, particularly at supplementary feeding places. In bodily contacts between young bucks and does, which rarely happened, the antlerless bucks were generally dominant over the adult does. The animals higher up the order were more often involved in contact than the others. The number of contacts was correlated more to the body weight than to the age of the animals. There was a significant connection between pecking order, number of contacts made, age and body weight, and the degree of tameness. It can be seen from this that the process of domestication is effective and lasts over several years. Tame animals would take more of the daily concentrates offered, or of the silage in winter, than the less tame ones. They came to the feeding stations straight away, whereas the less tame ones would wait until the keeper had moved away.

During the pre-rut the bucks spent about 4 per cent of their time on antler-rubbing, cleaning and clashing. Contacts with members of adjacent groups took place through the fence, with the antlers, or with the head if the antlers had been removed. As the rut proceeded the bucks would spend about 32 per cent of their time on clashing antlers, on contacts with other males, bellowing, approaching the hinds and mating. During the main period of the

Plate 5.13   Antler removal means less problems.

rut this proportion rose to between 51 and 64 per cent; 30 to 38 per cent of the daily activity was spent on rutting calls alone. There were no rutting fights observed between adult bucks and younger ones. Threatening and pushing always meant that the lower ranking bucks would immediately give way. Antler removal led neither to an increase nor to a complete absence of aggressive behaviour. The main activity was in lengthy attempts to mate with the does, less if there were no chaser bucks present.

During the main rut the buck would spend several hours close to the doe on heat. Before the end of mating the buck would mount the doe on average 16.5 times. Activity during the secondary rut was observed up to the middle of April; Pietrowski found that the conception rate was low at that time.

The does showed striking changes in behaviour patterns for about twenty-four hours before calving. Areas with tall grass were preferred. After rain showers newborn calves in tall grass were almost dry, so this obviously afforded good protection. During calving the amniotic sac and the afterbirth were eaten by the doe. When keepers or people with dogs approached, the animals showed signs of greater restlessness. When calves were being marked the usual distance to which people could approach before the animals took flight – 10–15 m – was lessened considerably. There were no problems with taking the calf away from the mother while it was being marked or its umbilical cord treated.

Loud calls were made by the doe during the first weeks of the calf's life to encourage it to suckle. By the third or fourth week the calf would itself seek out the doe to suckle. There was a significant link between the mother's calls and the frequency of suckling. From July to September calls from does and calves were recorded during 40–81 per cent of the day.

At every suckling period the doe would lick the calf. The most usual position of the calf while suckling is nose-to-tail, parallel with the mother. It is not often behind or under her. The average length of a suckling period was seventy-two

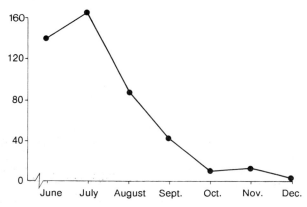

Figure 5.5 **Number of suckling periods in the herd per day (*Pietrowski*).**

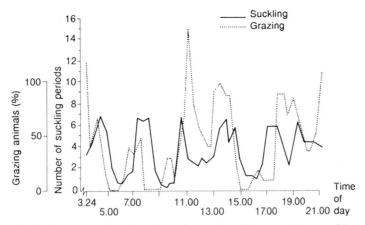

Figure 5.6   Daily schedule of feed intake and suckling activity on 25 June 1979 at Riswick House (*Pietrowski*).

seconds and the average number of periods per day 9.1, in calves at an average of eleven days old. After that the number of suckling periods decreased. As the calves grew older there were more instances of two calves suckling at the same time. At an average age of 23.3 days these were 18 per cent, at 29.2 days this was up to 25.8 per cent. In 11.6 per cent of cases, three calves would try to run up to the hind and suckle at the same time. The tolerance of the does towards strange calves varied. As a rule they were only accepted when the doe's own calf was already suckling. Even yearlings would try to suckle, but they were pushed away. Pietrowski thought that this incidence of suckling non-related calves had led to the over-estimation of twin births observed among wild herds. The mother would terminate the suckling period, and would then often turn and lick her calf. As the calf grew older the number of these contacts lessened.

The daily pattern of feed intake and suckling was remarkably similar at both sites, as shown in Figure 5.6. The frequency of suckling dropped in July and was very low in October and November – an important consideration when deciding whether the calves can be weaned before the beginning of the rutting season.

At two days calves could already be seen running (play behaviour) in the early evening. A week later running, jumping, leaping and mock fights were observed. At eleven days the first signs of riding were seen, with rolling over. At twenty-three days the maximum play time was reached: 4.2 per cent of the day.

Behaviour towards enemies was observed with dogs and cats. If these approached the farm, the hinds would goose-step up to them, even apart from calving time, and run along the fence (see Plate 5.14). It seemed that when the deer were lying down the body was positioned according to the wind direction. The head would be turned away from the wind, in spite of this limiting the visual and olfactory field. In both farms the direction in which the body lay was away from the neighbouring farm. Single does would spend an average of 0.6

Plate 5.14   Dogs and cats are driven off by kicking.

per cent of their time on spontaneous safety behaviour. When disturbed this was between 17 and 29 per cent, while with bucks it was between 16 and 36 per cent. Basically there was no difference to be seen between the behaviour of male and female animals. When disturbed they would gather in large, tight groups. If someone came nearer than 10–15 m, the animals would take flight, an adult doe always leading the group as it fled. The tamest animals did not always join the fleeing herd. Movement patterns, as with wild herds, were not observed. Stocking density and the size of the farm did not seem to influence the daily pattern of behaviour on either site.

Calves would take flight earlier than adults. They would form into groups to go to the feeding station, if the adults were gathered there and the keeper had left. The readiness to take flight and the degree of tameness were correlated with rank, age and body weight.

Between 4 and 5 per cent of the total time was spent on grooming, when lying or standing; most often this took the form of licking each other while standing (see Plate 5.12). The main period for this was in February and March. Defecating was while grazing or on the move in 42 per cent of the cases, 8 per cent during grooming. There were no sites particularly chosen, the animals defecating or urinating just where they happened to be.

The shelters provided on both sites were much used during periods of rain, especially sudden heavy showers. During prolonged rainy periods feeding would resume in the open, while in the period April to September the animals seemed to show a preference for areas of pasture which were in the shade.

As for the general influence of weather conditions on the animals' behaviour,

Plate 5.15   The older animals are first to feed from the hand.

Pietrowski found that there was a connection between air temperature, intensity of sunlight and humidity and their behaviour, but that wind and cloud seemed to have little effect.

The animals gradually became accustomed to the keeper through feeding with concentrates, bread, maize, sugar lumps, etc. The offering of tempting food accompanied by whistling or calling of names was effective. The animals could then be called up from a greater distance and tamed more easily. During feeding the animals should always be spoken to gently. Avoid all sudden movements, especially with younger animals, as they are timid and readily take flight. Older animals will take food first, and they are also the first to feed from the hand or a bucket. Be careful with antlered stags. As they become less timid they will push the keeper or the bucket away and can easily cause injuries, which is why it is always better to remove their antlers.

At the trials centre we were able to establish that animals rested and ruminated mostly in the open, even if woodland or shelters were available. Even when snow was lying 50 cm deep most of the herd would stay out in the open and scrape out resting places in the snow. Shelter from the wind is necessary, however. It is interesting to note that fallow deer apparently have premonitions about weather conditions well in advance: it was often noticed that they would find a place sheltered from the wind before the onset of severe storms or snowfall. They seek shade when it is very hot.

Even in herds with a high tolerance of humans, the approach of a stranger to within 30–50 m will cause animals to take flight. With young deer and calves the distance would be greater than with older animals. This behaviour

Plate 5.16 Take care! Stag with antlers!

Plate 5.17 Resting scrapes in the snow.

Plate 5.18 Little movement is made in snowy conditions, to conserve energy.

Plate 5.19 Young animals are very timid.

is an advantage on farms which are isolated, as it offers protection against poachers.

There seemed to be a tolerance for other farm animals, such as cattle, sheep and horses. However, caution is needed if they are grazing together at calving time, as the calves could be in danger from jealousy and biting by the other stock.

Opponents of deer farming might put forward arguments about the possible escape of deer, and associated problems such as cross-breeding with wild deer, claims for damages, traffic accidents, etc. In the trials and on the research farms escapes were due to gates and doors being left open, to land slips and in one case to poachers who had cut the fence and driven the herd out. In only one case was the cause of escape unknown. The deer always tried to get back into the paddock, to join the rest of the herd. Even those which had previously been on larger show farms would run up and down outside the fence. After poachers had let many of the deer out of the paddock, this behaviour occurred within one day. This conduct, along with the aggression shown towards dogs coming on to the farm, shows that the animals are familiar with their own territory. They can easily be led back if approached quietly and tempted with food.

Under no circumstances should deer be driven or scared. When attempts were made to gather deer by means of a net held over them by several men, it led to panicky flight, jumping at the fence, and finally as the chain of helpers drew closer, to the deer jumping over the nets and the men. Even at the height

Plate 5.20 The animals willingly come up to a keeper who is holding tempting food.

of their panic no deer jumped over the outer fence. It is therefore advisable for the keeper to catch the animals by using tempting food and a trusted voice and clothing. No more than one additional trusted person should help if the animals are calm: guide them without moving quickly or making wild gestures. Always remember that deer notice an intruder in the herd immediately, watch him constantly and react quickly to his presence. Flight may be started off by the leader of the herd, but also quite often by the most timid animal.

6 Grassland Husbandry

When fallow deer start grazing grassland and rough pasture which has previously been used for cattle, sheep or horses there are considerable changes. Fallow deer pastures have no manure heaps, dung and urine being spread evenly, so grass growing on these manured spots is eaten along with the rest. In wet weather and in winter the smaller hooves of the deer cause less damage than those of cattle or horses. This is especially noticeable on sloping land where, after a few years, the sward becomes thicker and the ground less bare. It is not advisable to have footpaths along the outside of the fence if the deer pastures are near busy roads or paths, however, as people might feed the animals.

6.1 Mowing

The growth profile of the sward is important. Under normal conditions grass begins to grow in March, reaching a peak at about the end of May. These dates are influenced by the soil temperature, soil type, drainage and pasture species, and they also differ according to region and altitude (see Figure 6.1). During the growing period the nutritional value of the pasture is continually changing. As the plants mature the water content decreases, the crude fibre content increases, and the digestibility, crude protein content and important minerals are all reduced.

Patchy and unproductive land should be reseeded, according to local conditions, in March–April or July–August, by over-sowing or shallow sod-seeding with a standard seed mixture at about 5–7 kg per ha. If, after several years' grazing, there are still some weedy areas with a high proportion of broadleaved weeds such as chickweed and buttercup, poor quality grasses, couch grass and docks, then a fresh sowing should be made in March–April in shallow drills 10–12 cm apart.

When planning the year's work it is important to remember that it is not necessary to mow pasture grazed by fallow deer until the beginning of July. There should still be enough growth at the beginning of winter to supply the animals with a part of their feed needs so this, together with some supplementary feeding, should carry them through to the beginning of spring growth.

Mowing is completely unnecessary if the stocking density is sufficient to keep down the heavy growth in April–June, and if the supplementary winter forage can be cut from outside fields. The beginning of July is the best time to cut for forage. Hay-making is a good idea if there are storage facilities nearby, otherwise silage-making should be undertaken. This is less labour intensive, usually

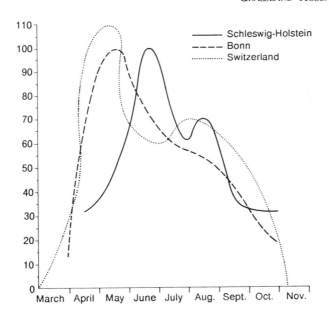

Figure 6.1   Grass growth on different sites (*Klapp, Knauer, Rieder*).

means lower nutrient losses and is also less dependent on the weather. A silo will be needed, but the crop can be harvested with a tractor and attachments if these are on the farm already. If the farm is too small to justify year-round tractor use, then hiring or borrowing machinery may be the answer.

In our experience, sloping land does not need to be mown if the right plans are made. The paddocks can be fenced off to ensure that the flush of grass in spring through to mid-July is fully utilised by the animals. Level fields could then be left ungrazed or only partly grazed, and cuts made from them for winter forage.

The aim should be to use as much home-grown forage as possible, and not only for husbandry reasons. The cost in Germany per MJ of Metabolisable Energy is about 7.5p for grassland, 12.4p for hay and about 24p for bought-in concentrates. If possible the feeding level should be uniform over the whole year, according to need, even when this is not always easy because of weather conditions.

The nutritional need per 'fallow deer unit' – hind + calf + yearling – is about 20,200 kJ ME per day from January to March, rising to about 20,600 kJ ME until sale or slaughter of the young animals, and falling considerably in the late autumn (see Figure 6.2). The figure is influenced by the animals' different needs at different times, for example the varying requirements of pregnant or suckling hinds.

If the nutritional needs of the deer and the growth of the pasture are compared, it is obvious that there is a surplus of forage in spring, a shortage in August and September if weather conditions are bad, and a sharply increased

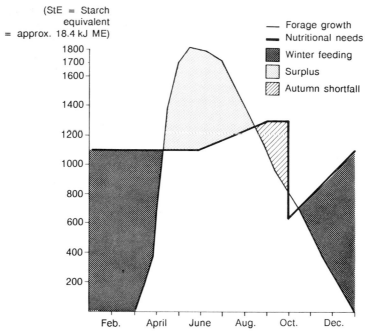

Figure 6.2 Forage growth and nutritional needs.

need for supplementary feeding in November to April. The surplus spring forage should be conserved for autumn and winter use. What is really vital is that there is sufficient growth of grass in August and September, otherwise supplementary feed must be offered.

6.2 Weed Control

Weeds which are seldom or never eaten, such as stinging nettles, should be cut down in the early years of the ley. Fallow deer will eat mown and wilted nettles and thistles, especially in autumn.

With smaller weeds which will not be eaten, chemical herbicides may be necessary. Our experience shows that it is very important to get the better of weeds in fields which have been neglected for years, by means of grazing, mowing, weed-killing methods and manuring.

6.3 Manuring

Manuring is important for several reasons. The quality of the sward and the nutritional value of the forage is dependent on the care given to the land and the efficiency of the fertilisers used. The animals' mineral needs should, if possible, be fully met by the forage.

The quality of the pasture is especially important when the fields are intensively stocked, however, as it affects the number of animals that can be grazed per hectare. The deer farmer must strive to produce as much fodder as possible from his own fields, to avoid the high cost of bought-in feed. Manuring can also influence the seasonal changes in the composition of the sward. If nitrogen applications are carefully timed, the natural fluctuations in growth can be levelled out a little. (Maximum growth occurs in May–June, as already mentioned.)

Before starting a deer farm it is advisable to test the soil for its clay, silt and humus content, while soil tests for potash, phosphorus, magnesium and lime are also recommended initially and then every three years. The levels of copper and sodium in the soil should be checked about every ten years.

Soil samples are usually taken to a depth of 10 cm over the relevant area and then sent to a laboratory for testing. It is best to do the tests between late autumn and spring, so as to have the information available before manuring is started. The farmer can do his own sampling. Forty core samples of 500 g, 10 cm deep should be taken over 1 ha; carefully mix them in a tub and send, packed in plastic bags or other containers, to a reputable laboratory. Areas near the field perimeter and those where there are piles of manure or feed residues should be excluded, as these can give false readings.

Recommended levels of nutritional content and pH value per 100 g of soil are:

Potash	15–20 mg (sand to sandy loam)
	15–28 mg (loam to clay)
Phosphorus	20–25 mg
Magnesium	8–12 mg
pH value	5.0 (sand to sandy loam)
	5.5 (loam)
	6.0 (clayey loam to clay)

The winter months are the best time for applying these fertilisers, but they can also be put on while the animals are grazing in the paddocks, with the exception, of course, of burnt lime. Fertilisers should not be spread on wet grass, if possible.

To provide potash, a material such as Kainite is best, while for magnesium deficiency Kainite, magnesium limestone should be used. There is a wide choice when it comes to phosphates such as Rock Phosphate or Triple Super. To give the values shown above a general application of 40 kg P_2O_5 and 60 kg K_2O per ha would be sufficient per year.

The first dressing of nitrogen – 40–60 kg per ha, applied as straight nitrogen – should be given with the first growth of forage in March–April. Later applications of nitrogen can be made at the same level, up to the middle of September, to satisfy forage needs. Reckon on a nitrogen requirement of 1–2 kg per ha per day between dressings, that is a total of 180–360 kg of nitrogen for the season, according to the stocking density and the quality of the sward.

Fischer's research has indicated that it is advisable, in areas which are mostly dry in summer, to apply nitrogen in winter so as to take advantage of damp weather and help towards accelerating the spring flush of growth. In those areas with higher levels of summer rainfall, however, application should be concentrated more in the summer months, to ensure a good level of forage spread over the season. In water-gathering and conservation areas nitrogen dressing must be kept within the maximum desirable levels as indicated by research and local regulations.

The equivalent of 1 kg nitrogen is about 80–90 kg of grass dry matter produced. The agriculturally viable limits of application are about 280 kg nitrogen per ha in upland areas and about 360 kg per ha in the lowlands. The figures will obviously be less in those pastures with more than 10 per cent of white clover in the sward.

Costs per kilogram of straight nitrogen vary according to the type of fertiliser used. Fertiliser prices vary considerably, so it is always best to obtain several quotations before purchase.

According to our experience so far, care must be taken with fertilisers containing copper, as fallow deer are very susceptible to a high level of copper.

6.4   Fencing and Equipment

Fencing, and particularly the outer fences, should be inspected at least once a week for damage and gaps near the ground. This is particularly vital near busy paths and roads. The strainers can also be adjusted then, as necessary, so it is useful if those checking the fences carry with them tools such as hammers, pincers, strainers, nails and wire. Every few weeks make sure that the nails on the inside of the fence are still secure.

At least once a year check the posts – particularly the corner posts, but also the intermediates – by applying strong pressure to make sure they are firm and sound. Gates and doors which are in constant use need a specially careful and regular check, particularly the locks and fasteners. (Gates are often the weak points in fencing, as was mentioned earlier.)

To make sure the animals have a constant supply of clear drinking water check drinking points daily or every few days. These can be contaminated with soil, dung or feed residue, supply and drain pipes may be blocked, and in winter they can freeze.

The state of feeding areas is most important, particularly in winter. Feed residue should not be left lying on the ground, but removed because decaying or rotten foodstuffs can lead to ill-health, or even the death of animals. Under no circumstances should leftovers be put back into the racks: this is false economy. Leftover feed and dung should be collected up weekly from the hard standing and taken away. It is a good idea to scatter lime lightly on the area, and also round the feeding troughs, as this acts as a disinfectant.

7 Nutrition and Feeding

by Professor Dr W. Hartfiel

An animal's life system is shaped by various chemical and physiological processes, and the intake of a great variety of nutrients is necessary for these to function properly. Nutrients serve both to build the body and to supply energy. As the food eaten has a high molecular structure it must be broken down by enzymes before it can be absorbed into the body. These processes differ between animals. Ruminants, the group to which fallow deer belong, possess four stomachs and so are much more successful in breaking down food than those animals, such as pigs and poultry, which have only one stomach. In particular, ruminants are able to make good use of foodstuffs containing cellulose.

The particular food needs of the fallow deer are still relatively unknown. Present details are incomplete and much information is borrowed from what is known about other ruminating wild or farmed animals, such as sheep. Some of the following observations, therefore, are partly based on data which have not come from fallow deer.

7.1 Physiology of the Digestive System and its Function in Ruminants

Nutrients in food should be supplied in certain quantities and the ration must also be balanced. After the intake of unchopped forage, the following breaking-down processes occur in the ruminant: salivating and swallowing the coarsely chopped forage; the partial digestion of this in the rumen by bacteria; this is interspersed with much ruminating to make the pieces smaller; and mixing with saliva. Then the contents pass to the omasum and finally through the abomasum, where they are broken down by enzymes, to the small intestine. Feed material still not digested is separated off into the rectum, where a further breaking-down process takes place.

The ruminant's saliva is formed in various glands in the region of the mouth. With the adult animal there is a continual secretion of saliva during ruminating and when eating (Brüggemann et al.). This varies in level according to the type of fodder, its dry matter content, its structure and its digestibility. The apparent function of the saliva in ruminants is partly to give the food to be swallowed a better consistency and partly to neutralise the volatile fatty acids which are formed in the rumen. This is possible because of the saliva's quite alkaline pH of 8–9. The inorganic contents of the saliva are mainly bicarbonates of sodium and potassium, phosphate and chloride. Organic constituents include proteins and other nitrogen compounds of which an important one may be urea.

117

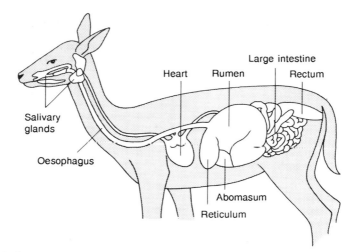

Figure 7.2   Diagram of the stomach of ruminants (*Geiger et al.*).

The fodder of the ruminant is roughly masticated, salivated and swallowed into the rumen, where micro-organisms begin the digestive process. About 20–40 minutes after the end of feeding there is usually a first period of rumination, when whole boluses are regurgitated into the mouth through the gullet. This process is sub-divided into phases of sucking in and expelling. Regurgitation occurs as a reflex action controlled by the nervous system and can be influenced by both internal or external factors. The most important factor is the structure and digestibility of the fodder. Rough forage such as hay and straw promotes rumination and increases its duration, whereas finely structured foodstuffs greatly reduce the length of rumination. There is also a change in the pH, to the acid or the alkaline side, depending upon the contraction of the reticulum and rumen and the ruminating process. This often occurs when there is a sharp drop in the pH level following a build up of lactic acid, which may arise after eating foodstuffs containing a lot of easily digested carbohydrates (e.g. starches, sugar).

During rumination the food is broken down, mixed with saliva and then regurgitated to undergo further fermentative microbial processes in the rumen. The refining process is initiated mainly by means of several different stomach gases. The most important of these are carbon dioxide (CO_2), methane (CH_4) and hydrogen (H_2), which bring about the formation of monosaccharide sugars (the end-products of the breakdown of carbohydrates). Methane, which is of high energy value, is produced by special methane-forming bacteria which are present in large numbers in the rumen. The mixture of salivated gases builds to a certain level of pressure in the rumen until it is finally expelled in rhythmic bursts (eructation) through the oesophagus. In cattle, quantities of 45 litres of methane have been recorded over a period of twenty-four hours. Figures for fallow deer are not available, but are obviously much lower.

After food particles have been broken down and partly digested in the rumen, they are passed continually through the omasum. This organ consists of sheets of fibrous tissue (leaf-like internal walls) which draw off a large proportion of the water, volatile fatty acids, minerals salts, ammonia and CO_2 from the mixture leaving the rumen. The concentrated mass of food then goes to the abomasum, which secretes an acid digestive juice, and there begins the breakdown of the food by enzymes produced by the organisms themselves and separated off in the abomasum.

The end-products of this process are mainly amino acids, monosaccharides and free fatty acids, which pass through the gut wall into the body. With the help of the bloodstream and lymph glands they pass through the liver and other glands to be used for the various bodily functions, to be stored as fat or to provide for the production of meat, or milk, when lactating.

The absorption of the food which has been broken down by enzymes is mainly completed in the duodenum, while in the final intestine a thickening of the remaining food mass takes place as the liquid is drawn off. The microbiological changes which take place here are of little importance for the nutrition of the animal, as the products formed in this area, with few exceptions, are little used and are shortly excreted along with the undigested material.

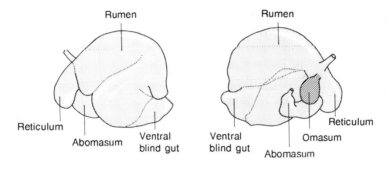

Figure 7.2 Diagram of the stomach of ruminants (*Geiger et al.*).

Together with the food nutrients reaching the abomasum, the bacteria and protozoa formed in the rumen have an important role to play in a ruminant's nourishment. These micro-organisms are constantly carried with the food flow to the abomasum and digested by the body's own enzymes, as mentioned above. The importance of these tiny organisms lies mainly in their high protein content – but it is not only their quantity but also their quality and biological value which is important. The formation of body-building proteins needs essential amino acids; these cannot generally be created by the body itself, but are taken in as protein contained in the foodstuffs. Only ruminants (and horses, which have a large blind gut) are the exception to this rule, in that they are able to synthesise these essential amino acids themselves, by means of the micro-organisms which are present in the rumen, where they multiply rapidly.

Table 7.1   Amino acid content in the protein of rumen bacteria and protozoa and of meadow grass and maize (g amino acids/100 g protein)

Essential amino acids	Protozoa[1]	Bacteria[1]	Rye grass[2]	Maize[2]
Lysin	8.9	6.7	5.6	2.9
Methionin	1.1	4.4	2.3	1.9
Cystin	2.2	3.2	1.4	2.0
Tyrosin	4.5	6.6	4.6	4.1
Arginin	3.2	3.7	8.8	4.6
Histidin	1 4	3.2	2.0	2.7
Isoleucin	5.8	5.4		3.7
Leucin	6.8	7.0		11.5
Phenylalanin	4.9	4.8	4.2	4.7
Valin	4.7	5.3	6.4	4.5
Threonin	4.4	5.3	4.1	3.5

Sources: [1] B. Piatrowski; [2] DLG Tables of Food Values.

Table 7.1 enables a comparison to be made between the amino acid content of the bacteria and protozoa proteins and that of the generally high level of grass and the lower level of maize or other crops. Note the importance of the amino acid lysin, which occurs in large amounts in the protein of the micro-organisms, in the digestive system of the ruminant.

The rumen, with the reticulum, is the largest organ of the ruminant's digestive tract. Its size is essential for the ruminant's intake of bulk forage, which contains only a small percentage of nutrients and thus a large proportion of highly indigestible matter, compared with the food ration of animals with only one stomach. Figure 7.3 shows the size of rumen and reticulum reached

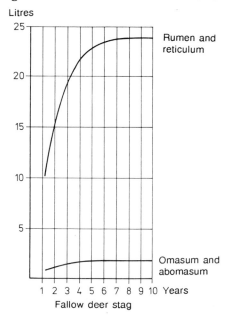

Figure 7.3   Growth of the capacity of the digestive organs (*Bubenik*).

in the fallow deer, compared with that of the omasum and abomasum. The rumen and reticulum can reach a capacity of 23–4 litres, that of the omasum and abomasum 1.8–2 litres. According to Drescher-Kaden this maximum volume would be reached at a body weight of 100 kg. As the average weight of a fallow deer is about 70 kg (54–102 kg), the capacity of the rumen would usually be about 17 litres. However, according to Drescher-Kaden, only about 44 per cent (plus or minus 10 per cent) of this capacity is used when deer are grazing freely. As the stomach capacity as compared with the body weight is a measure of the speed at which microbial changes take place, the ability of the fallow deer to break down feedstuffs high in crude fibre content is very good (Hungate). A comparison made by Nagy and Regelin between roe, fallow and red deer showed the rumen and omasum of the fallow deer to have the largest volume compared with body weight.

A special peculiarity of the ruminant, apart from the size of the rumen, is its lining with a membrane which has a large number of soft hairs called villi. These increase the surface area of the stomach lining, and cause a better and quicker absorption of the products of the breakdown of material by the digestive fluids. The length of an individual villus varies from 0.01–1.0 mm at the lower end of the scale to 10.51–12.00 mm at the top, according to Langer's classification. Most of them are between 1.5 and 6.0 mm long. With fallow deer, Langer reckoned that the mean factor of increase of the surface area was 5–6, but that there were large variations which could be caused by different circumstances (age, regional and seasonal influences, effect of the biotope), as the animals examined had been killed in different parts of Schleswig-Holstein and at different times. It was apparent, however, that there were differences, in the fallow deer, between the various areas of the digestive system as to the separation of differently structured food components. From our own research we discovered that the villi are longer in the bottom area of the rumen than at the top, but the longest ones are to be found in the omasum (Enzinger and Hartfiel).

Changes in the rumen villi according to food intake can also be seen in cattle and sheep. There was a positive correlation between the length of the villi with the fodder consumption, and of the length and thickness of the hairs with the DM intake (Kunkel *et al.*). High proportions (70 per cent) of rough fodder lead to shorter hairs in cattle, according to Bleichner and Ellis. With sheep, under similar conditions, a thinning of these hairs was noticed (Nockels *et al.*). Under similar conditions of feeding and husbandry, the numbers of villi per square centimetre at various identical areas of the rumen were measured at 80–140 with fallow deer and 54–79 with sheep (Enzinger and Hartfiel).

However, Kauffold found no change in the stomach lining after feeding a ration with 65 per cent straw, as against one of hay. After several years of adding urea to the feed there was also no deviation from the normal condition. After feeding rations lacking in fibre, however, detrimental changes were noted in the stomach's mucous membrane. After a barley feed, a hard coating on the mucous membrane (hyperkeratose) occurred in nearly all the animals. Also noticed were clusters of villi (49 per cent), losses of villi (29 per cent), atrophy of villi (43 per cent) and inflammation of the stomach lining (Fell *et al.*). Feeding dry, chopped forage only, according to Vidacs and Ward, led to hardening of the mucous membrane and also to atrophy in some areas after only four to six days.

These observations on the changes in the stomach lining are very important for the feeding of ruminants in general. Many mistakes may be made because of lack of knowledge about correct nutrition, which could lead to a deterioration in the performance and health of the animals.

7.2   Digestion by Micro-organisms in the Rumen

Enzyme reactions are made possible by the secretions of the body's glands. The rumen does not have glands in the mucous membrane, so such reactions cannot take place there. Rather, the rumen is to be seen as a large fermenting chamber, in which considerable microbial breaking-down and building-up processes take place. As this first organ of the digestive tract has an important part to play, which cannot be observed, or only to a lesser extent in the relatively small abomasum, the ruminant's food must be suitable for the microbial processes which take place in the rumen. To put this briefly, one must first satisfy the living conditions of the microflora of the rumen and then apply oneself to the nutritional needs of the animal.

The siting of micro-organisms in the stomach occurs soon after birth, by transfer from the mother (licking) and by early eating of green material which contains these tiny living cells. There is no evidence at present about the number and type of bacteria in farmed fallow deer, but there has been comparable research with wild deer. Crha found there to be 447,000 cells per ml of digestive fluid (plus or minus 58,500). Our own first results gave a rather higher figure, depending on type and quantity of feed, of 4,000,000–5,400,000 cells per ml (Enzinger and Hartfiel).

During their comparative research on red and fallow deer, and also roe deer, Prins and Geelen found the overall figures and proportions of species for protozoa shown in Table 7.2. From this we see that there are more protozoa in the rumen of the fallow deer than in the red deer, and many more than

Table 7.2   Numbers and types of protozoa in the rumen of red, fallow and roe deer

	Red deer	Fallow deer	Roe deer
Number of animals	10	16	6
Total protozoa	4.22	5.91	1.64
$(\times 10^5/ml)$	(1.62–9.50)	(1.06–22.30)	(0–2.60)
Percentage			
Dasytricha	0–1.6	nil	nil
Isotricha	0–1.6	nil	nil
Entodinium	84.0–99.3	84.5–100	0–100
Diplodinium	0–3.5	0–5.5	nil
Eudiplodinium	0–8.0	0–15.5	nil
Elytroplastron	0–0.05	nil	nil
Epidinium	0–6.5	nil	nil

Source: Prins and Geelen.

Table 7.3 Micro-organisms in the rumen of roe deer, fallow deer and mouflon

	Roe deer	Fallow deer	Mouflon
Number of animals	13	10	7
Animals without protozoa	9	0	0
∅ number of protozoa × 10^3/g rumen content	62	1,325 ± 263	730 ± 208
∅ number of bacteria × 10^{10}/g rumen content	3.0 ± 1.5	1.8 ± 1.3	1.9 ± 0.8

Source: Drescher-Kaden and Seifelnasr.

in the roe deer. The differences between the deer species are probably due to different feeding habits. Our researches also found the species dasytricha, isotricha and epidinium in fallow deer rumen (Enzinger and Hartfiel).

Similar research was undertaken by Drescher-Kaden and Seifelnasr on roe deer, fallow stags and mouflon (Table 7.3). From this it appeared that the animals, from various woodland areas in southern Germany, showed big differences in the total numbers of protozoa. Thus on one site the fallow deer figures were 1,325,000 per gram stomach content, and on another only 115,000 per gram. The bacteria in the rumen were generally more numerous than the protozoa. The figures for fallow deer were somewhat similar to those for the mouflon, which is a grazing animal eating grass or rough forage, as do sheep or cattle (Hofmann). When the fallow deer is eating hay and/or straw, the number of protozoa in the rumen is smaller than when it is fed on green forages and concentrates (Enzinger and Hartfiel).

These figures on the microflora are important, as one is able to ascertain by microbial means whether or not an animal is capable of breaking down this or that food material efficiently in the rumen. Samples were always taken from a carcass of the wild animals in the experiments, although it would appear that there was no influence on the microflora present in the rumen, in spite of the trouble taken to undertake research immediately after death. This is emphasised by Treichler's similar comparative tests on living animals.

Fallow deer have a large stomach for their body weight and similar microflora to the red deer (Nagy and Regelin). This underlines the fact that the ruminating ungulates are separated into grazing types, and the fallow deer is classified as a mixed grazer which tends to prefer grass, but cannot survive without a high fibre content in its diet. According to Drescher-Kaden, however, this classification does not always mean that the animals show typical feeding habits and digestive processes under different environmental conditions. It must be said that ruminants, in spite of differences in their rumen size and other variations in this area, can cope very well with a feeding regime which distinguishes them from other groups of grazing animals.

For the microflora of the rumen to be effective, it is important that conditions are just right. There are two main needs: a constant availability of nutrients and a precise level of acidity in the stomach contents. With the continual passage of digestive fluids from the rumen to the abomasum, following the grinding and breaking down of cellulose-rich food particles, there is a drop in the level of nutrients available to the bacteria and protozoa. The ruminant must therefore eat large amounts of food to prevent the loss of these nutrients leading to a decline in the number of organisms and so to an interruption in the breakdown of further food intake. If a break of 36–48 hours in feeding were to occur, it would mean an immediate loss of function in the stomach of the ruminant, unlike those animals with a single stomach system, such as pigs or hens. Similar results follow sudden changes in feeding regimes, as the micro-organisms can react only slowly to the different nutrients, which they do by increasing the population of specific types. According to the type of fodder, this can take up to six weeks.

The level of acidity (pH value) is the second factor to be considered. In general the normal pH value in the stomach of ruminating farm animals is in the slightly acidic region of 6.2–6.8. Research with dead wild deer indicated the lower level of 5.7–5.9, however. According to Short the levels are similar in white-tailed deer. Prins and Geelen attribute this lower level to the higher proportion of lactic acid in the stomach. Treichler, on the other hand, puts the view that they may be due to changes occurring in the rumen after the death of the beast. Another, perhaps better explanation is that the fodder eaten by animals examined, which had come from the wild, contained less fibre and more carbohydrates. This would lead to higher quantities of lactic acid being produced, and at the same time a reduction in alkaline saliva because of the lower level of ruminating activity in the rumen. It would be wrong to assume, though, that because the protozoa and bacteria of the rumen of ruminating farm animals survive best in a pH level of about 6.2–6.8, those in the fallow deer need a more acidic environment. The feeding of the deer should be monitored to ensure a sufficient proportion of fibre content so that there is a good level of rumination and thus a better secretion of saliva. This is the way to keep the pH value of the digestive fluids at its most efficient level.

The reason for over-acidity in the stomach is the presence of volatile fatty acids produced there, of which acetic acid is in the greatest quantity, but lactic acid leads to the severest lowering of the pH level. Details are given in later sections of this chapter.

7.3   Metabolism in the Rumen

What are the functions of the microflora in the rumen? They can be divided into three main areas:

- Breakdown of carbohydrates.
- Breakdown of nitrogen.
- Breakdown of fats.

Carbohydrates are mostly broken down by the micro-organisms in the rumen. However, there are big differences between the various types of carbohydrates, shown in the speed at which breakdown occurs and in the resulting end-products.

Starches are broken down quite quickly in the rumen, by enzymes. The resulting fermentation leads to a release of energy, mainly in the form of

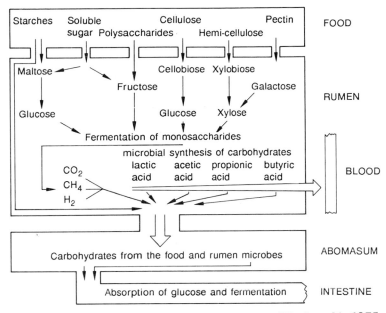

Figure 7.4   Metabolism of carbohydrates in ruminants (*Piatkowski 1975, revised*).

methane and heat. Material end-products are volatile fatty acids, particularly acetic, lactic and propionic acids. Lactic acid especially leads to a drop in the pH level in the rumen, as we have just mentioned. If large quantities of starchy food are eaten there may be over-acidity, which will affect the function of the bacteria and protozoa acting on cellulose. The result is often an upset in the functioning of the rumen due to an acidic stomach, and this can lead to the animal going off its food and showing other symptoms of ill-health.

Sugars are used by the microflora as a source of energy for the building of their body tissue. They also build up carbohydrates which can be stored in the abomasum of the ruminant as glycogen after they have been broken down. The direct absorption of monosaccharides (simple sugars) through the stomach wall only happens rarely.

Polysaccharides are soluble carbohydrates. These are broken down, passing through fructose to volatile fatty acids.

Cellulose is broken down by specific bacteria and protozoa, along with which the enzymes glucosidate and cellobiate are essential. Cellobiose and glucose are intermediate and end-products of this process. The monosaccharide glucose serves primarily to create more volatile fatty acids.

To enable the growth of these micro-organisms, easily digested carbohydrates and, above all, nitrogen-containing substances are essential. Free ammonia (NH_3) must always be available as a source of the nitrogen necessary for life (Bryant). This ammonia can be produced by the liberation of amino acids from the food protein or else from urea added to the feed by the action of the urea enzymes of the rumen's micro-organisms.

Hemicellulose and pentosan are broken down largely by microbes in the rumen. With both substances – cellulose and hemicellulose – the degree of fibre, i.e. the lignum content, is important for the level of digestibility.

The last group of carbohydrates shown in Figure 7.4 is the pectins. These are also broken down by enzymes with the help of bacteria and are utilised by the ruminant. The last stages of the process are the formation of monosaccharides and finally free fatty acids.

The synthesised volatile fatty acids, which arise from the action of the bacteria and protozoa on the carbohydrates in the rumen, can pass directly through the walls of the rumen, reticulum and abomasum into the veins of the bloodstream. The speed of this transfer depends on the pH value and on the 'chain length' of the fatty acids. According to Aafjes's research, a maximum concentration of these could be found in the blood thirty minutes, at the most, after the intake of free fatty acids into the rumen. It was shown that lactic acid passes into the blood more quickly than propionic acid, and this in its turn is quicker than acetic acid. Lactic acid, formed in large quantities by the breaking down of easily digested carbohydrates, shows a speed of absorption only one-tenth that of the suitably named volatile fatty acids.

The protein in fodder is largely broken down in the rumen of the ruminant via the intermediate steps of peptide and then amino acids. These processes allow the micro-organisms to build up their own bodies from the synthesised protein. However, deaminisation by the enzymes also takes place, in which the amino acids (NH_2) are split up and processed into ammonia.

This breaking down of protein is a relatively swift process, the maximum

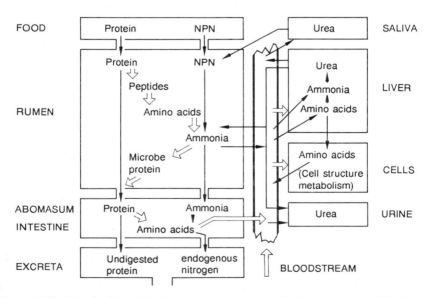

Figure 7.5 Metabolism of nitrogenous compounds in ruminants (*Piatkowski 1975, revised*).

being reached within two to four hours of food intake. The quantity of ammonia formed is, however, dependent on the type of food protein. Thus there is a lower concentration of NH_3 after an intake of protein in the form of fish meal, maize or rape than, for example, with groundnuts and above all milk protein, which has a very high content (Gürtler). There are also big differences between silage and hay. With a feed containing cocksfoot grass silage the NH_3 concentration in the rumen was double that after an intake of hay made from the same type of grass. Also young, protein-rich grass means a higher concentration of ammonia in the rumen than does older grass with higher crude fibre (Piatkowski).

Part of the ammonia is used and developed by the microflora of the rumen for the synthesising of protein for their body building. The surplus passes through the stomach wall into the bloodstream and so to the liver. As a high concentration of NH_3 is toxic when it builds up in the body, it is synthesised into urea in the liver. From here it passes back through the stomach wall in the bloodstream or back into the omasum in the saliva. In this way a continual balance is kept between the level of the NH_3 in the rumen and the urea in the blood. The urea passing into the rumen is changed back to ammonia by the ureal enzymes formed in the vicinity of the stomach wall. The same reaction takes place in the rumen following the intake of urea with the fodder.

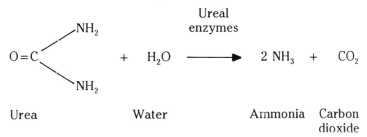

| Urea | Water | Ammonia | Carbon dioxide |

Part of the urea, i.e. the surplus, is voided through the kidneys in urine. Undigested nitrogen-containing substances are excreted.

Too high an intake of protein-rich fodder rarely leads to ammonia poisoning; the cause of this is more likely to be infrequent, too large, doses of urea or similar substances. If the microflora of the rumen is allowed to absorb these doses gradually, however, so that they can cope with the input, the danger of toxicity is much reduced. Also, with large quantities of easily digested carbohydrates in the ration, an increase in the NH_3 level in the rumen and also in the blood can be prevented, as there is a quicker and higher rate of synthesising of protein by the microflora.

Some of the symptoms of ammonia poisoning are restlessness, muscle twitching and increased saliva flow. Also urinating and defecating are more frequent. A dose of diluted acetic acid has proved to be a very effective antidote.

Special attention should be given to supplementary feeding of fats to ruminants. The three fatty acids, usually with the addition of one molecule of glycerine, are partially hydrolised by the bacteria enzymes in the rumen, so free fatty acids are formed when water is added. The glycerine released in this process is used by the micro-organisms in the building up of volatile fatty acids.

The free fatty acids separate in the area of the rumen. Those with fourteen and more carbon atoms (long-chained fatty acids) go through the digestive tract via the abomasum to the upper small intestine, where their final absorption takes place. They undergo no further changes during their passage.

Medium-length chain fatty acids with up to ten carbon atoms pass straight through the stomach wall into the bloodstream. Only about 30 per cent of lauric acid (twelve carbon atoms), according to researches on dairy cows by Hagemeister *et al.*, is passed through the stomach wall, while the remaining larger percentage is taken through the abomasum for absorption in the small intestine, as with the long-chained fatty acids.

The action of the rumen bacteria is important for the unsaturated fatty acids. They can hydrogenise fats by their own enzymes, i.e. with the carbon atoms in the area of a double bond about one atom of hydrogen is accumulated. In this way, for example, oily acids with a partial hydrogenising process can be produced from the essential linoleic acid with two double bonds, and stearin acids with the full process. Researches by Hagemeister and Kaufmann, using stomach tubes and catheters to by-pass the intestines, showed that linoleic acid with two double bonds was hydrogenised up to about 75 per cent in the rumen of dairy cattle. With the unsaturated fatty acids of about C-18 (18:1, 18:2, 18:3), the rate was about 60 per cent. The critical factor is whether the fats or fatty acids are compatible with the enzymes of the rumen's microflora, in which case they can be subjected to the enzymatic process, or whether they are protected in the cells of the foodstuffs during their passage through the rumen and reach the abomasum, where the enzymatic digestive process takes place. In this way unsaturated fatty acids which are in fodder that has been only roughly chewed are much less hydrogenised than those which are added as pure oils or fats. Fatty acids which have undergone this process of change reach the abomasum and small intestine where digestion and absorption take place.

The rumen's micro-organisms themselves synthesise long-chain fatty acids. According to Hagemeister and Kaufmann, the stomach microflora form fats with varying patterns of fatty acids. The bacterial fats thus include mainly the saturated stearin, palmitin and oily acids, while the protozoa synthesise chiefly palmitin acids. But the characteristic microbial fats are the specific fatty acids with uneven C-atoms (C-15 and C-17), which otherwise occur in traces in vegetable and animal fats and oils.

The level of fat synthesis by micro-organisms in the rumen is negatively influenced by a higher proportion of fat in the diet. Large intakes of dry matter, usually leading to an increase in the number of micro-organisms, bring about more fat synthesis in the rumen (Hagemeister and Kaufmann).

If fats are added to the diet of ruminants, the digestibility of the crude fibre is lessened. According to Czerkawski *et al.* long-chain fatty acids have the effect of checking the cellulitic activity of the rumen's microflora, which is strengthened with the saturation level of the fatty acids. Similar observations were made by Rohr and Okubo and Rohr *et al.* Østergaard *et al.* demonstrated that, with an increased intake of fats, not only is the digestibility of crude fibre lessened but also, at the same time, there is a relative drop in the concentration of acetic and butyric acids and an increase in propionic acid. It is hardly worthwhile, therefore, to raise the fat content in the deer's diet; it is much more important to ensure that their energy needs are satisfied through the breaking down of cellulose-rich fodder.

7.4 Live Weight Gain

The birth weight of deer calves averages about 5 kg (Reinken), and they grow quickly due to the high nutritive content of the doe's milk which, according to Drescher-Kaden, may contain 6.4 per cent crude protein and 7.9 per cent fat. After the early suckling period the calves soon begin to eat forage, and by the end of grass growth in late autumn the animals will have reached weights of 20–26 kg (Reinken). At this stage the female calves will have gained more slowly than the males, and weigh on average 5 kg less.

Following this period, in the winter, there is a sharp decline, almost to a standstill, in the growth rate, which is regulated by the body's hormones – prolactin, testosterone, oestradiol and thyroxin. These processes coincide with the shortening of daylight hours in winter, and it is not clear whether the changing hormone secretions and growth pattern lead to a smaller intake of food or whether it is the lowered feed intake which brings about the metabolic changes (Kay). Only when the days grow longer and warmer and the vegetation begins its spring growth in March–April is there a resumption of live weight gain. The weight difference between males and females continues to increase.

Trials by Möhlenbruch have shown that there is a loss of weight in winter if insufficient food is offered (Figure 7.6). Those calves which had adequate grazing and a supplement of 100 g concentrates and 400 g straw per animal

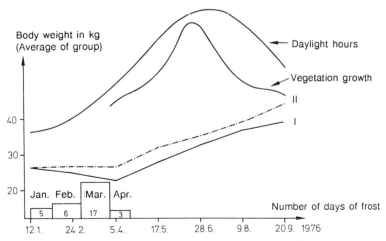

Figure 7.6 Live weight gain in deer calves (Möhlenbruch).

per day from 12 January to 5 April showed (I) a clear loss of weight averaging 45.5 g per animal per day, a total of 4.1 kg. Where supplementary feeding was at the level of 450 g concentrates and 250 g straw there were losses in weight by only one or two calves, and an average slight gain in weight of 2.9 g (II).

Adult animals may also show weight losses if inadequately fed. This is seen too in ruminants which live in the wild. Drew noticed similar results in red deer in New Zealand during the autumn and winter months. Feeding must be appropriate to the specific needs of the animals during this period, which means that there should be a lower protein level and a relatively higher level of energy-giving foods.

It would be wrong to assume, when losses in weight have occurred, that winter live weight losses are made good by larger gains in the following grazing period. With two selected groups which had started at the same weights, Möhlenbruch shows that the weight differential in winter was almost the same at the end of the trial period (20 September). This is because the genetically controlled growth potential is limited for each period of life, and so once weight losses have occurred they cannot be made up again within the space of one year. As the animals grow older these differences in weight are not apparent.

The recommended levels of daily supplementary feeding are:

Winter
I = 100 g feed mix + 400 g straw.
II = 450 g feed mix + 250 g straw.

Summer
I = 100 g feed mix + pasture.
II = 450 g feed mix + pasture.

It follows that calves for fattening should receive sufficient and well-balanced supplementary feeding during the period when pasture growth is low, to enable their final slaughter weight to be higher. In this connection the results obtained by Möhlenbruch are important. He showed that female animals lost less weight than males, so it would be cost-effective to segregate the sexes at the beginning of winter so as to allow the feeding of a larger ration to those male calves destined for slaughter.

Foodstuffs with a high energy content are suitable supplementary feeds, as grass contains a surplus of crude protein. Recommended foods are crushed cereals, dried and molassed sugar beet pulp and energy-rich finishing mixtures from the trade. They should be offered in such a way that the adults cannot reach them. This could be accomplished by dividing off the feeding area with several narrow passages which cannot be passed through by the adult animals. The feeding could also be automated.

Möhlenbruch also recorded interesting results from a farm where the fallow deer were in an open-fronted shed. These housed calves, with supplementary feeding of 250 g straw and 600 g feed mix, or 400 g straw and 450 g feed mix per animal per day showed weight gains over a trial eight-month period (12 January–20 September) of 9.3 kg and 5.3 kg respectively. This compared with those calves remaining at pasture and with supplementary feeding of 100 g (I) or 450 g (II) feed mix and 400 g or 250 g straw. This latter group showed gains of 12.3 kg (I) and 18.0 kg (II) (see Figure 7.6). This housing of ruminants, which is a widespread practice on farms, has been shown to be a poor way of using fodder, at least from these experiments. The range of individual live weight gains within the groups was wide, as some of the animals did not have their fair share of food, in spite of the trough frontage being adequate. The varying results have shown, however, that such housing of deer is possible. Since the aim of fallow deer farming is the utilisation of pastures, the year-round feeding of these animals indoors has no significance.

7.5 Digestibility of Foodstuffs

The digestion of food by ruminants is closely linked to the microflora of the rumen, as we have seen. Within the group, animals can be differentiated by the size of the rumen and the type and quantity of food consumed. As deer are similar to sheep and cattle in their forage-eating habits there should not be much difference in the way they utilise the food which is eaten – but statements by various authors contradict this. One reason is that the results are often based on examinations of carcasses of wild deer which, in addition, have come from different feeding grounds, so generalisations from these results can lead to false conclusions being drawn.

Table 7.4 Digestion quotients of hay in dairy cows and wethers

Type of animal	Organic matter	Crude protein	Crude fibre	NFE
Dairy cow	67.9	58.1	70.5	68.5
Wether sheep	67.1	59.5	69.1	67.5

Source: Dijkstra et al.

To obtain more exact comparisons on the efficiency of food digestion by deer and by other farm animals, Möhlenbruch used sheep in his trials. These were chosen for the experiments as they are very similar to cattle in their digestive processes, and the results obtained can be extended to the larger types of ruminant. Results obtained by Dykstra et al. show that the digestive processes of cattle and sheep are very similar. It appears that there is a slightly higher proportion of crude fibre digestibility in cattle, who have a larger rumen, whereas there is a slightly lower figure for protein.

Maloiy and Kay made further comparisons in red deer and sheep, with different forage. From Table 7.5 we can see a clear similarity in the digestive processes of the two types of animal, if we take into account the variation and the number of trial dates. Further experiments by Maloiy and Kay on red deer and sheep after feeding a straw plus urea ration showed the same pattern.

Comparative trials on the digestibility of raw fodder in roe deer and goats were undertaken by Dissen, and Dissen and Hartfiel. It is true that these

Table 7.5   Dry matter intake and apparent digestibility of dry matter and cellulose in red deer and sheep

Animal	Ration	Live weight in kg	Dry matter intake g/day	Digestibility Dry matter	Cellulose
Red deer	Grass hay 1	53	996	62	64
	Grass hay 1	51	882	61	57
	Grass hay 1	45	1,031	60	52
	Grass hay 2	53	1,229	56	54
	Grass hay 2	50	1,229	58	56
	Lucerne hay	50	1,049	53	56
Sheep	Grass hay 1	38	857	63	60
	Grass hay 2	46	878	65	64
	Grass hay 2	40	878	60	62
	Lucerne hay	40	872	50	52

Source: Maloiy and Kay.

showed generally lower digestion quotients for roe deer, but the differences were quite small and in the case of nitrogen-free extracts not statistically proven.

Möhlenbruch's experiments went on to make a comparison of the digestibility of fodder in fallow deer and sheep. The animals chosen for this trial were male (buck) calves, 27–32 kg in weight, and black-faced wether lambs, 32–39 kg in weight. The rations consisted of dried grass pellets and two combinations of the same pellets with feed mix in the ratios of 1:1 and 1:3. The average digestion quotients from these trials are shown in Table 7.6.

Table 7.6   Comparison of digestion quotients for grass pellets and grass pellets/concentrates from trials with deer calves and lambs

Feed	Organic matter	Crude protein	Total fats	Crude fibre	N-free extracts	Digestible foodstuff (TDN)
Deer calves						
Grass pellets (February)	58.1	57.9	46.5	53.3	61.9	525
+ Grass pellets (June)	58.1	60.2	48.2	52.4	61.8	522
Grass pellets/ concentrates 1:1	69.5	67.6	58.1	49.9	77.8	542
Grass pellets/ concentrates 1:3	75.7	73.1	75.7	48.4	82.0	710
Lambs						
Grass pellets	65.4	62.6	62.7	60.3	58.5	593
Grass pellets/ concentrates 1:1	69.7	64.5	71.2	51.9	76.6	648
Grass pellets/ concentrates 1:3	78.7	75.0	78.7	54.9	84.7	740

Source: Möhlenbruch.

Table 7.7 Comparison of digestion quotients of food mix, calculated as the difference in the results (Table 7.6) from trials with deer calves and lambs

Feed	Organic matter	Crude protein	Total fats	Crude fibre	N-free extracts	Digestible foodstuff (TDN)
Deer calves						
Grass pellets/	80.4	74.9[a]	67.6	35.9	86.8	759[a]
concentrates 1:1		73.9[b]				755[b]
Grass pellets/	81.3	77.4[a]	83.7	41.7	86.4	771[a]
concentrates 1:3		76.7[b]				770[b]
Lambs						
Grass pellets/	73.9	66.3	80.4	15.2	82.1	700
concentrates 1:1						
Grass pellets/	83.1	78.6	84.4	48.4	88.3	790
concentrates 1:3						

[a] Calculated from February results; [b] Calculated from June results.
Source: Möhlenbruch.

In general the lambs were shown to achieve better digestibility of the dried grass pellet feed and of the pellets/concentrate 1:3 ration, which with few exceptions was statistically significant. There was no significant difference between the two types of animal with the ration of pellets and mixed feed in equal quantities. Möhlenbruch also then calculated the digestibility of the mixed feed. The values thus obtained show only small statistically insignificant differences in the digestive ability of the bucks and lambs which were tested (see Table 7.7). We may conclude from this that the digestibility of the pellets with a high crude fibre content of 28 per cent and only 42 per cent NFE (N-free extract) was rather worse with the deer calves, whereas that of the concentrates with only 7 per cent crude fibre and 65 per cent NFE was about the same with the two types of animal.

The repetition of dried grass pellet feeding for the deer calves during the period in February when they were not growing, and again in June, showed, apart from a slight improvement in the digestion of protein (Table 7.6), a rise in nitrogen retention of 0.23 to 1.16 g N per beast per day.

In general these trials have shown that fallow deer have a somewhat lower efficiency of digestion of fodder high in crude fibre. The reason is their smaller rumen when compared with the sheep, which means that the speed of passage through this important part of the digestive tract is quicker (Short, and Maloiy and Kay). Dissen also showed that there was a quicker passage of fodder with roe deer than with goats. However, this does not mean that fallow deer should be fed less forage. Since food passes through more quickly, these animals are able to take in more of the forage, so that in the end the quantity of digested nutrients may reach the same level. In connection with Möhlenbruch's experimental results, however, mention should be made that sheep also show better digestion than cattle. However, cattle compensate for this by means of a bigger build-up of gases and the loss of energy with the urine is about levelled out again (Jentsch *et al.*). It is not known how far similar conditions prevail in comparisons between fallow deer and sheep.

7.6 Nutritional Requirements, including Minerals, Trace Elements and Vitamins

The feed requirements of deer must be suitable, above all, for the special demands of a ruminant, i.e. the crude fibre content should make up at least 10 per cent of the total ration. This requirement must also be taken care of when deer are at pasture because, for example, young spring grass has a high protein content and insufficient fibre. Supplementary feeding with hay and/or ammonia-treated straw, which is much more palatable than untreated straw, can help to bridge the gap in this period.

When forage is growing well the animals should receive sufficient nutrients from the pasture. This is only possible if the stocking rate is not too high, however, and the sward is adequately fertilised. In this way not only will the pasture be sufficient, but there will be an adequate level of minerals and trace elements. A chemical analysis of the forage, which can be undertaken by the agricultural farm research and investigation centres, will reveal the levels. Such an analysis should be carried out just before setting up the deer farm, and subsequently at two–three year intervals, testing for the most important elements such as calcium, magnesium, phosphorus, manganese and zinc. A planned fertiliser programme can be followed on the basis of the results to supply the necessary plant nutrients.

Supplementary feeding, starting with the slowing down of grass growth in autumn, should be fitted as nearly as possible to the nutritional needs of the animals. On the one hand deficiencies in the rations should be avoided, but on the other hand feed costs should not be excessive. It is necessary to know the facts about nutritional needs and the nutritional content of the fodder. As specific levels for fallow deer are not available, we have adapted the figures from other farm animals, particularly sheep. However, it should be noted that in winter deer have a much slower rate of growth, perhaps none at all, so that even with calves the needs are only for maintenance. This applies particularly to protein requirements, since with little body building there is practically no requirement for nitrogen. The supplementary feeding of protein with fodder is only necessary to fuel the constant turnover of nitrogen-containing compounds in the body and to nourish the microflora of the rumen.

In calculating the level of protein needed, it should be remembered that ruminants in general have the ability greatly to reduce nitrogen loss in the urine through the kidneys because of a higher rate of reabsorption. According to Eisfeld's research, the protein requirements of the selective feeding roe deer are about the same as those of the less selective farm animals, so there is no reason for assuming that wild ruminants have different protein needs from those of farm animals. This general view also applies to the feeding of fallow deer, so, particularly in winter, the protein content of the fodder can be greatly reduced for all age groups. From the above-mentioned research by Eisfeld, a roe deer needs only 24.3 g of crude protein in a food intake of 440 g dry matter. This is in line with more recent trials on the utilisation of the ammonia formed as a result of the deaminising of amino acids by the bacteria in the rumen. If these micro-organisms are fed an adequate amount of available energy, there is an increased rate of microbial growth and so better conversion through increased synthesis of protein. Menke has had results showing that with sheep the level of digestible crude protein needed dropped from 83 g to 55 g per animal per day if the ratio of energy to digestible protein was raised from eight to ten. From this we can deduce that fallow deer should receive a plentiful supply of carbohydrates, particularly those rich in cellulose.

However, the energy needs of fallow deer are greater in relation to size than those of other farmed ruminants. This is partly due to the fact that more energy is expended on account of their being outside, without the protection of buildings. In addition, compared with sheep, they have less protection against heat loss because their hide and the thin layer of fat under it do not provide such good insulation. In this respect the research by Hartfiel *et al.* on roe deer and sheep, using quantitative thermography, is of interest. Measurements demonstrated that when the outside temperature was $-1°C$, roe deer showed higher heat reflections than sheep. The mean levels on the upper body were $+1.9°C$ with a four-year-old deer and $+2.9°C$ with an eight-month-old kid, while with a two-year-old sheep it was only $+0.4°C$. Similar levels could be expected with fallow deer. This means that heat losses in these animals in winter are certainly greater than in sheep, so that there will be an increased need for energy-giving foods (see Table 7.8). There has been no specific research on the energy needs of fallow deer living at various outside temperatures, so this finding is important. There are only Moen's results with white-tailed deer, according to which heat losses were as high as 60 per cent as the winter temperatures dropped (from $-1.8°C$ to $-23.9°C$). With this considerable increase in energy needs there was also less activity by the animals, which were moving more slowly to reduce energy loss.

In addition, comparative research by Simpson *et al.*, with sheep and wild red deer, has shown that the maintenance requirement of the wild deer, weighing on average 35–45 kg, was about 20–50 per cent higher than that of sheep. According to body weight – with an average of 35–50 kg – the levels were 99–122 k cal/kg$^{0.75}$ per day (415–509 kJ). There are also recommendations by Menke on the subsistence needs of adult sheep, depending on living conditions. According to these the levels at optimum temperature ($+20°C$) are 370 kJ and they rise to about 50 per cent higher under unfavourable grazing conditions (Table 7.8).

On the basis of these figures it can be seen that the subsistence needs of deer

Table 7.8 Recommendations on maintenance requirements of adult sheep depending on husbandry

Husbandry		Increase in requirement %	Maintenance requirement KJ
In pens	Neutral temperature/optimal conditions (20°C)	0	370
In pens	Actual conditions	10	407
At pasture	Favourable weather conditions	20	444
At pasture	Unfavourable weather conditions	50	555

Source: Menke.

in winter can be put at about 50 per cent more than those of sheep. From this we have the recommended figures for different age groups (see Table 7.13 on p. 152). When the temperature drops below zero there is an increased energy need.

To relate these figures to bought-in fodder, the requirements for crude protein are given, in which the average digestibility is set at 65 per cent. This relatively low figure was chosen because the supplementary feeds added to the fallow deer ration are low in energy concentration and this means lower digestibility. In addition, Menke's recommendations should be noted, according to which, with ruminants, when there is a ratio of 10:1 energy:digestible protein, there is a higher utilisation of nitrogen. On the other hand, a better availability of nitrogen has the effect of saving energy, so that the utilisation of more protein by the animal is possible. As, with few exceptions, such as various types of straw, most foodstuffs have a closer ratio than 10:1 of energy:digestible protein, lower levels of crude protein in the ration are not a practicable proposition.

Along with the intake of organic foodstuffs, inorganic elements are vital for the animals' well-being as there is also a constant turnover of these taking place in the body. Among the more important effects can be a reserve of certain minerals (calcium and phosphorus), especially in the bones, which can be drawn upon in periods of greatest demand, especially when suckling.

Of the multiplicity of other necessary elements, only the minerals calcium, magnesium, phosphorus and sodium and the trace elements manganese, cobalt, zinc, copper and selenium are of interest, since all the rest are present in adequate quantities in the feed. As there are no figures available on the requirements of minerals and trace elements for fallow deer, the subsistence requirements of sheep have been used. The quantities shown in Tables 7.9 and 7.10 per 10 kg body weight should be given daily with the fodder.

Manganese and cobalt are important for enzyme activity and the specific synthesis of vitamin B_{12}. Zinc deficiency can cause parakeratose (changes in

Table 7.9 Maintenance requirements of minerals per 10 kg live weight in g per beast per day (sheep)

Calcium Ca	Phosphorus P	Magnesium Mg	Sodium Na
1.0	0.73	0.12	0.21

Source: Animal Nutrition Group.

Table 7.10 Maintenance requirements of trace elements per 10 kg live weight in mg per beast per day (sheep)

Cobalt Co	Copper Cu	Manganese Mn	Selenium Se	Zinc Zn
0.02–0.04	0.4–0.7	5–7	0.1–0.2	5–7

Source: Agricultural Research Council, calculated.

the skin). As far as the tolerance of both sheep and deer to copper is concerned, there are as yet no definite figures. However, it would seem advisable to assume a low initial requirement, as there have been cases of calf fatalities when they and their dams received higher quantities of copper in their feed.

It is not always necessary to add vitamin A to the fallow deer diet. When grass growth is good, in late spring, summer and early autumn, there is enough of the provitamin beta-carotin taken in with the grass. Sufficient vitamin A can then be produced in the body for current needs and for a surplus to store in the liver and fat cells.

In late autumn, winter and early spring grass growth is usually too sparse to support the animals, however. (This is clearly shown in the growth chart in Figure 6.2.) Also, if there is snow on the ground in winter there is little or no possibility of grazing, so that the supply of vitamin A through beta-carotin may not be sufficient and the reserves built up in the body may soon be exhausted.

Supplementary feeding is therefore necessary from autumn to spring because of the general shortage of grazing, but unfortunately most of the farm-produced fodder is also low in beta-carotin. Straw contains no provitamin A, and even the content in well-made hay is lowered quickly when stored, due to oxidisation. Much of the beta-carotin is also lost with the present-day practice of wilting grass before ensiling. The content of rape silage is insufficient to supply needs, and chopped turnips, potatoes, apples and sugar beet are low in beta-carotin content. Concentrates supplied by the trade, however, always have vitamin A added. The only way to ensure sufficient quantities of the vitamin is to feed these products.

Why is vitamin A intake essential? First, for the maintenance of the membranes of the breathing and digestive tracts. Second, the body's immune system is improved: with a lack of the vitamin the body is more susceptible to attack by infections and virus-borne diseases. Third, in young animals a deficiency can cause retarded growth, and there may be cases of malformed foetuses, and premature or still-births.

Fulfilling the other vitamin requirements of ruminants is made easier because the group of water-soluble substances of the B-complex and vitamin K are synthesised by the microflora of the rumen and from there are supplied to the body's system. Only the fat-soluble vitamins A and E need to be added with fodder. When the animals are not housed, vitamin D_3, which also belongs to this latter group, can be produced from the effects of ultra-violet rays on the animal's skin reacting with the body's own provitamin 7-dehydrocholesterol. As there is sufficient vitamin D_2 present in pasture, where it is synthesised by plants, there is hardly any need to provide this as a supplement.

The supply of vitamin E from the pasture is similar to that of beta-carotin. This substance is only formed in green plants and is stored up especially in those seeds with a high fat content. The animal's system can supply the body's needs from its intake of green matter. The vitamin E content is higher in young grass and clover than in old. When there is enough growth on the pasture there is sufficient supply of this vitamin.

As with beta-carotin there is a loss of vitamin E in storage, however, due to oxidisation, for example with hay, silage or cereals. The supply does not meet the requirements of the animal because of this, and the body's reserves are soon used up. The necessary additional supply is best met by giving a trade-supplied feed mix with vitamin E additive.

The major importance of vitamin E lies in its biochemical function as a 'redox' system. By means of this, unsaturated fatty acids (membrane lipids), beta-carotin and vitamin A are protected from oxidisation. In addition, vitamin E also helps to improve the body's immune system, i.e. it helps ward off infectious diseases.

In this connection the trace element selenium (Se) must also be mentioned. It is effective through the Se – containing glutathion – peroxide. With the help of this enzyme, the oxidised compounds such as essential linoleic acids or the hydrogen peroxide produced by the red corpuscles can be reduced. In cases of selenium deficiency these reactions are impaired, leading to severe illnesses. With calves and lambs this can mean bodily weakness such as muscular dystrophy, liver abscesses and a reduced immunity against bacterial infections.

The supply of selenium to the deer can be through pasture and other fodder. According to results of soil samples, however, there is a general selenium deficiency in Germany (Hartfiel and Bahners), so that there is not enough directly available through farm-produced fodder. For this reason make sure that the purchased concentrates used contain at least 0.5 mg selenium/kg. As selenium is only stored in the body in small quantities, a deficiency can soon arise, so if possible there should be a constant intake of a sufficient quantity of the element by the animal (0.2 mg/kg in the total ration).

Bacterial infection can damage the membranes of the gums, tongue, throat and larynx. There is an association here between the effects of vitamins A and E and of selenium in protecting the membranes of the breathing and digestive tracts, so enabling the animals better to resist any bacterial infection and inflammation.

As a preventive against such infection, a special supplementary feed was first introduced in 1980 on a deer farm where there had been particularly high losses of calves over several years due to this disease (Hartfiel). No further losses occurred, and the treatment was also effective with other herds. From our experience, then, a regular medication against infection should be given by including vitamins A and E and selenium in the feed.

Even a foetus can be affected by deficiencies due to lack of nourishment in winter and spring, so the addition of the special supplement should start about six weeks before calving and be continued through to about eight weeks after calving. This ensures an improved supply of the substance before birth, and then again in the dam's milk. (This is also the period during which most of the calves were infected.)

According to our experiments up to now, the daily intake of substances through the dam should be in the following quantities:

30,000 IU vitamin A
30 mg vitamin E
0.4 mg selenium

They should be given with simple feeds or compound mixes, in such a way that the required amount is received by all pregnant animals, but the concentration must finally depend on the quantity of compound which will be eaten per hind per day. The greater the ration of feed, the greater the certainty of equal shares being received. At a ration of under 100 g per day the proposed dose per animal should not be added, however, otherwise the concentration of the substance is very high and there is the danger of too great an intake by some individuals. Great care is needed in this respect, since an overdose of selenium can have toxic effects.

A recommended mix is one with the following amounts of vitamins and selenium:

$$\left.\begin{array}{l} 6{,}000{,}000 \text{ IU vitamin A} \\ 6{,}000 \text{ mg vitamin E} \\ 80 \text{ mg selenium} \end{array}\right\} \text{ in } 100 \text{ kg feed mix}$$

Each pregnant animal should receive a daily allowance of 500 g of the feed mix, if possible split into two feeds daily. A lower concentration of supplement could be given (but not a higher one), with larger quantities of feed mix. The supplementary feed is best given in combination with other feed, e.g. silage. It should also be put out in several feed troughs or feeding areas on the ground.

Calculations for ordering the special supplement are made as follows: 100 days × number of pregnant hinds × proposed amount of feed (calculating the duration of the treatment as fourteen weeks, as mentioned on p. 138).

Money and time must be spent on these measures to combat necrobacilli, but it must be taken into account that the expenditure of both is low in comparison with the value of calves which might be lost. Also, pregnant hinds have a greater need for good nutrition in the later stages of pregnancy and in the suckling period, and this is well taken care of by this supplemented feed mix ration.

7.7 Water Requirements

There are only a few detailed figures on the fallow deer's needs for water. While Nordenflycht-Lödderitz reported that only once had a direct intake of water been made by the deer he was studying, Möhlenbruch reported regular drinking during his trials. According to him, the daily water intake varied with the air temperature and the moisture content of the feed. In winter, during frosty and snowy periods, when the calves were being fed mainly on dry concentrates and straw, the quantity of water drunk was 1–1.5 litres per beast per day. With the increased intake of grass in spring and summer, the quantity dropped to 0.5 litre (spring) and 1.0 litre (summer), i.e. there was still a considerable amount drunk in spite of the high moisture content of the fodder.

Pietrowski observed more drinking when there was less pasture, and dry supplements were being fed. There was a need to drink, depending on the moisture content of the fodder, even when there was snow lying in winter, as the animals rarely ate snow. With snow and dry, cold weather there was even increased drinking of water by fallow deer (Enzinger and Hartfiel).

Feeding trials by Dissen with roe deer showed that the requirement for water depends on the quantity of food eaten and on its moisture content. Thus, for example, when eating silage with 75 per cent moisture content, the animal's need for liquid was fully met. The air temperature was also an important factor. At a live weight of 10 kg, the ratio of dry matter to water intake was 1:2.2 at 4.3°C, 1:3.4 at 11.7°C and 1:4.0 at 25.2°C, i.e. between the lowest and highest temperature there was almost double the need for liquid per kg dry matter content of the fodder eaten. Similar results apply to fallow deer, which have a water requirement of 4–5 litres per animal per day (Enzinger and Hartfiel).

The requirements of a suckling hind for water are greater. However, drinking water must always also be available for the calves, especially when they are being fed dry rations (Reinken).

Linked with water requirements is the quantity of sodium (salt) which is taken in. Salt blocks are often provided to supply this mineral. This method is not recommended, however, as the animals vary in their use of the blocks, some using them very often and others not at all. Also the salt licks often contain quite large amounts of sodium, which must be processed through the kidneys and voided again in the urine. When there is a high intake of sodium combined with insufficient liquid, there can be an imbalance of the water and salt intake, which in extreme cases can lead to poisoning.

It must be a priority for a deer farm to maintain a constant supply of fresh drinking water.

7.8   Feeding

The previous sections contain basic facts on the nutrition of the ruminant, as well as the special features which need attention when feeding this group of animals. The deer farmer who starts off thinking that the feeding of deer is the simplest thing in the world, with grass in summer and hay in winter plus a few concentrates being sufficient, is making a big mistake (Rüssmann). Some knowledge of nutrition and feeding is obviously a sound basis for a successful deer farming enterprise, but the farmer who wants good performance from his herd, whether in terms of live weight gains or breeding efficiency, must also provide his animals with the necessary nutrients and minerals, trace elements and vitamins in their feed. The special demands of the ruminant must be borne in mind: first the rumen and its microflora must be 'properly fed', and after that one can think about the animal itself. If the rumen is not functioning correctly, the deer will not reach its full potential and, in addition, illness may follow.

Supplementary feeding of the fallow deer herd must start as soon as the pasture is no longer capable of supplying the requisite nutrients. The timing depends on the climatic conditions of the site, including temperature, the amount of rainfall and its frequency during the growing period, and also the fertiliser programme (i.e. quantity and frequency of fertiliser applications).

Figure 6.1 shows how much the growth of pastures can differ. The stocking density is also important in working out the food available. This applies especially in spring and autumn, when the animals' growth rate is slow or even at a standstill. All these factors are important when beginning to reckon up the

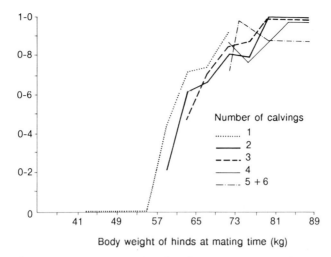

Body weight of hinds at mating time (kg)

Figure 7.7 Condition of red deer hinds of various ages, and calving numbers related to their body weight (*Hamilton and Blaxter*).

duration and amount of supplementary feeding. Finally the economics of the exercise must be taken into account.

A positive factor in such calculations is the expected improvement in profit from the sale of a greater number of calves following a higher live weight gain, and also the improved health of the herd as a whole. The good feeding of the hinds leads to better fertility, according to trials by Hamilton and Blaxter with farmed red deer (Figure 7.7). These results show that none of the hinds under 53 kg at mating time produced a calf, whereas all those weighing over 87 kg did so. This connection between the weight at mating and the hind's calving rate should also apply to fallow deer.

A further advantage of better nutrition is the improved birth weight of the calves. The figures from Blaxter and Hamilton for red deer show clearly that there is a positive correlation between the mother's weight at the time of mating and the birth weight of her calf (see Table 7.11). This is not dependent on the age of the hind at calving time.

In addition, there is a correlation between the birth weight of the calves and their survival rate. In trials over seven years it was shown that calves which were underweight when they were born had a much smaller chance of survival (see Table 7.12). As has already been mentioned, there is a link between the weight of the hind and that of her calf. The nutrition of the hinds as early as mating time and right through to calving down is therefore of very great importance for their successful breeding, and also for the profitability of the deer farm.

There is yet another advantage to be gained from the correct feeding of the hinds. It is obvious from Figure 7.8 that there is a clear link between the weight of the hinds at rutting time and that of the calves when weaned (at an age of 104 days). This shows that if the hind is heavier at mating time, her calf will

Table 7.11   Birth weights of male and female calves from red deer with live weights of 60 kg and 80 kg at mating, divided according to age

Age of hind at calving time (years)	Birth weight (kg) of male calves, when the live weight of the hind was:		Birth weight (kg) of female calves, when the live weight of the hind was:	
	60 kg	80 kg	60 kg	80 kg
2	6.21	7.20	5.80	6.79
3	6.79	7.31	5.93	6.75
4	6.23	7.15	6.06	6.98
5	6.32	7.40	5.80	6.88
6	6.20	7.12	5.64	6.56
7	6.03	7.60	5.56	7.13

Source: Blaxter and Hamilton.

Table 7.12   Deaths of red deer calves at (perinatal) and after (postnatal) birth, given in relation to birth weight

Weight of calf at birth (in kg)	Perinatal Number of calves		Postnatal Number of calves		Total death rate %
	Male	Female	Male	Female	
2.0– 2.9	3	—	—	—	100
3.0– 3.9	1	—	—	3	100
4.0– 4.9	5	2	2	2	46
5.0– 5.9	3	1	2	1	7
6.0– 6.9	3	—	1	2	5
7.0– 7.9	2	—	4	2	6
8.0– 8.9	—	—	5	1	13
9.0– 9.9	—	—	1	1	28
10.0–10.9	—	—	—	—	
11.0–11.9	—	—	—	—	

Source: Blaxter and Hamilton.

be heavier when born and this advantage will continue through to the end of the suckling period.

These results can also be applied to fallow deer. Möhlenbruch was able to show in his trials that stronger calves showed better live weight gains than those with lower birth weights. Also, those calves or yearlings of low weight at birth or which suffered weight loss due to insufficient nourishment in winter do not appear to make up the loss in the following summer at pasture (see Figure 7.6). The reason is the genetically limited potential for processing protein, i.e. body growth cannot be increased above a certain level.

On the basis of these facts, it is certainly an advantage to maintain the nutrition of the deer herd at a good level. The animals need an adequate supply of all the necessary nutrients, minerals, trace elements and vitamins for this. Most of these needs should be met from the pasture, at times of good growth, if it has had fertiliser applied according to soil test results. Schick's experiments showed that following a higher rate of nitrogen application (increased from 58 to 104 kg N per ha), a 50 per cent better stocking rate and a shortening of the

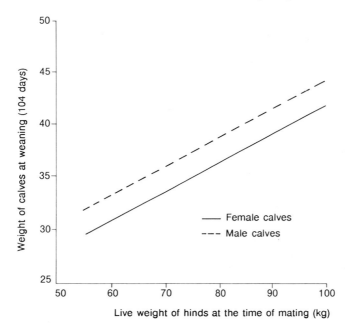

Figure 7.8 Correlation between the weight of red deer hinds at mating in October and the weight of their calves at weaning in the following October (*Hamilton and Blaxter*).

duration of supplementary feeding were possible.

The animals should be conditioned gradually to supplements and to winter fodder, so that the rumen's microflora can adapt to the change of foodstuffs. This is also true in the spring, when the intake of large quantities of young green forage can lead to stomach upsets. As for feeding arrangements, it is important to provide sufficient troughs and racks to enable all the beasts to have equal access and therefore sufficient quantities of fodder.

7.8.1 Fodder

During the period from autumn to spring, farm-produced conserved forages (silage, hay, straw) should be used as much as possible. The advantage of these bulk fodders is that they can normally be offered *ad lib* to the animals, without danger of too great an intake causing digestive upsets. Exceptions to this are turnip tops and silage made from them or from other brassica leaves. All the rest have the necessary fibre structure, i.e. after their intake there follows rumination and salivation, by means of which the fatty acids formed in the stomach are broken down.

Pasture
The nutritive content of pasture is influenced by its botanical analysis and the condition of the sward. Some swards may be grass alone, and others may have proportions of legumes and weeds. Usually, intensive grazing, together with

applications of fertiliser, results in a more or less exclusively grass pasture. The nutritive content of a well-grown pasture is amply sufficient for the needs of deer, but the pasture's condition during grazing periods is very important. While young grass has only a low content of dry matter and crude fibre and a high proportion of protein, these values change greatly as the season advances through to flowering and seeding. It is preferable, therefore, not to start using the grassland too early, and if possible not until the flowering period. Grass conservation policy must also be decided, remembering that the energy content of grass silage made from an autumn cut is lower than that from the first cuts in spring, while the conversion of protein has been shown to be lower due to the greater elimination of nitrogen in the urine (Ribeiro *et al.*).

Green crops for pasture can include various types of cereals, legumes and the cruciferous plants. Forage used includes rye grass and, above all, forage maize. The best time for using such forage is at the ear emergence stage, but if silage is to be made, then the best time (for whole plant silage) is at the 'milk-ripe' stage of the grains, because there is a better level of nutritive content then. If possible, the material should be chopped into 4–6 cm lengths, otherwise there will be difficulties with making the silage. (Insufficient depth of the store leads, among other things, to the formation of mould and to poor fermentation.)

Maize-growing is popular nowadays, mainly because of its high nutritive value, and it generally makes good silage. However, it must be remembered that it is low in protein, calcium, phosphorus and sodium, although it is rich in energy.

Other forage plants are the cruciferous types, including field mustard, oil-seed rape and marrow-stem kale. If well fertilised, they can produce good crops, which can be fed fresh, but usually in Germany they are ensiled. The time at which these crops are harvested is important, because they soon become woody and lose their nutritive value and digestibility. Feeding too large amounts of these crops should be avoided because they contain glucosinolate, which can be toxic in high concentrations. Too high a level of feeding kale can lead, among other things, to a lowering of the iodine and vitamin A content of the blood plasma, leading to anaemia.

Silage
Silage is an excellent feed for deer, provided it is well made from good quality material. It can be stored on the fields so as to make daily feeding in troughs or feeding belts easier, but it is also possible to open one side of the silage clamp and put in a suitable feeding grid, so that the animals can be self-fed. Care must be taken, though, because if there is a lot of waste silage lying on the ground, mould quickly forms which contains toxic material (aflatoxin). This waste must always be discarded.

When feeding wild deer, a silage container has proved efficient (see Figure 7.9). The animals can eat from it at any time, and it only needs filling up every two days, according to its capacity, from a larger store of silage. Care must be taken when loading the silage that it is well compacted, however; if the air gets to it, there will be secondary fermentation and mould forming after only a few days. As the animals take the silage from the top, the upper boards can be removed from time to time (Hartfiel).

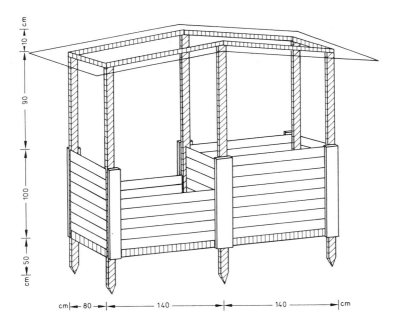

Figure 7.9 Silage feeding facility.

When making silage there are several basic rules to follow, to ensure successful conservation of the fodder. These are:

1. Do not use grass which is wet after rain or dew, because of its high moisture content. Also there would be a larger quantity of sap, and the concentration of nutrients which are needed for quick bacterial growth would be weaker.
2. When stacking the green matter, care should be taken to exclude as much air as possible. Compaction can be achieved by means of a tractor driving to and fro, or by treading down well. Unwieldly material, which will not compact well, should be chopped into about 5 cm lengths; this will reduce air penetration to a minimum while still retaining fibre structure.
3. Filling and compacting the silo should be done as quickly as possible, so as to enable it to be made airtight by enclosure under plastic sheeting. This is important to cut short the respiration of the forage and prevent over-heating of the silage.
4. The ensilage of plant material such as young grass, which is rich in protein, is not always successful. A commercial silage additive can be used to achieve better fermentation.

The best fermentation, achieved through a good build-up of lactic acid, is completed in about four to six weeks, after which the silage can be fed to the animals. It must be remembered that silage made from sugar beet tops, young grass or finely chopped maize does not have sufficient fibre structure for a ruminant's needs so hay or straw should be fed as a supplement.

Hay and Straw

According to Kossow, hay is the feed most frequently used by deer farmers, and the chief methods of drying it are on the ground or on racks. Drying on the ground is the most commonly used method, although in a western European climate conditions are often unfavourable and it is difficult to get the moisture level down to 20 or 18 per cent. If this is not achieved quickly then, with rain, constant turning and oxidation losses of nutrients occur which can reach 50 per cent. Such hay is also unpalatable and its nutritive value (high crude fibre content, and a sharp drop in beta-carotin content) is inadequate. Tripods are an advantage in uncertain weather, because the drying material can then be placed on them, even with a moisture content of 50 per cent, for further drying. However, this practice is labour intensive.

It is dangerous to store hay which has not been properly cured, whether loose, or in flat or round bales, because mould can often form quickly and there may be a build-up of aflatoxins. Such hay should not be used as feed, as it can lead to illness, especially in pregnant hinds, when abortion may occur.

Insufficiently dried hay can be stored if it is treated with ammonia (gas or liquid) (NH_3 – content about 25 per cent) and covered with opaque plastic sheeting (see Figures 7.10 and 7.11). For general conservation, however, an addition of 1 per cent NH_3 is sufficient.

In contrast to hay, straw is not found palatable by many animals, and they only eat it in small quantities, although oat straw is an exception. Straw has a high level of cellulose, hemi-cellulose and lignum (this last being difficult to digest) and a low level of proteins, minerals and trace elements. It is still good fodder for deer, however, since cellulose and hemi-cellulose can be broken down by the rumen's microflora, and the good fibre structure of straw leads to frequent rumination (Kossow).

Even with low intakes, though, the digestibility of straw is only moderate. It can be improved by using additives of sodium hydroxide (3 per cent Na OH) or ammonia (3 per cent NH_3), but the preparation and use of Na OH-treated straw is not really to be recommended, as the technical and financial outlay is very high and there are often difficulties with the acceptability of the treated forage. There is an increased need for drinking water when large quantities are being eaten.

Treatment with ammonia (gas or liquid) is better. The most suitable straw is wheat straw (Hartfiel). After NH_3 treatment the intake and digestibility of the straw are both much improved. There is also an increase in the protein content, to about 7–10 per cent (Nx 6.25), so that this straw can be used on its own for the addition of minerals, trace elements and vitamins. Adding molassed sugar beet pulp or a 'fodder completer' improves the digestibility still further.

Straw can be treated with either gaseous or liquid ammonia (25 per cent NH_3), but the stack must be kept airtight afterwards, with a covering of 0.2 mm-thick polythene sheeting, because ammonia is very volatile. The polythene should be spread on the ground with round or square wooden laths, about 3–5 cm in diameter, laid on it. The straw bales are then stacked on top of and at right angles to these, leaving 0.7 m width clear all round. Finally a

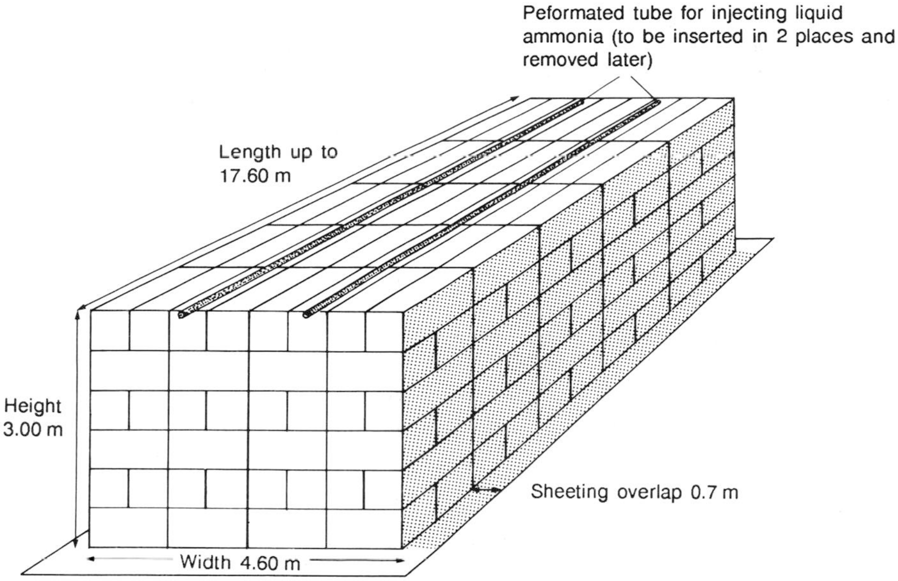

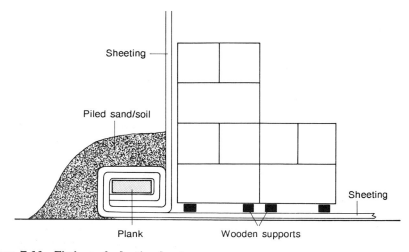

Peformated tube for injecting liquid ammonia (to be inserted in 2 places and removed later)

Length up to 17.60 m

Height 3.00 m

Sheeting overlap 0.7 m

Width 4.60 m

Figure 7.10 Straw clamp built on plastic sheeting and with perforating tubes for distributing liquid ammonia.

large polythene sheet is laid on top, also overlapping by 0.7 m (Figure 7.10). Both outer edges arc folded tightly together (using a pole makes this task easier), and earth or sand piled on top to keep them in place (Figure 7.11). A polythene sheet 12 × 25 m (not including the bottom sheet) will enclose a straw stack of maximum width 4.60 m, height of 3.00 m and length of 17.60 m.

Sheeting

Piled sand/soil

Sheeting

Plank   Wooden supports

Figure 7.11 Fitting of plastic sheet.

A more convenient stack, however, would be one of the same width and height but only 8–10 m long.

Gaseous ammonia comes in special pressurised containers, delivered by professional firms. The NH$_3$ is injected through a lance into the straw stack, which should not be tightly sealed, as the volume increases with the change from a liquid to a gaseous state.

Liquid ammonia is added by using a small pump (not corroded by caustic) and extendable plastic tubing with many perforations along the sides. The tubing is pushed through the sheet on top of the stack and laid on top of the straw (see Figure 7.10). After the NH$_3$ treatment has finished the tubes are withdrawn and the holes immediately sealed with self-adhesive plastic.

Liquid ammonia, which is also used as a fertiliser, can be transported in screw-capped drums by the farmer himself, so there is the advantage of being able to choose one's own time to inject the straw so that it can be made airtight immediately after treatment. (If this is not done, mould growth may develop and the contaminated straw cannot be fed. This effect is worse if the straw is damp or wet (the ideal is about 30 per cent moisture content). Using gaseous ammonia one is dependent on the delivery dates of the firm, which have to be fixed in advance.

Bacteria and fungi cannot develop under the effects of ammonia, so even straw with a high moisture content can be preserved by this treatment.

The stack can be opened up after about four–six weeks if the outside temperature is over 15°C; otherwise it takes eight–ten weeks. It is better not to remove the sheeting completely, but to take straw from one end, removing a sufficient length for several days' feeding requirements. The stack can then be re-covered and the plastic temporarily re-fixed so that most of the ammonia remains in the stack. Conservation of the straw is thus continued and its ammonia content stays high. Feeding trials have shown that even when the ammonia level in such straw is still high, it is eaten willingly by the deer, and moister feed leads to an increased intake (Hartfiel).

Cereals

Barley, oats, wheat and maize can all be fed to deer, but their digestibility is improved if the grains are crushed or rolled. As these cereals are high in starch they serve primarily to provide energy, i.e. proteins must also be supplied, together with certain minerals, trace elements and vitamins. Special grain balancers, which can be obtained from the trade, are most suitable, and can be mixed with farm-grown cereals.

It should be noted that the feeding of cereals, and particularly maize, should be limited because over-use can lead to an undesirable build-up of fatty acids in the rumen. If there is not enough fibre-rich fodder taken as well (i.e. hay or straw), rumination may be reduced leading to insufficient alkaline saliva being formed which can easily cause over-acidity in the stomach and perhaps even death.

Take care that the cereal grains are not damaged or diseased on the stem or in storage. Cereals which are sprouting or stored damp lose their nutritive value and become subject to microbial attack, which can lead to illness (aflatoxin).

Roots
This group of farm-produced feeds consists mainly of fodder beet, turnips, sugar beet, kohlrabi, swedes, late turnips, carrots and potatoes. They are all high in moisture so have a relatively low concentration of nutrients (proteins, minerals and trace elements). Also, their shelf life is limited: if not fed soon after harvesting they must be stored in a building or outside clamp at a temperature between 0°C and 5°C. Even then supplementary feeding will be needed in the spring, when the limit of their keeping time will have been reached. Frozen turnips deteriorate quickly after thawing and should not be fed (they cause stomach disorders).

Also be careful, when feeding roots, to give them along with fibre-rich forages (hay, straw or grass silage), to promote rumination in the animals. Single-crop silage (potatoes or carrots) can be made in combination with other crops (wilted grass, maize).

By-products of Industrial Processing
One popular feed is a by-product of the processing of sugar beet. It can be obtained as 'wet or squeezed' pulp, the difference being in the moisture content. Pressed pulp with a dry matter percentage of 20–24 per cent is commonly sold but this has only a short storage life (two–three days), quickly fermenting and forming moulds which can cause disorders in the stomach and upset the metabolism when fed. Larger quantities of the pulp should therefore be conserved straight away in a movable or self-fed silo. Fermentation will take place without the need of a silage additive. However, when the material is only loosely stacked, enclosure with a plastic sheet to keep it airtight is necessary. If moulds still form, the affected portions must always be thrown away.

Dried and molassed pulps are almost always sold in pellet form. They keep well in dry stores and are very palatable. Care should be taken to avoid feeding large quantities, however, as they swell in the stomach. Nutritive content, as with the 'wet or pressed' pulp, is mainly carbohydrates (i.e. the cell wall structure of the beet and traces of sugar, partly from the addition of molasses).

Another by-product, brewer's grains, comes from the brewing industry. Mainly from fermented barley, this is relatively rich in protein (23–25 per cent in the DM) and is a good supplement for feeds such as roots and beet pulp. With their content of barley husks, the brewer's grains have a high crude fibre content (17–20 per cent in the DM) but a relatively low level of dry matter (20–25 per cent). Like wet and crushed beet pulp, therefore, brewer's grains have only a short storage life, so if large quantities are bought they should be ensiled as quickly as possible.

Care should also be taken with this product, as today much preparation work at the brewery is done in copper containers, and the product could have an increased copper content. Fallow deer have only a low tolerance of copper, as has already been mentioned, so large quantities of the product fed over a long period could lead to the danger of copper poisoning.

When barley is prepared for malting by brewers, sprouts are produced by the grains, which are usually supplied in a dried state. This by-product contains about 20–25 per cent crude protein and 12–15 per cent crude fibre (mostly easily soluble carbohydrates). Because of its nutritive content, malt barley, like brewer's grains, can be added to feed to improve the protein content of roots such as beets, which are high in carbohydrates.

Extracted soya-bean meal has a crude protein content of about 42–44 per cent, and is especially useful. It can be purchased from most suppliers and stored in a dry place for a long time, as its moisture level is a maximum of 13 per cent.

Fruits and Vegetables

Fallow deer are very fond of apples. They can be stored in large quantities in season, but their keeping quality is limited. Some farmers simply tip apples out on the ground for the deer to feed from them at will, but this method has led to losses of animals. The reason is that there is a build-up of volatile fatty acids in the rumen, which cannot be dispersed owing to insufficient rumination.

The same considerations apply to the feeding of apple pomace or other general by-products from the preparation of fruit. Because of their relatively high content of easily digested carbohydrates, but low protein level and usually indigestibility, intake can lead quickly to severe over-acidity of the stomach. Another disadvantage is their lack of keeping quality because, like beet pulp and brewer's grains, they are soon liable to ferment and form moulds. When large quantities are involved, they must be ensiled straight away, which can be done in plastic sacks (watch out for damage by mice). The conservation process is very speedy and efficient when air is excluded, owing to the high sugar content of the product.

Vegetable residue from industrial preparation or obtained directly from growers can also be used. Mostly it is a case of brassica leaves (cauliflower, red, white or green cabbage). These have a high moisture content (82–86 per cent), so they can either be fed direct or made into silage. Depending on their dry matter content, they can be quite high in nutritive value. They should not, however, be fed in large quantities over a long period, because this could lead to illnesses such as kale anaemia, blood disorders and damage to the thyroid glands.

Horse Chestnuts and Acorns

Horse chestnuts are palatable to deer, in spite of their bitter taste, and can be given in limited quantities. The carbohydrate content is very high (78 per cent in the DM) and crude protein content low (7.8 per cent in the DM). Digestibility is good. Horse chestnuts should be treated against fungal attack, which occurs readily when they are stored.

Acorns are known to be a favourite food of wild deer, even though, like horse chestnuts, they contain a lot of tannic acid. Their nutritive content is similar to that of horse chestnuts (73 per cent carbohydrate, 6.3 per cent crude protein in the DM). The deer can be fed at the level of about 1 kg (kernels) per beast per day, as with horse chestnuts.

Bread and Other Bakery Waste

Using bread and confectionery crumbs to feed deer is a possibility. The nutritive and energy content are about the same as with cereals, but care should be taken that individual animals do not eat too much, or they may quickly develop over-acidity of the stomach. Also they must be given with other fodder (hay, straw or silage), and mouldy bread or confectionery crumbs must never be fed.

Purchased Compounds
Various commercial feed mixes are available for adding to deer fodder. Like cereals, proteins and the by-products from industrial processing, they usually contain a certain amount of minerals, trace elements and vitamins, so that all nutritional requirements are met. This is a big advantage over the other feedstuffs mentioned above, which on the whole do not contain all the nutrients required.

The main disadvantage of such concentrates is that they contain very little fibre, so they must always be offered with hay, straw or silage. Deer are not difficult to feed in this respect, so long as the forage is of good quality.

In addition, the energy concentration in the mixed feed is quite high (about 12–13 MJ ME), so that the requirement is soon exceeded when large quantities are fed. To limit the intake per animal and yet ensure that all receive sufficient quantities, it is advisable to spread the feed over several feed troughs or feed belts. It also helps to split the daily ration into two parts. Even when these measures are taken, however, it is difficult to prevent the stronger beasts taking more food than the weaker ones.

When choosing concentrates, ensure that the copper content is below the maximum allowed in the rations for sheep (15 mg per kg). It is also wise to use only those mineral additives which are suitable for sheep.

Minerals and trace element mixtures on their own are not palatable to the deer, so choose mixes containing an adequate content of these inorganic additives. When mineral licks are put out, there is the danger of uneven take-up, with not all the animals getting sufficient for their needs.

7.8.2   Calculating Rations and Fodder Requirements

The basic figures for calculating rations are, on the one hand, the animal's needs for the various nutrients (including crude protein, energy and minerals) and, on the other hand, the analysis of the available fodder. With the aid of this information it is quite easy to calculate the daily rations for the deer and then, on the basis of this, to provide for feed needs over a certain period of time.

Necessary nutritional levels for fallow deer were discussed in section 7.6. Since there are few important differences between deer and sheep in the digestion of food, according to comparative research, the data for sheep can be applied to deer as a basis for calculating the rations. It must be borne in mind, however, that deer graze outdoors all the time, in bad weather (wind, rain and cold), in late autumn, winter and spring, often with little available shelter and there are greater demands for energy in these conditions. The details given in Table 7.8, based on Menke's figures, give an estimate of this increased need for energy in unfavourable conditions: the maintenance requirement is up 50 per cent if the animals are grazing outdoors in bad weather. Because deer apparently lose body heat (and so energy) more quickly than sheep (section

7.6 showed that roe deer suffered higher losses), an additional energy need of about 30 per cent should be provided when deer are out at grass in low temperatures in winter.

Schick put together figures from wild-living ruminants, and came up with an approximate average energy need of between 23 and 25 MJ ME, for a live weight of about 100 kg. For fallow deer the somewhat higher figures given in Table 7.13 are much more realistic. In fulfilling these needs, too, a higher number of calves and increased live weight gains can be achieved. It is also a good idea to feed the animals well in winter to avoid weight losses, which are hard to make up again in the following season at pasture.

Table 7.13   Recommended requirements for crude protein, energy (kJ), calcium and phosphorus per fallow deer per day in winter

Age		Live weight kg	Crude protein g	Energy kJ[1] (approx.)	Ca g	P g
1 year	female	22 (7– 31)	60	7,200	2.2	1.6
	male	20 (5– 25)	60	7,000	2.0	1.5
1/2 years	female	31 (18– 47)	80	10,000	3.1	2.3
	male	43 (16– 57)	110	13,500	4.3	3.1
2/3 years and over	female	38 (23– 54)	85	11,000	3.8	2.8
	male	50 (28– 78)	110	14,000	5.0	3.7
Over 5 years	male	70 (43–103)	120	16,000	7.0	5.1

[1] When temperature drops below freezing, energy requirements will be up to 30 per cent higher.

A popular practice must be mentioned where the animals are given a high ration of concentrates rich in minerals, trace elements and vitamins from autumn until the onset of winter. After this, maintenance rations should suffice for the winter season.

It was stated earlier that grass growth is already starting to slow in August–September, and there are also frequent periods of drought which means a shortage of forage for the animals. In addition, there is often only over-mature material in the pasture. This can give the impression that there is sufficient grazing, but the nutritive value is lacking. Under these conditions, and especially when the pasture is densely stocked, supplementary feeding should be started in good time in the autumn. This will put the herd in better condition for the winter, with the probability that there will be an improvement in fertility, in the number of calves born and also in their birth weights.

It is well known that feed costs are the largest element of expense for the animal producer, but consideration must also be given to the fact that high supplementary feeding with concentrates in autumn may not be an economic measure on nutrition and physiology grounds. This is because the surplus nutrients are metabolised into body fat deposits. The increase in thermal energy which comes from these metabolic processes cannot be fully exploited by the animal in the autumn, but it is a different matter in winter when temperatures are low, loss of body heat is much greater and the fat laid

Table 7.14   Contents in foodstuffs of dry matter, crude protein, energy, calcium and phosphorus

	Dry matter g	Crude protein g	Energy kJ (approx.)	Calcium g	Phosphorus g
1,000 g (fresh) foodstuffs contains:					
Forage					
Meadow hay					
1st cut − (Begin/Middle Heading)	860	96	6,400	6.0	2.0
2nd cut − (4−6 weeks later)	860	119	6,800	4.1	2.1
Barley straw	860	33	5,800	4.1	0.6
Oat straw	860	30	5,200	3.5	1.2
Wheat straw	860	28	5,400	2.7	0.7
Wheat straw, NH_3 treated	860	64	6,450	2.7	0.7
Silage					
Grass silage					
1st cut (Begin/Middle Heading)	350	53	3,200	2.6	1.1
2nd cut (4−6 weeks later)	350	55	3,250	4.1	1.2
Rye, milk ripe	195	17	2,000	0.9	0.7
Maize, dough ripe	270	24	3,195	1.1	0.7
Brassica leaves, clean	160	21	1,990	2.1	0.4
Cereals					
Winter barley	880	105	13,900	0.6	3.6
Oats	884	110	12,300	1.1	3.1
Maize	879	95	16,000	0.4	2.8
Winter wheat	876	119	15,200	0.6	3.3
Bakery crumbs	877	106	16,800		
By-products					
Brewer's grains, fresh	237	59	2,800	0.9	1.6
Brewer's grains, silage	267	64	2,850	0.9	1.5
Brewer's grains, dried	904	227	9,900	4.1	6.5
Malted kernels	920	279	9,750	2.4	7.5
Whole soya extract husks	883	454	14,000	2.7	6.2
Sugar beet, fresh silage	130	13	1,600	1.3	0.2
Sugar beet, crushed silage	184	22	2,600	1.8	0.2
Sugar beet, dried	916	54	14,200	8.9	1.0
Sugar beet, dried, molassed	907	112	13,000	7.3	0.9
Fruit and vegetable waste					
Apples, fresh	152	3	2,590	0.1	0.1
Apples, pomace	253	10	2,850	2.0	0.7
Cauliflower (leaves only)	121	28	1,590	0.7	0.5
Red cabbage (stalk and leaves)	144	31	1,900	1.3	0.5
Roots etc.					
Fodder beet	146	12	2,000	3.0	0.4
Sugar beet	232	13	3,250	0.5	0.3
Potatoes	219	20	3,260	0.1	0.5
Carrots	119	11	1,670	0.5	0.4
Late turnips (no leaves)	81	11	1,100	0.4	0.3
Rape, kohlrabi, swede	110	12	1,630	0.6	0.4
Field mustard	127	27	1,400	2.0	0.4
Green rape, summer	110	25	1,620	2.1	0.5
Marrow-stem kale	124	21	1,600	2.4	0.4

Source: DLG Tables of Food Values.

down is needed mainly for metabolising into thermal energy. At the same time the functions of the rumen must be maintained even when forage is sparse in winter, and there must be a minimum intake of protein to keep the rumen's microflora fully active even though the body weight is not increasing.

It is therefore more sensible to offer only a moderate level of supplementary feed in autumn when there is not enough grazing. A maintenance feed must then be given in winter, which supplies the needs of both the rumen's microflora and the animal itself, so as to avoid weight losses as far as possible. Offering poor quality hay or straw is not good enough.

The necessary data to calculate the rations for fallow deer are given in Table 7.13, which shows the nutritive needs for proteins and energy as well as for calcium and phosphorus, related to the body weight. The contents of the various forages are given in Table 7.14. When using these figures, it should be noted that they are averaged, and that there are great differences in the products, which are influenced by soil conditions, fertiliser applications, time of harvest, storage and processing (of silage etc.). For this reason it is advisable, if large quantities of hay or silage, for example, are made, to send samples to the local agricultural laboratory for analysis. The costs involved will be recovered from the more accurate feeding which will result.

The best way to calculate the rations is to take the quantity of nutrients contained in the proposed daily ration of, for example, hay or straw (Table 7.15), then add the value of the cereals or silage (always multiplying quantity of fodder by value of nutrients). From various combinations of feed quantities

Table 7.15 Calculations of rations for fallow deer of various ages and live weights

	Dry matter g	Crude protein g	Energy kJ (approx.)	Calcium g	Phosphorus g
Ration 1: 1-year-old calves					
0.2 kg meadow hay, 1st cut	172	19.2	1,200	1.20	0.40
0.3 kg winter wheat	263	35.7	4,450	0.18	0.99
0.1 kg (chopped) sugar beet pulp (dried molassed)	91	11.2	1,250	0.73	0.09
	526	66.1	6,900	2.11	1.48
Requirement at 20–22 kg live weight		60	6,800–7,200	2.0–2.2	1.5–1.6
Ration 2: 1–2-year-old female					
0.3 kg hay, 2nd cut	258	35.7	2,000	1.23	0.63
0.3 kg winter barley	264	31.5	4,150	0.18	1.08
1.5 kg (chopped) sugar beet (crushed, ensiled)	276	33.0	4,100	2.70	0.30
	798	100.2	10,250	4.11	2.01
Requirement at 31 kg live weight		80	10,000	3.1	2.3

Ration 3: 1–2-year-old male					
1.0 kg grass silage, 1st cut	350	53.0	3,200	2.60	1.10
0.3 kg winter wheat	263	35.7	4,450	0.18	0.99
0.2 kg (chopped) sugar beet (dried, molassed)	181	22.0	2,590	1.46	0.28
0.5 kg oat straw	430	15.0	2,600	1.75	0.60
	1,224	125.7	12,840	5.99	2.97
Requirement at 43 kg live weight		110.0	13,000	4.3	3.1
Ration 4: 2–3-year-old female					
0.5 kg hay, 2nd cut	430	58.5	3,255	2.05	1.05
0.5 kg potatoes	110	10.0	1,700	0.05	0.25
0.2 kg winter wheat	175	23.8	2,860	0.12	0.66
0.2 kg sugar beet pulp (dried)	183	10.8	2,820	1.78	0.20
	898	103.1	10,635	4.00	2.16
Requirement at 38 kg live weight		85	10,500	3.8	2.8
Ration 5: 2–3-year-old male					
1.0 kg wheat straw, NH₃ treated	860	64.0	6,450	2.70	0.70
0.3 kg winter barley	264	31.5	4,020	0.18	1.08
1.0 kg maize silage	270	24.0	3,200	1.10	0.70
	1,394	119.5	13,670	3.98	2.48
Requirement at 50 kg live weight		110	14,000	5.0	3.7

With rations made up solely of home-grown forage, a winter supplementary feed (sheep) with vitamins A and E and selenium is successful. Also good straw should be readily available, preferably ammonia-treated.

a balance can finally be arrived at between the required levels and the values contained in the ration.

There are obviously variations in live weight in different herds and at different times of year. To ensure a level suitable for both below average and above average live weights, the figures given in Table 7.13 for the low and high weight groups can be averaged. To give an example: the one- to two-year-old does, starting at 31 kg, have an average weight of 35 kg. The recommended requirements for this weight are about 82 g protein and approximately 10:4–10:6 MJ ME per animal per day. Figures for minerals and trace elements can be calculated in the same way.

When choosing winter forage, it must be remembered that silage may often be frozen when the weather is cold (especially in hilly areas), and the animals find it difficult to eat. Frozen fodder can also cause harm to the rumen microflora when the temperature of the stomach contents is lowered. Dry concentrates are a more suitable feed under these conditions but there is, of course, a greater need for drinking water if these are fed.

In Table 7.15 five calculations of rations are set out. Using these examples for various age and weight classes it is possible to work out suitable rations, making the best use of fodder produced on the farm. When buying in fodder, it is important to make sure the analysis is good, as this makes sound economic sense. The figures are rather different for deer than other farm animals, because they put on very little weight in winter and so need food with a higher energy level rather than protein-rich food in their rations. Table 7.15 also shows that with a satisfied energy requirement there is usually a surplus of crude protein.

It is often more difficult to achieve the correct balance with minerals in a ration (see Ration 5). Some individual foodstuffs contain more phosphorus than calcium (particularly cereals and cereal by-products), but the majority contain more calcium. To get the balance right, there is a choice of mineral supplements and feed mixes with a close or wide Ca:P ratio. The choice of supplement is important because deer, as has already been mentioned, do not usually have sufficient vitamin A and E and selenium from late autumn until spring, and the deficiency can be rectified in this way.

According to Kossow's information, the most common mineral supplements given are one designed for sheep and one for game. The one for sheep is preferable because it should contain only a little copper and it will usually have the necessary levels of vitamins A and E. Make sure that the compounder also adds 0.3 mg selenium per kg feed (to prevent muscular dystrophy).

In practice most deer herds have a range of age and live weight groups. It is a good policy to separate the deer into small groups of similar age and sex, and weight as they have different nutritional requirements. In this way rations suitable for each particular group's requirements can be given. It is especially recommended in the case of growing calves, which are often pushed away from the feeding troughs when in a larger herd and so will not show good live weight gains. It is also an advantage to be able to feed groups of similar weight separately, because the rations can be computed more accurately.

Hay is the first choice fodder for a deer herd, with straw as second (Kossow, Schick). In addition fodder beet and maize silage are often added. With lower cereal prices the use of milled or preferably crushed wheat, oats and barley is favoured. Then there is a large number of alternatives which can be added to the feed (see Table 7.14).

It is advisable to do an estimate of the fodder which will be needed for feeding the herd from autumn to spring, and the duration of winter feeding is obviously a factor which must enter into this calculation. Schick suggests 111 or 136 days, for two different areas. According to Kossow's researches the average was 136 days, varying from a minimum of 105 to a maximum of 240 days. It is clear from this that it is not possible to reach figures for feed requirements which will meet all conditions. Each farm must calculate its own plan, using past experience when applicable, although extreme weather conditions such as droughts or periods of cold weather cannot be foreseen or taken into account in the calculations. The farmer will know the approximate number of animals and their weight range, and whether it will be possible to separate the herd into groups.

After decisions about grouping the herd have been made, the various rations can be worked out. The basic quantities of each food per beast per day should be multiplied by the number of animals and the number of days of feeding. This will give the amount of each food which will be needed. When using one's own crops for hay or straw or silage-making, there are figures for expected yields per hectare. Calculations are easier with bought-in feeds such as dried or pressed sugar beet pulp or brewer's grains for silage.

As it impossible to be absolutely accurate in estimating requirements, always have in stock a reserve of fodder which stores well, particularly hay and straw (if possible ammonia-treated), dried sugar beet pulp or cereals. If necessary, or if one's own forage is insufficient, a supplementary feed mix suitable for sheep may be used but care should still be taken to feed fibre-rich matter (hay, straw) at the same time, and to make sure all the beasts have enough, otherwise stomach disorders and damage to health could follow.

7.9 Rearing Orphan Calves

In the rare cases when the doe dies while giving birth, or shortly before or after calving, it may be necessary to rear orphan calves. This artificial rearing might also have to be considered for weak calves or those born during a period of continuous heavy rain. However, in general, strange calves will be accepted by other hinds and will survive.

At the Rowett Research Institute in Scotland, red deer calves were taken from wild herds at a few days old and were artificially reared. The object was to have tame animals, which would be used to handling by humans. However, losses, averaged over three years, reached 11–22 per cent. An important factor in this was colostrum consumption prior to artificial rearing (Buckland, Abler, Kirkpatrick and Whelan), as this contains the necessary immunity factors for the calf, unobtainable through medication or injections.

The colostrum must be taken about six times a day for the first two days of life. If the hind has died and there is no deer colostrum available, that from recently calved cows should be used. Quantities of colostrum should be frozen, to ensure a good supply for the deer calves.

In New Zealand, agricultural advisers have issued special recommendations for a colostrum-substitute mixture, after widespread trials with red deer calves. This is: 0.7 litre pasteurised cows' milk, 1 egg, 1 teaspoon cod liver oil, 1 dessertspoon glucose, all to be mixed and stirred well and fed to the calves in a feeding bottle. It should be given so that each calf receives one egg per day. For the first five days the calves also receive one teaspoonful daily of a sulphonamide preparation.

At first the calves should have 20 cc every hour of the colostrum mix, gradually reducing to a feed every two–four hours. The calves will wake up if they are hungry, and one feed should be given during the night.

Hygiene of the navel region is important with newborn calves. After breaking – never cutting – the cord, the remaining blood in it should be squeezed out with the fingers so that no clots will be formed there. If the navel is treated with tincture of iodine the scar will heal and dry up quickly, so bacteria cannot get in and multiply. It is important to massage the rectum and anal regions so that any residual discharge and urine can be excreted.

It is difficult to get the calves to drink for the first few days, according to our experience. Freericks, at the Teaching and Research Centre at Riswick House, had good results using a teat on a lemonade bottle. This was about 8 cm long, and can be obtained from any supplier of veterinary products (Plate 7.1). The hole at the end of the teat should be the size of a pin-head, and a little milk should drip from it when the bottle is up-ended. This will ensure that the calf takes in a little at a time for the first few days. To ensure a sufficient quantity of milk at about three to four weeks of age, another hole should be made in the end of the teat so that the sides do not stick together when the calf is sucking vigorously.

If the calves will not drink by themselves, in the first few days, they should be encouraged to do so by means of stroking or rubbing the back and crotch, speaking to them and, if all else fails, by holding them and feeding them from the bottle. The head should be held, the teat inserted into the mouth and small quantities given at intervals, with short pauses (Plate 7.2). Care should be taken that the calf is swallowing naturally. If it coughs, spits or swallows the wrong way, it should be released immediately: milk should never be allowed to get into the lungs. As soon as the calves are drinking by themselves, they should be given milk to appetite or till they refuse to drink. Information on the quantities of liquid required are given below.

A great deal of patience and a love of animals is needed to rear calves in this way. If possible the handler should not change. Calmness – especially when giving milk – is most important. Strange noises or people will frighten the animals.

Plate 7.1 Feeding orphan calves from the bottle.

Plate 7.2 Feeding orphan calves (holding method).

NUTRITION AND FEEDING 159

Ulmenstein noticed when rearing calves that the lachrymal glands had a signalling function; this had been suggested earlier by Wölfel, working with red deer calves. A new calf will open the lachrymal glands as early as six minutes after birth, while it is being licked dry by its mother. It is believed that this wide opening increases the hind's milk flow. When the red deer calves were drinking the openings gradually grew smaller. In the first weeks of life there were already signs of behavioural habits such as raising of the tail preparatory to taking flight, running games and early grooming behaviour. According to observations made by Krzwinski, Niedbalska and Twardowski, hand-reared fallow deer calves are not so tame as red deer, red deer/wapiti hybrids or roe deer, but they do have a greater herd instinct.

The composition of the milk is very important, especially in the first days and weeks. According to our research, the doe's colostrum milk contains 22.6 per cent dry matter, 3.0 per cent inorganic substances, 10.4 per cent crude protein, 2.0 per cent fat, and 2.4 per cent crude sugar. In Table 7.16 figures are given comparing milk from different deer species with that of cows, sheep and goats. These show that the milk from the deer species has higher fat and protein levels; sheep's milk is the most similar. During the lactation period, according to Blaxter's red deer trials, the dry matter, fat and protein levels increase, while those of lactose, inorganic matter and minerals generally

Table 7.16 Composition of milk of various types of animals and milk substitutes (in %)

Type		Inorganic substances	Dry matter	Fat	Crude protein	Total sugar (lactose)
Roe deer	[2]	1.1	20.4	6.7	8.8	3.8
Sika deer	[1]		36.1	19.0	12.4	3.4
White-tailed deer	[1]		21.0	6.0	7.8	4.6
Red deer 1st lact. month	[3]	1.0	20.5	6.9	7.7	5.1
2nd lact. month	[3]	1.3	25.4	10.6	8.9	4.5
3rd–30th day	[4]	1.2	21.1	8.5	7.1	4.5
31st–100th day	[4]	1.1	23.5	10.3	7.6	4.5
101+	[4]	1.1	27.1	13.1	8.6	4.5
	[6]	1.4	34.1	19.7	10.4	2.6
Fallow deer colostral		3.0	22.6	2.0	10.4	2.4
5th day	[5]			8.8	7.9	
3rd day	[3]			7.9	6.4	
	[1]		25.3	12.6	6.5	6.1
Cow	[6]	0.7	12.5	3.5	3.5	4.7
Sheep	[7]	1.1	17.0	6.0	5.1	4.5
Goat	[6]	0.7	14.5	4.8	5.0	4.0
Milk substitute		Crude fibre, max.				
Lamb Feed mixture		3	15–30	20		
Calf		1	5–30	20		

Sources: [1] Chapman; [2] Pinter; [3] Drescher-Kaden; [4] Blaxter; [5] Zwirner; [6] Dairy directory; [7] Haring.

remain the same from the third day of lactation until after the hundredth day.

When rearing orphans it is therefore important, from the third day and after feeding colostrum, to use a milk substitute suitable for deer. There are several ways of providing this:

- Enriching cow's milk with fat and protein, using condensed milk (4:1).
- Thinning condensed milk with milk substitute.
- Using milk substitute produced for cattle or lambs.
- Purchase of a specially formulated milk substitute.

There were good results from all these with roe deer calves. White-tailed deer were reared on cow's milk. In Scotland, based on several years of trials, sheep's milk substitute was recommended for red deer calves.

Table 7.17   Rearing fallow deer calves

Age	Number of drinking periods	Quantity of milk g per day	Food	Special treatment
1st day	7 6.00–22.00	300–400		Massage intestine and rectum. Watch out for diarrhoea!
2nd day	7	300–450		
3rd day	6	500		
4th–6th day	6	520–600		
2nd week	6	800–1,200	grass,	Faeces like adults
3rd–9th weeks	3–4	1,000–1,500 Drinks may be given cold	concentrates water soil	(dark, hard, holds shape). Hardening off of
10th week at the latest			*ad libitum*	calves.
14th week		Turning out with herd		

Source: Eurostat.

In our trials, sheep's milk substitute (25 per cent) and a mixture of 7.5 per cent tinned cream and cow's milk in a ratio of 1:4 were equally effective. The daily number of feeds, quantities and the supplements given at various ages are given in Table 7.17. From nine feeds a day, given between 06.00 and 22.00 hours, the intervals between feeds can be increased as the quantity of feed intake grows. For the first three weeks the milk should be given warm – 38°–40° – after which it can be given cold.

Cleanliness in all the containers used is most important. If several calves are drinking from a container, ensure that each drinks a sufficient quantity.

If diarrhoea is a problem, feeds and fat intake should be decreased, and strong tea or special medicine given. Calves with diarrhoea should be separated from the others. Weak calves should usually be given an antibiotic and some vitamin preparation, following advice from a veterinary surgeon. This is especially recommended if a tinned milk mixture is being given; milk substitutes usually contain sufficient doses of these medicaments.

Weak and backward animals should be examined by a veterinary surgeon for coccidiosis and bacterial infection. Lung infection is a frequent cause of calf death, and can occur if the animals are too cold or – from our experience – if they have been kept too warm before being turned out with the herd.

In their second week the calves will begin to take solid food. They like to eat earth regularly, and clean damp earth should be provided in a dish. (The reason for this habit is not yet clear.) Hay, young grass and fresh drinking water should also be available at all times. When using concentrates, those meant for lambs or sheep should be chosen, and of those compared, according to Freerick's trials, the preference was for barley- and oat-based feeds rather than wheat. Regulations for these set a maximum level for copper content of 12 mg per kg. As our tests have proved, deer, and in particular deer calves, are as sensitive to copper as lambs are. If a different concentrate is chosen, this maximum copper content of 12 mg per kg should be guaranteed by the supplier. Calves will also eat small, sweet twigs. The consistency of the faeces should be checked regularly.

At the age of three–four weeks the first molars are visible. After nine weeks, at the latest, the feeding of milk should have finished completely. Fodder – grass and concentrates – as well as water, should be given *ad lib.*

After about twelve weeks the calves can be put out to pasture with the herd, but at least two weeks before this the temperature of the shed should be equalised with that outside, as far as possible, by opening doors and windows (without causing draughts), so as to harden off the calves. This is the only way to avoid setbacks or even losses. The animals will still be very tame for the first few days after being turned out, so it is easy to go on checking them and giving supplementary feed. Marking the calves with a different coloured collar from the other animals makes it easier to look after them separately.

The space needed for rearing calves is about 1 sq m of floor space per animal in a dry, sheltered shed. As the calf will not have the benefit of the hind's body heat, there should be a good layer of straw bedding and an infra-red lamp can be installed about 1 m above ground level. These measures should ensure the calf's welfare during the first fourteen days without the doe. The rearing pen should be separated from the rest of the building by a wooden or chipboard partition. Do not use wire: in our experience timid calves will run into the fence if they are disturbed, and may injure themselves. From about eight days the calves will start to romp about, so it is sensible to cut down space from then onwards.

Cleanliness and hygiene in the rearing shed are essential. Wet bedding, dung and feed leftovers must be regularly removed. Cold, draughts and all sources of infection are a danger to the vulnerable calf. The feeding of milk substitute and other foods is best carried out within the pen. Preparation of the liquid feed will be easier if electricity and water supplies are handy.

Rearing orphan calves was the subject of research by Klopfer. This showed that calves which were separated from their mothers between twelve and twenty-four hours after birth settled down and behaved calmly within the first thirty-six hours. Later they would stand up, walk about and call loudly and often. They soon lost their fear of people and dogs moving about in the building in which they were housed. After the first few days they would lie

Plate 7.3 Growth of the capacity of the digestive organs (Bubenik).

Plate 7.4 Paring of the hooves may be necessary when in pens.

quietly between feeds, and only call if they were hungry. From the second week onwards they started to show interest in each other, apparent in the increasing tendency to sleep close together. In the third week, fights between male calves were observed: they would butt heads, as the older males do. In general, however, the calves were timid and nervous, and their temperament did not change as they grew older.

Gilbert took calves from their mothers between one and forty-eight hours after birth, reared them as orphans or on a nanny goat, and kept them either in groups or partly on their own. At four to seven months of age they were compared with normally reared calves as regards their tolerance to humans and their behaviour in the herd. Gilbert stated that the calves brought up on their own showed the closest contact with humans. The human 'imprint' was increased in line with the early separation of calves from their hinds. The first day was particularly important in later behaviour. Calves reared separately were tamer with humans than those which remained with other calves for a period. Their behaviour toward others – social grouping, or aggressiveness – is dependent on the time of separation from the mother and the manner of their rearing, and is the opposite of their behaviour towards humans. A male calf which had been fostered on a nanny goat, for instance, was 'imprinted' with goat behaviour when adult, including its sexual behaviour.

The development of calves reared as orphans is usually slower, and only occasionally as good as that of those remaining with the mother. These latter calves also show fewer losses. When the increased expenditure on housing, feeding, hygiene and especially the higher labour costs are taken into account, it is obvious that artificial rearing is only viable as an emergency measure to save deer calves.

The calves which were reared at the Teaching and Research Centre at Riswick House by Freericks showed no behavioural disturbances when on show on open days, with the public viewing and taking photographs and with TV filming.

8 Health

by Dr E. Körner

Preventive health care plays an important part in all areas of animal husbandry, ensuring efficiency and good results, and enabling the production of good quality beasts. Knowledge of the most important diseases and their treatment is essential if health care is to be successfully integrated into the overall management of the deer farm.

As deer farming is one of the newer branches of animal husbandry, there is only a limited background of experience to draw on. At first, data had to be based partly on literature concerning deer in the wild, in parks or on hunting estates, or in show herds or other similar groups. Our own knowledge comes mainly from veterinary research and experimental herds on grassland in the region of the Agricultural Office of the Rhineland, and on our experience of various deer farms over the last ten years.

8.1 Illnesses and Their Causes

Authors from all over the world are unanimous in their view that deer in the wild, in parks and on estates are very resistant to disease, although there are no accurate statistics about the losses due to illness. Wetzel and Rieck, in their standard text on the diseases of wild animals, stated that wild deer suffered very few losses through illness and were apparently very resistant to parasites and infectious diseases. Research by Chapman and Chapman on 115 deer which were found dead, ill or injured in Richmond Park, in England, between 1967 and 1973 showed that 61 per cent had been killed in accidents, mostly on the roads. About 25 per cent of the animals which were the subject of the research had died of natural causes, or had been shot because they were ill (see Table 8.1).

Up to the present there have been no overall figures published on the causes of death in deer herds. Several state associations, however, have undertaken surveys among their members, sending out questionnaires on causes of death. Since 1974 the Animal Health Department of the Agricultural Office of the Rhineland in Bonn has made enquiries about the causes of death of those animals which had died on agricultural holdings and which were available to their laboratories for research. A summary of the replies is given in Table 8.2.

The ratio of the sexes in the sample and the ages of the animals examined are given in Table 8.3.

The diagnoses given are summarised in Table 8.4, and it is clear from them that illnesses of the digestive tract and bacterial infections are the most

164

Table 8.1   Causes of death of 115 deer in Richmond Park, 1967–73

Cause of death	Proportion %	
	Male	Female
Road accident	43	55
Other accident	18	6
Illness	26	24
Injury caused by dog	4	11
Injury caused by stag	2	2
Unknown cause	7	2
Total	100% = 57 deer	100% = 58 deer

Source: Chapman and Chapman.

Table 8.2   Replies sent to animal health office, Bonn, 1974–85

Year	1974–6	1977–9	1980–2	1983–5	Total
Number of animals	18	64	70	31	183

Table 8.3   Samples sent to animal health office, Bonn, since 1974 classified according to sex and age

Total animals	Sex		Age		Yearlings	Adults
	Male	Female	Calves 4 weeks	1 year		
183	78	105	45	95	12	31

frequent in farmed deer, while accidents and other external circumstances cause only a small proportion of deaths.

Along with information on the causes of death, regular parasitological observations have been carried out since 1974, and the results are shown in Tables 8.5 and 8.6.

In addition to the laboratory tests on dead deer and on faeces samples, between 1983 and 1985 blood samples were taken from 4½–5-month-old male deer calves when their antlers were being removed. These blood samples were laboratory-tested both haematologically and chemically, and the results are collated in Tables 8.7 and 8.8.

In 1981 Matzke was able to confirm the results gathered in the Rhineland since 1974, on the basis of his own veterinary observations on wild deer herds, and there was close similarity in their findings and in their opinions. Matzke also pointed to the necessity for hoof treatment when the deer were kept in certain conditions.

In 1982 Schellner evaluated the results of information sent to the Agricultural Research Unit of the Health Department of Southern Bavaria between 1 January 1977 and 31 March 1982. One hundred and twenty-five carcasses

Table 8.4 Classified diagnoses of 183 deer samples, animal health office, Bonn

Illness in digestive system	67	Inflammation of abomasum	29
		Haemorrhaging inflammation of intestine	22
		Catarrhal inflammation of intestine	13
		Over-acid rumen	1
		Over-full rumen	1
		Bleeding in omasum	1
Bacterial infections	98	E. coli/clostridii	46
		Necrobacilli	32
		E. coli	15
		Clostridial entero-toxaemia	2
		Streptococci	2
		Puerperal septicaemia	1
External causes	26	External injury/accident*	8
		Foreign bodies in stomach	6
		Heart circulation difficulties after stress	3
		Inflammation of jaw	3
		Hypothermia	3
		Technopathy	2
		Ruptured stomach	1
Parasites	30	Lung worm pneumonia	24
		Stomach/intestinal worm infestation	13
		External parasites	3
Upset metabolism/poisoning	6	Copper poisoning	6
Premature births (calves not capable of surviving)	12	Copper poisoning	9
		Stress	3
Other diagnoses	43	Inflammation of lungs	12
		Inflammation of stomach lining	5
		Liver abscess	4
		Infected navel	4
		Gangrenous inflammation of throat	3
		Infection of throat	2
		Heart-circulation-failure	2
		Inflammation of brain (encephalitis)	1
		Dislocation of jaw	1
		Throat and tongue abscesses	1
		Lung mycosis	1
		Fluid on lung	1
		Parasitic inflammation of liver	1
		No reason found (illness)	1
		Not suitable for examination (cadaverous)	5

* Fractured skull, brain haemorrhage, trauma (chest and stomach), bleeding in flanks (from tranquillising projectile), putrid inflammation of joints, inflammation of hooves.

and organs, mainly from farmed deer, were divided according to cause of death from parasitic, microbial or non-infectious sources. Internal parasites were the main cause of illness in 40 per cent of the animals, while in 20 per cent it was microbial infection. In herds fed on silage seven cases of listeriosis were found, thirteen cases of coliform septicaemia, and three cases of pasteurellosis, actinomycosis in one case and one infection with *Salmonella dublin*. Among

Table 8.5 Parasitological findings 1974–85, animal health office, Bonn

Diagnoses	1974–6	1977–9	1980–2	1983–5	1974–85	
Number of samples	286	522	257	104	1,169	%
Eggs of stomach/ intestinal worms	219	316	161	52	748	64
Eggs of thread worms	70	71	69	23	233	19.9
Eggs of tape worms	9	6	—	—	15	1.2
Eggs of liver fluke	1	4	16	—	21	1.8
Larvae of lung worms	29	81	55	7	172	14.7
Coccidialoocysts	139	191	157	41	528	45.2
Negative	33	107	49	39	228	19.5

Table 8.6 Results of parasitological tests 1974–85, animal health office, Bonn

Year	Total samples	Negative samples %	Positive samples %
1974	30	20	80
1975	55	0	100
1976	181	15	85
1977	342	25	75
1978	137	16	84
1979	43	0	100
1980	96	14	86
1981	58	24	76
1982	103	21	79
1983	89	39	61
1984	6	—	100
1985	9	44	56
1974–85	1,149	19.5	80.5

Table 8.7 Haematology test results in fallow deer

	Average value	Standard deviation n=36
Haemoglobin g/%	17.87	2.13
Haematocrite %	49.92	3.71
Erythrocite Mio/µl	13.71	1.44
Leucocite Mio/µl	3,622.22	99.99
long kernel %	2.46	1.68
segmented kernel %	64.47	10.52
eosinophile %	1.83	1.47
basophile %	0.08	0.27
Monocite %	1.18	0.40
Lymphocite %	32.22	10.13

fifty 'other causes of illness' were eight cases of unnatural substances being found in the contents of the stomach and four cases of bleeding after being gored by antlers.

Table 8.8 Clinical chemistry test results in fallow deer

	Average value	Standard deviation n=58
GOT U/1	74.48	24.23
γ-GT U/1	11.64	11.26
Urea mg/100 ml	57.73	17.75
Phosphorus mmol/1	3.37	0.6
Calcium mmol/1	2.27	0.16
Copper μg/100 ml	129.29	29.93

* GOT = Glutamate–Oxalacetate–Transaminase.
γ-GT = Gamma–Glutamyl–Transferase.

In 1985 Davidson, Crum, Blue, Sharp and Phillips found in the two male and three female deer which were infected out of a herd of 200 head, that two of them had antibodies against 'epizootic-haemorrhagic-disease-virus', one had antibodies against bluetongue virus, and there were nine different types of internal parasite. All the animals examined by them showed at post-mortem that they had previously been infected by the internal parasite *Parelaphostrongylus tenuis*, without clinical symptoms having been apparent.

8.2 Infectious Diseases

Diseases which originate from the presence of infection-causing organisms in the host organs – viruses, bacteria, fungi – are called infectious diseases. The receptiveness of the host organ is a crucial factor in whether the organism precipitates the effects of the disease.

Many of these diseases originate from a combination of various factors conducive to illness, and they are therefore called factoral diseases. Many living creatures, because of their species or individual characteristics, are resistant to certain of these stimuli. This seems to be the case with deer, in present-day circumstances.

Viral Diseases
Deer may be receptive to the viral infections which are the subject of this section, although most of the following have never been observed or described in them: foot and mouth disease, rabies, mucosal disease, viral diarrhoea, catarrhal fever, rinderpest, Aujeszky's disease, 'Q' fever, vesicular stomatitis, epizootic haemorrhage, bluetongue virus and enzootic ataxia.

There are regulations governing cases of foot and mouth disease, rabies and mucosal disease. Enzootic ataxia (hip lameness in red deer) has been observed on rare occasions in fallow deer, according to English researchers. The symptoms are progressive weakness and lack of co-ordination of the hind quarters (Chapman and Chapman).

Foot and mouth disease used to be found occasionally in wild deer but, according to present research, it has not been of any significance. Apparently fallow deer, along with wild ungulates in general, are very resistant to the infection. According to numerous observations, fallow deer do not even succumb to the disease when in contact with infected cattle.

In 1975 Gibbs, Hernimann, Lawman and Sellers infected various wild species artificially, by giving them two hours' contact with cattle infected with foot and mouth disease. In most cases the fallow deer in the test showed only sub-clinical symptoms, but the virus was transmitted to other animals such as cattle and sheep. The results of blood samples and samples taken from the mouth and throat, as well as the viruses spread by aerosol in the course of the infection, were the same as those found in sheep and cattle during the experiments. In fallow deer the infection was still present in the throat more than twenty-six days after infection. In an epidemic of foot and mouth disease it is improbable that there would be such close contact with other farm animals as was brought about in this experiment, and the authors concluded that – in spite of the receptivity to foot and mouth disease of the various wild species – this would not be a major factor in the spread of the infection during an epidemic among farm animals. In 1978 Lawman, Evans, Gibbs, McDiarmid and Rowe found no foot and mouth antibodies in fifty blood samples from fallow deer and concluded that these animals – as well as other species of deer – had no significance as carriers of the virus.

A foot and mouth virus attack usually follows grazing on infected pasture. The incubation period is about two days, rarely going up to seven days. The progress of the disease is generally steady, lasting about one to two weeks, the infection being spread through the whole body via the bloodstream. In severe cases, if the infection leads to degeneration of the heart muscles, the disease may be fatal. Hard blisters containing red fluid form on the stomach lining. A rash occurs at the site of the infection, mainly in the gums, inside the lips and on the edge of the tongue. The liquid in this, which is clear and yellowish, contains the virus. Following the rash there are scars on the skin with a dark red base which later scab over and then heal up. Infected animals show heavy salivation and, if the hooves are affected, will be very lame. Splitting of the hoof may occur; this can gradually grow out, but a badly affected animal might shed the sole of its foot.

Foot and mouth is a notifiable disease and treatment is prohibited. In Germany there is a preventive/protective injection against it.

Rabies is an almost world-wide, fatal contagious disease of the central nervous system, which is of especial importance as it is a zoonotic infection, i.e. it can be transmitted either way between humans and animals. Deer in western Europe are probably mainly at risk from rabies-carrying foxes and other carnivores.

The disease has been known since early times. It was more closely re-searched in the nineteenth century, and was described as a dramatically spreading disease in wild deer by Fleming at the beginning of the last century. In 1886 many deer in Richmond Park died of rabies. Research by Horsley showed that infected animals could spread the disease to every other animal by biting. In 1889, within a period of three months, 450 of the 600–700 wild deer population of Ickworth Park, Suffolk, died in an outbreak of the disease (Chapman and Chapman).

The virus is usually spread through the saliva of infected animals; the incubation period is put at two–ten weeks (usually three–four weeks) but it can also be only a matter of days. The course of the disease depends on the site of the infection, the amount of virus and the virulence (i.e. total disease-carrying characteristics) of the germ. The virus spreads and multiplies along the nervous system until it reaches the brain and spinal cord. The most obvious symptoms are aggressiveness following a loss of the animal's natural timidity, jealousy and restlessness, and the length of the illness can be anything from one day to about four weeks.

There will be increased saliva flow, stark appearance and loss of appetite, followed by lameness, lying still and difficulties in swallowing, with eventual paralysis and weakness. Death comes from the damage to the central nervous system and paralysis of the respiratory system. There are no special changes to be found by post-mortem examination, although diagnosis can be made by examining certain antigens in the brain, and also through histological examination of the nerve cells. Rabies is a notifiable disease and treatment of affected animals is forbidden. There is an injection available of a dead vaccine.

Mucosal disease (MD) was found by Munday in Tasmania in eleven out of seventy-six deer examined, and is a world-wide infectious disease of cattle. Its symptoms are acute septic inflammation of the membranes of the digestive organs and, occasionally, of the skin near the hooves. (In Germany, about 50 per cent of all cattle carry antibodies, without having shown signs of the disease.) From present knowledge mucosal disease is not a significant illness of European deer. There is a vaccine available which is sometimes used for cattle, but its use is not really necessary. Mucosal disease is notifiable, however.

Lawman, Evans, Gibbs, McDiarmid and Rowe found, after examining blood samples from different species of deer, that they had antibodies against many of the different viral illnesses of domestic animals: IBR (infectious bovine rhinotracheitis) antibodies in red deer, mucosal disease and virus diarrhoea antibodies in red, fallow and sika deer, and reovirus and adenovirus antibodies in red, fallow, sika and Chinese water deer. They did not find antibodies against the sources of the following viral infections: foot and mouth disease, swine vesicular fever, EHD (enzootic haemorrhage), bluetongue, bovine herpes-mammillitis or PI3 (para-influenza 3).

There are no figures available for whether deer are susceptible to viral infections of the smaller farmed ruminants such as Borna disease, Louping ill, a contagious skin inflammation (*Ecthyma contagiosum*) and 'viral'-abortion (Chlamydia abortion).

Bacterial Diseases
Many bacterial infectious diseases have been observed and described in wild deer, and some have also been confirmed in farmed deer. From evaluating the literature and from our own experience, however, it can be stated that there are no known specific bacterial infectious diseases of deer. Of the bacterial diseases mentioned in the following sections, therefore, only a few of the particularly important ones will be dealt with in connection with deer. Those mentioned in the literature are: anthrax, pasteurellosis, tuberculosis, clostridial infection, brucellosis, salmonellosis, *B. coli* infection, necrobacillosis, red fever, heptospirosis, histeriosis, paratuberculosis and actinomycosis.

Anthrax has been known from early days, and is a world-wide disease; it has caused great losses of animals in the past and is also important because it may be transmitted to humans (i.e. it is a zoonotic disease). It was formerly the most important disease of wild animals, including deer, causing heavy losses. In the summer of 1874, in Prussia alone, about 2,000 head of red and fallow deer died because of it.

Basically infection follows the intake of anthrax germs from the ground with the forage, where the source is a very resistant, spore-forming and encapsulated ground seed. The spores develop and multiply in the alimentary canal and from there spread through the bloodstream and lymph glands to the whole body. It can take from one–fourteen days from intake of the germs to the first signs of illness, but the course of the disease is very swift: death comes after one–three days. The most significant symptom is a bloody discharge from the orifices of the body; there are also breathing difficulties and distension will be noted. From dissection the following picture emerges: the blood is tarlike, thick and not fluid, there is a lot of bleeding and a very swollen spleen, and the lymph nodules are swollen and bloody. The opening up of anthrax-infected carcasses is extremely dangerous and therefore prohibited. An injection against anthrax is possible; but it is not usually necessary to use this preventive measure as, thanks to measures taken by veterinary authorities and to generally improved hygiene, the disease is now very rare in Europe. Anthrax is a notifiable disease.

The name 'pasteurellosis' encompasses all those diseases which are caused by pasteurella appearing as haemorraghic septicaemia (food poisoning circulating with the blood). They often have the characteristics of factoral diseases: the causal organism is widespread in healthy animals and apparently requires a deterioration in condition or special environmental circumstances to trigger the onset of the disease. In the second half of the nineteenth century and up to the start of the First World War, pasteurellosis was identified as the cause of high losses among red and fallow deer. There have been no further outbreaks confirmed in Germany in this century, so the disease can be regarded as eradicated. Vaccines are available, but there is no need for immunisation.

Tuberculosis used to be an important disease among farm animals, and is also well known as a zoonotic disease. TB occurred in wild deer and also in estate and park deer; it counts as a 'genetic' disease to which wild deer are frequently susceptible. Of the three species of bacteria (*Mycobacterium bovis*, *M. humanus* and *M. avium*), avian TB and bovine TB germs have appeared in wild deer. Wilson and Harrington supplied information about a death from bovine TB of a deer in the wild in England. In the 1960s, in England, McDiarmid confirmed avian TB among various wild deer, in the open in 14 per cent of the animals examined, and in the parks in 28 per cent of animals (tests on the lymph nodules), and in 13 per cent of the wild deer tested in the New Forest.

Infection usually arises from grazing on pasture which has been infected by germs excreted in the faeces of diseased cattle or birds. When there are herds running together on estates and parks, there may also be cross-infection from close contact between the animals and from the faeces of other animals in the herd.

The course of the disease is usually slow, and it begins in the organ first infected, mainly as lung or intestinal TB. It can either be localised here, with scarring, hardening and healing according to circumstances, or it can spread through the organ's cells and affect the whole body. Affected beasts lose weight, and early symptoms are coughing with lung TB and diarrhoea, which is often chronic, with intestinal TB. General body condition gradually deteriorates. Treatment is not advised: affected animals should be slaughtered as quickly as possible. There are ways of testing live animals (TB tests), but no preventive inoculation. Poultry, as a likely source of infection, should not be kept close to a herd.

Occasionally there has also been mention of the presence of atypical *Mycobacteria* (germs similar to those causing TB) among fallow deer.

B. coli infection was a frequent cause of death among deer calves, as we noted from our own research with farmed deer. This disease is known world-wide among farm animals as a cause of losses and as an infection which appears in various forms in young animals. The causal organism, *Escheria coli*, appears in the intestinal tract of healthy animals, who can then develop debilitating characteristics if unfavourable environmental conditions apply (poor nutrition, cold, damp, or bad hygiene). *B. coli* infection is usually a causative disease. The incubation period is between a few hours and about three days. Peracute coli-septicaemia, which is known in calves as a feverishly progressive illness, has not yet been identified in deer calves. But acute progressive types have been noted, in which thin, light yellow, foamy faeces, severe body wasting and rapid dehydration of the body are symptoms. If the beasts are not treated, death can occur from a few days to about a week. The stomach and intestinal lining of the beast is inflamed, the intestinal lymph glands swollen, and the organs show signs of higher blood content. Diagnosis can be confirmed by bacteriological tests; if possible, the isolated virus should be tested for antibiotic resistance, to enable the necessary treatment to be put in hand.

The preventive measures taken with other farm animals (vaccination of the dams, treating the newborn animals) are not always suitable for deer, or indeed may not be necessary, but attention must be paid to ensuring the most hygienic conditions and the feeding of balanced rations, as well as disinfecting the navel at the same time as calves are marked on their first day of life. There are no proprietary vaccines specially prepared for deer; if needed, specific vaccines can be made up.

Necrobacillosis, a microbial infection caused by thread-like bacilli, which is widespread, has also been found among deer both in the wild and on estates. In the early autumn of 1978 it led to several deaths among 8–10-week-old deer calves in an experimental station's herd.

Necrosal bacteria are found in the soil and in the intestines of healthy animals, developing in darkness and under suitable circumstances, into sources of infection which can cause more or less serious, discharging ulcers and changes in the organs concerned. Frequently these are in the mouth, tongue and larynx membranes, but are also found in the cleft of the hooves, the frog and the coronary cushion. The disease is often encountered in ungulates. Fatal cases among deer calves were observed on a pasture which had for some years previously been grazed by sheep that had suffered from foot-rot.

The infection is apparently spread in the feed and symptoms are septic inflammation of the mouth and throat membranes (diphtheroid). Putrid-smelling sores appear on the tongue and larynx and also in the liver. As the disease is often only confirmed at a late stage of its progress, a proportion of calves cannot be saved: they will die within three–four weeks, since they can no longer swallow because of serious inflammation of the mouth and throat.

In the past several cases have been diagnosed at various sites. The disease always affected young beasts and on occasion caused heavy losses. Medical treatment is difficult; quick action is necessary. Veterinary measures include careful cleaning and washing of equipment, also spraying suitable disinfectants on the sores, and the usual dosing with sulphonamides and/or antibiotics. There are no injections available.

Isolating the affected beasts and putting them on clean pasture has proved worthwhile. Pastures which have been infected by sheep with foot-rot should be particularly avoided. Scrupulous hygiene precautions should be taken by those dealing with infected beasts: stalls, feeding and sleeping areas, drinking troughs and all equipment should be disinfected. On farms at risk, strict hygiene at calving and during calf rearing should be observed.

The germs can enter the body through small lesions in the membrane of the mouth, tongue, throat and oesophagus. The resistance of the membrane to these attacks can be boosted by intakes of beta-carotin and vitamin A. The addition of special supplementary feed with a high level of vitamin A is therefore recommended as a precaution against microbial infections.

Several other bacterial infections have been mentioned in the literature as affecting deer:

1. Erysipelas (red murrain) – in Tasmania, in two out of seventy-four deer tested (Munday).
2. Leptospirosis in one out of ninety-four fallow deer in southern England (Twigg and colleagues); no report of leptospirosis in New Zealand (Daniel); one out of 127 in Tasmania.
3. Actinomycosis in one fallow deer in the wild in Germany (Kober).
4. Brucellosis antibodies were never found to be at high levels in thousands of blood samples taken by McDiarmid. Also no brucellosis antibodies were found by Roberts, McDiarmid and Gleed in 670 serum tests in different areas of England, although they suspected that fallow deer were susceptible to brucellosis.
5. Pseudo-tuberculosis was established as the cause of death in one deer in a zoo (Zwart and Poelma).

Clostridia was found several times when we were investigating the cause of death in deer, but to date it cannot be determined whether these alone are significant sources of disease among fallow deer, or whether they are only to be regarded as contributory factors. Listerii are the cause of a disease (listeriosis) which is increasingly to be found in sheep, and which affects the brain in particular. It is a germ found widely in the soil, to which many types of animal are susceptible, but it is not known whether this also applies to deer. Listerii have optimum conditions for multiplying in poor quality silage which has not fermented properly, or soil-contaminated silage. Such forage is often responsible for outbreaks of sickness and is, therefore, to be avoided. Cases of listeriosis were reported by Schneller in fallow deer in West Germany.

Fungal Infections
Illnesses due to fungal infection have been found in one or two instances among wild deer. The fungi were mainly aspergillus and mucor types, and chiefly concern diseases of the respiratory tract. Infection is through mouldy fodder. The progress of the disease is chronic, with the formation of tubercles and tumours in the lungs. There is nothing to be gained by treatment; a precautionary step is to avoid feeding mouldy fodder.

Ringworm is a fungal infection of the skin, which occurs in all domestic animals and also in wild animals. It can be transmitted to humans, too. Infection is through fungal spores occurring in the environment, or it may be transmitted from one animal to another. Damp conditions encourage the onset of the infection. The spores attack the roots of the hair or the follicles: hair and scales fall from the scalp, and itchiness occurs. Ringworm is mainly found on the head and neck, and circular bald patches are to be noticed.

If cases are suspected, the vet can take scrapings of the skin and send them for analysis. Precautions and treatment are possible with specific preparations (antimycotics).

8.3   Digestive Illnesses and Poisoning

According to all the literature about animal health, farmed deer do not seem to suffer much from illnesses caused by the intake of various toxic substances (inorganic fertilisers, insecticides, seed dressings, etc.), or the digestive illnesses which affect the smaller farmed ruminants (tetanus, myositis and pregnancy toxicosis). They have certainly not been observed or described up to the present.

Digestive upsets, particularly in the rumen, were found in the herds tested if feeding regimes were changed when the herds were moved to other sites. These upsets took the form of acid stomach (over-acidity) or alkaline stomach (alkaline content of the omasum). The causes included sudden switching to silage as the basic fodder, insufficient provision of crude fibre on lush grass pasture, and feeding a lot of potatoes following grazing only on pasture. They were in part similar in spread to the occurrences of factoral diseases.

It can be seen from this that it is advisable to avoid any drastic change in feeding regimes, and to make sure that the rumen's microflora is very gradually adjusted to the new diet, over a period of about fourteen days, on average, with fallow deer.

Our own research shows that copper poisoning is an important digestive illness with deer. As with sheep, the feeding of concentrates with a high copper content is thought to be responsible for the onset of the illness, but copper-containing forage and soils can also cause this poisoning. Significant factors in this are the content of both geogens and antropogens.

There were many losses in deer calves at different farms, following the intake of large quantities of copper-containing concentrates and mineral supplements. The calves were either born too early and were therefore very weak, or else they died at only a few days old. The animals were insufficiently developed, showed a lack of vitality, looked jaundiced and sometimes had diarrhoea. On dissection there was much yellowing of the fatty tissues and particularly of the liver. On histological examination the liver tissue was shown to be greatly affected by the toxin, and chemical analysis of the livers of these animals showed readings of 1,300–1,450 mg copper per kg dry matter. As there were no figures for normal levels, many samples of liver tissue were taken from animals which had died from other causes, and from slaughtered deer, and the copper levels were tested. In young, healthy deer the values were 11–57 mg copper (average 25.5 mg) per kg dry matter.

No treatment is possible for copper poisoning; precautionary measures are to use only those concentrates and mineral mixes which are low in copper content, which are the ones generally recommended for sheep. It is very difficult to take precautions, though, if the grassland or other forages used have high copper levels – which depends, of course, on the particular environmental circumstances of the farm.

8.4 Parasitic Diseases

The presence of temporary or permanent parasites in or on the body, and the evidence of their eggs, larvae or other stages of development are not to be confused with the presence of a parasitic illness. The effects of the parasite population depend upon its strength and numbers, on the resistance of the host animal or its immunity, and on various other external factors, such as environmental conditions. Under natural conditions there is almost always a parasitic population associated with ruminants; there is usually a balance between the host and its burden of parasites.

The farming of large numbers of animals on a limited acreage creates favourable conditions for parasites to thrive, and for their disease-bearing or toxic effects to be increased, with consequences for the health of the herd. In wild herds, or in those farmed under proper hygienic conditions, the numbers of parasites are often only low or moderate, in spite of there being opportunities for infection. Animals carrying a low parasite burden may show no visible symptoms of disease, but sub-clinical infection can cause lasting damage, affecting the development, fertility/bearing ability and genetics of the host. Apart from this, an infected animal can spread the infectious material (eggs and larvae of the parasite). If the balance between the host and its burden of parasites is disturbed, this can lead to serious health upsets and to the progression of disease, and may have severe effects, particularly on young animals.

Attack by Single-celled Parasites (Protozoa)
The presence of coccidia has been noted in wild deer, without these having caused disease epidemics; coccidiosis is not apparent in farmed deer either, according to the relevant literature. The evidence of coccidial oozysts in excreta found in parasitological examination of fallow deer bore no relationship to any symptoms of disease present.

Coccidiosis is an important disease when lambs are kept indoors, close together. It affects the intestinal membranes and can often lead to death following weight loss and bloody diarrhoea. Strict cleanliness and hygiene in the living area are necessary precautions. Sulphonamides and coccidiostats have proved to be worthwhile additives.

Even if no previous cases of the disease have appeared in deer calves, however, it is advisable for the deer farmer to be on the alert.

As regards other protozoan parasites, there have been reports of:

- Babesis – a rare case with sub-clinical effects (Klös and Lang).
- One case of toxoplasmosis in Czechoslovakia.
- One report of sarcosporidies in Germany (Drost).

All these reports concern fallow deer.

Attacks by Worms

Those parasitic diseases which are caused by worms are the most important. Much has been written about the many types of worms found in both wild and farmed animals. The main species are shown in Table 8.9 and they are separated into the groups *nematodes* (round worms), *trematodes* (sucking worms) and *cestodes* (tape worms). The diseases caused by them which particularly

Table 8.9 Commonest parasitic worms in wild fallow deer

Name of species	English name	Part of body affected	Germany	Europe	Elsewhere
Nematodes	*Round worms*				
Bunostomum	Hook worms	Small intestine	×	×	×
Capillaria	Hair worms		×	×	×
Chabertia	Large intestine worms	Large intestine	×	×	
Cooperia	Small intestine worms	Small intestine	×	×	×
Dictyocaulus	Large lung worms	Lungs	×	×	
Haemonchus	Twisted stomach worms	Abomasum	×	×	×
Muellerius	Small lung worms	Lungs	×		
Nematodirus	Small thread worms	Small intestine	×	×	
Oesophagostomum	Small knot worms	Large intestine	×	×	×
Onchocerca		Connective tissue	×	×	
Ostertagia	Brown stomach worms	Abomasum	×	×	
Spiculopteragia	Stomach worms	Stomach/small intestine	×	×	×
Strongyloides	Small thread worms	Small intestine	×		
Trichostrongylus	Stomach thread worms	Stomach/small intestine	×	×	
Trichuris	Whip worms	Large intestine	×	×	
Trematodes	*Sucking worms*				
Dicrocoelium	Small liver fluke	Liver	×	×	
Fasciola	Large liver fluke	Liver	×	×	
Paramphistomum		Rumen	×	×	
Cestodes	*Tape worms*				
Moniezia	Tape worm	Small intestine	×	×	
Tape worm parts					
Echinococcus		Liver	×		
Taenia	Dog tape worm	Musculature	×	×	×

apply to farmed deer will be dealt with in the following pages.

Stomach and intestinal worms are widespread in both wild and farmed deer and can lead, if the infection is severe, to many cases of loss of condition and sometimes even death. The abomasum is often the host to large worms (twisted stomach worms – haemonchus) and/or small worms (brown stomach worms – ostertagia), and stomach thread worms (trichostrongylus), while the small intestine has small thread worms (nematodirus), whip worms (trichuris), hook worms (bunostomum) and other types of round worm. Usually there is multiple infection by different species, and there are often lung worms present, too (dictyocaulus and muellerius). Some types of worm are visible to the naked eye when dissecting the abomasum or intestines, such as the 2–3 cm long twisted stomach worm; others are only a few millimetres in length and as fine as hair, so that they are often overlooked or only detected by a specialist. The oval, thin-shelled eggs of the stomach and intestine worms are excreted, and they can be detected in faeces samples subjected to parasitological examination.

As a rule there is no cross-infection between farmed ruminants and wild ruminants such as deer, because most types of parasite have a specific host animal. From the eggs of the worm emerge larvae which are capable of becoming infective, externally and without needing an interim host, within one–two weeks. This infective period lasts for up to four months. Infection occurs from the pasture: the active larvae move up the grass stems and are

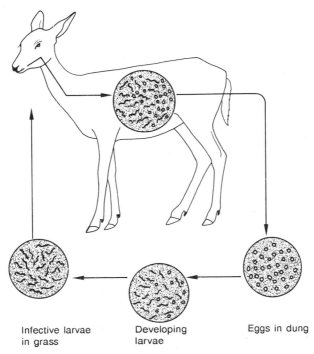

Infective larvae   Developing   Eggs in dung
in grass   larvae

Figure 8.1 Life cycle of the stomach/intestinal worm.

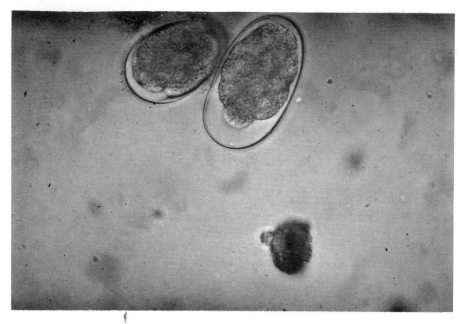

Plate 8.1   Eggs of stomach/intestinal works, magnified.

eaten with the forage. They develop into fertile worms in the alimentary canal, and can begin their cycle of egg-laying as early as three weeks after infection. The ill effects they can cause include the abstraction of blood and nutrients, damage to the membranes, and supplying toxic metabolic products. Sick animals show symptoms of anaemia, with loss of condition, thin, almost liquid faeces, a lack-lustre coat and, in severe attacks, throat oedema. Fatalities can occur, particularly with young animals.

Safe and effective medicines are available, which will be mentioned later along with worm treatments. One important precaution would be to avoid using wet or marshy grassland for grazing, and to use this grass for hay or other purposes. Regular dosing of all animals in the herd, after testing faeces samples, is recommended and should be done as a routine measure at least four times a year.

Lung worm attack is often linked with attack by stomach and intestinal worms. Severe infection can lead to serious disease symptoms, even death, especially with young animals. There are two types of lung worms, large and small.

Large lung worms (dictyocaulus) grow to about 6–10 cm in length and live in the air passages in the large bronchial tubes; their development cycle, like that of the stomach and the intestinal worm, proceeds without an intermediate host. (The larvae, which can be detected in the faeces under a microscope, emerge from the eggs which are coughed out or excreted.) Treatment is the same as for stomach and intestinal worms.

The various types of small lung worm are only 1–1.5 cm in length and live in the smaller bronchial tubes and in the surrounding lung tissues. Their larvae

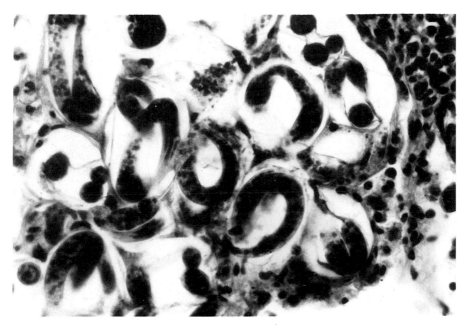

Plate 8.2   Larvae of lung works, magnified.

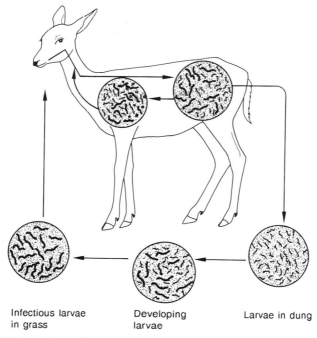

Infectious larvae
in grass

Developing
larvae

Larvae in dung

Figure 8.2 Life cycle of the large lung worm

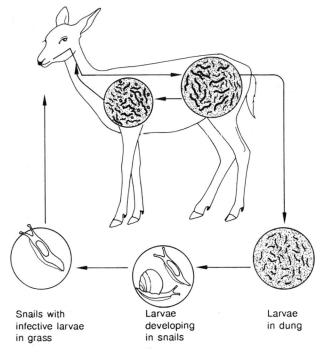

Snails with
infective larvae
in grass

Larvae
developing
in snails

Larvae
in dung

Figure 8.3 Life cycle of the small lung worm.

need particular snails as intermediate hosts in their development cycle. They enter the foot of the snail, develop into infective larvae and the snails are then eaten with the grass on damp pasture. Once inside the body of the host the larvae pass from the intestine to the lungs.

Large lung worms lead to more or less apparent inflammation of the bronchial membranes (bronchitis) and the nearby lung tissues (lung worm pneumonia). Affected animals will cough, usually a short, dry cough which in the advanced stages sounds strained and painful. With severe cases, the animals will lose condition and weight, and there is a nasal discharge. Death sometimes follows from the inflammation of the lungs. Infection by the small lung worm may remain undetected for a long time, but the overall health of the animal can be affected and symptoms are exacerbated by unfavourable environmental conditions, dampness and simultaneous attack by stomach and intestinal worms.

The normal stomach or intestinal worm treatment is not effective against the small lung worm, but there are specific remedies available. Preventive measures are the same as for stomach or intestinal worms.

Liver fluke is a problem with both wild and farmed animals in susceptible areas, and there are many instances cited in the literature. There are both large (fasciola) and small (dicrocoelium) liver flukes. The former is about 3 cm long, a dark grey, broad flat worm, which lives in the gall ducts of the liver; its eggs are excreted, and can be seen in faeces under a microscope. The

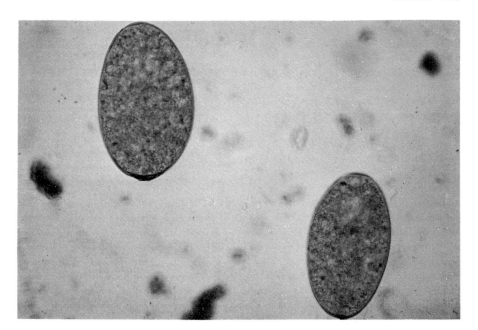

Plate 8.3 Liver fluke eggs, magnified.

larvae which emerge from the eggs have a lengthy (i.e. several months) and complicated life cycle, depending on small mud snails as intermediate hosts. In the following stage the young worms, encapsulated in a bubble, are taken in as the animal grazes. Mud snails live on the edges of ponds or on muddy areas in damp pastureland, so deer grazing such places are particularly vulnerable to liver fluke infestation. Affected animals show signs of loss of appetite, pale membranes, loss of weight, sometimes diarrhoea and, in severe infestation, throat oedema.

There are special preparations available, which are also partly effective against the immature stages of the liver fluke, and they should be given if the vet has found evidence of the fluke in parasitological examinations after dissection or in faeces samples. Prevention includes field hygiene measures such as flood and drainage precautions, combating the snails either with chemicals (but beware the danger to the environment) or dressing the pasture with calcium nitrate (about 300 kg per ha) at the start of grass growth. If faeces samples have shown positive results, all the animals on the farm can be treated as a precaution at the same time.

There are special characteristics to note with the small liver fluke. This approximately 1 cm long dark brown or black flat worm is only found on chalky, dry soils, where its intermediate hosts, snails and ants, have their habitat.

Tape worms are of little significance as instigators of disease, according to the literature and also from our own experience, although there may often be evidence of their presence when eggs are found in faeces. If there are a lot of

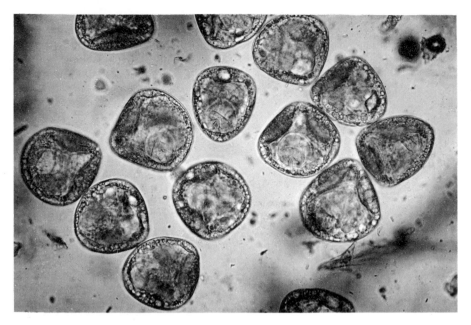

Plate 8.4 Tape worm eggs, magnified.

them, treatment with proprietary preparations can be given, as is the practice in sheep farming. Overall preventive measures are not usually necessary; infestation with tape worms, which can often be found in wild deer, is not of any significance when deer are farmed. The presence of tape worms in deer is linked with the presence of moss mites as intermediate hosts.

Medicinal Treatment of a Worm Burden
Until lately, specific medicines were needed for the various worm infections (endo-parasites) or a mixture of these, but now there are very effective and acceptable broad-spectrum anthelmintics on the market. There is the obvious advantage of their wide effectiveness, but they are also easier to use and economically priced. A selection is given in Table 8.10. This only includes a few of the older, well-known medicines which have limited effectiveness, because dosing with the new broad-spectrum anthelmintics is the more common practice today. In Germany, all the medicines named must be obtained from the vet under prescription, and veterinary advice should be taken on methods of treatment and choosing the most appropriate materials. In our own experience granules and tablets are preferred, if the animals are used to being given 'tempting food', as they will take the dose along with this.

Worming treatment should always be considered for the herd in general, i.e. it should encompass all the animals; individual treatment is usually pointless and uneconomic. Medicinal remedies on their own are not enough to solve parasite problems: the health programme must also include regulation of the herd's environmental conditions and taking general hygiene measures.

Table 8.10 Some of the commonest worming medicines for small ruminants

Name	Manufacturer	Worms combated
Bayvern	Bayer	Gut worms, lung worms, tape worms
Ovitelmin	Janssen	Gut worms, lung worms, tape worms
Panacur drench or in feed	Hoechst	Gut worms, lung worms, tape worms, liver fluke
Oramec (drench)	MSD	Gut worms, lung worms, tape worms
Ivomec (injection)		Liver fluke
Fasinec	Ciba Geigy	Liver fluke
Vermadax	RMB	Gut worms, liver fluke
Valbazen	Smith Kline	Gut worms, lung worms, tape worms, liver fluke
Levacide	Norbrook	Gut worms, lung worms

Infestation with External Parasites

Parasites present in wild and farmed deer include lice, fleas, mites and ticks, but these seem to cause no serious damage to the health of the host animal. Lice were found on wild deer in various parks in England (Chapman and Chapman), and have been known on truly wild deer for many years. Fleas — blood-sucking wingless flies — have been noted as summer parasites in various European countries but are apparently not very common on wild deer. Ticks are often found on both wild and farmed deer, but the transmission of pathogenic micro-organisms by them as they suck blood has not been conclusively proved. Mange mites are apparently not an important factor with deer, as only one report of a case of sarcoptes mites has been noted (Chapman and Chapman).

The presence of these ecto-parasites in or on the skin or hair is not usually of any importance, but a severe infestation can lead to restlessness and sometimes to weakness due to loss of blood. Insect bites cause much itchiness, however, and can lead to a deterioration in the animal's general condition. Inflammation of the skin or hair loss may occur through rubbing, scratching or biting the affected area but, as a rule, serious cases of infestation only affect weak, sickly or aged beasts. There are contact insecticides available in spray or powder form for treating the infestation, and these can be used as a precaution on susceptible sites. It is not practicable to wash, dip or bathe fallow deer as a precaution, as is the practice with other farm animals.

Finally, mention must be made of botflies, warble flies and tongue worm attacks. Botfly or deer botfly larvae are the young stage of a botfly development, of which there has been an occasional isolated case affecting fallow deer. They pass through several stages of development in the upper section of the nasal passages and in the throat, causing inflammation of the membranes. The animal's overall condition can be severely affected, with coughing spasms, and fatal cases have been observed in wild animals. Treatment for botfly attack can be carried out successfully by giving the preparation Flukamide (MSD) or similar.

Warble flies have been reported in various types of deer, but so far not in fallow deer.

There have been very rare instances of the thread-like capsules of the larvae of the tongue worm (*Linguatula*) having been found in deer, which function as an intermediate host. This is of no practical significance, and preventive measures and treatment are not necessary.

8.5   Preventive Measures

Health problems increase with the denser stocking rate of farmed animals, with the greater possibility of contagious diseases spreading. Environmental conditions also have a lot of influence on the animals' resistance or vulnerability to disease. Farming deer obviously carries a similar risk of such health problems arising, and there are also on-going economic demands, such as buying and selling the beasts, and farming the acreage to the best advantage. The husbandry of the animals must, therefore, include a planned health programme. All aspects of animal hygiene must be taken care of when planning and then using the farm's facilities, as they are of vital importance, but measures to combat infectious illnesses and parasites should be the central aim.

Nursing a single sick animal back to health is often difficult on a farm; apart from special circumstances (such as the case of a valuable breeding animal), treatment of an isolated case when farming extensively can hardly be economically valid.

Veterinary surgeons are, therefore, almost exclusively geared to the preventive health care of the whole farm population, and a trusted vet should be seen as a knowledgeable adviser. Such matters as feeding and breeding hygiene demand specialised knowledge and experience of the biology of deer and their practical farming.

Dangers to health fall into three categories: those caused by infection, parasites and contaminated fodder. The losses suffered are not only from fatal cases; much more important are the effects of appetite loss, weight loss and the way in which resistance to disease and also fertility are affected. There may be a link between diseases in animals and in humans, with the possibility of cross-infection, and the health of the animal can also have subsequent effects on food quality and hygiene. Thus careful health precautions have to be taken on both ethical and economic grounds on the deer farm.

The measures which are necessary depend mainly on the size of the farm and the type of enterprise (breeding, rearing or meat production). Topographical and other local conditions and stocking density are also factors to consider. Some of the more important prophylactic measures are discussed below.

Fencing is one means of ensuring against the unwanted entry of other animals and protecting the deer from infections and parasites entering the area. Because of the danger of rabies in certain parts of western Europe, a special watch must be kept there on foxes, stray dogs and other potential carriers of the disease. The fencing must be so constructed that it will not be liable to injure any deer which take flight when startled.

Setting up a quarantine area for inspecting and examining new arrivals guards against introducing infection. The animals should be kept there in isolation for about four weeks and, during this time, clinical, blood, parasito-logical and other tests can be done as well as necessary treatments and injections given. The quarantine area should be secure against breaking in or out, should keep the deer from contact with other animals, and should be sited so that it is not necessary to pass through the main grazing area to reach it. The entry should be furnished with a disinfectant mat or preferably a dip, which should be regularly cleaned out and renewed. The site should be on dry hard ground and this and equipment in the area must be kept clean and disinfected.

Sick animals should be brought into a separate paddock or stall for examination and treatment, which should be equipped like the quarantine area. These measures make handling easier and guard against infecting the rest of the herd.

An on-going health control programme is vital and should cover the systematic examination of all dead animals, the planned testing of faeces samples (at least four times a year) and, where necessary, the catching and isolating of animals which look ill, to enable a diagnosis to be carried out. To make sure this programme is successful, preventive and curative measures should be planned and carried out with full knowledge of all the facts. This is particularly the case when dealing with parasitology. A regular laboratory test of fresh faeces samples at a veterinary centre will give information on the type and extent of parasitic infestation. If single samples are sent in only occasionally, it is difficult to form a complete picture. The measures necessary to treat an outbreak will depend on the results of the examination, and the vet will help with the choice of suitable medicaments, dosages required and the method of administering them.

A long-term systematic programme of health care will not only include the medicinal treatment of affected animals, but also the interruption of the development cycle of the parasites. This is done by alternating the use of pastureland (rotational grazing, cutting for hay or silage), and measures to ensure land hygiene. Attacking the intermediate host can be effective against certain types of parasite, as mentioned earlier, and attention should also be paid to flood precautions, drainage and the disposal of parasites or intermediate hosts as well as the treatment of parasite-infected pastureland. There is a range of effective, harmless medicines available which are suitable for use with deer, and which can be given in pellet form with the food, with appetisers or as a licking block.

Attention must be paid when moving dead animals, and care is also necessary with animals showing apparent signs of infection. Cutting up, skinning, removing offal, etc. can help spread infection. (The possibility of infection with rabies or other serious contagious diseases must be borne in mind.) A definite diagnosis of the cause of death can only be made if the whole carcass is sent as quickly as possible to the veterinary laboratory for examination. When sending in samples, these guidelines should be followed:

1. Only fresh samples, and in the case of faeces samples a sufficient quantity, should be sent by the quickest means possible (express parcels or messenger delivery).

2. If the outside temperature is above 10°C, samples will deteriorate within a day.
3. Carcasses, faeces and other samples should be packed in waterproof plastic and sent in rigid containers.
4. With them should be a note of the name and address of the sender, details of the farm, the number of diseased animals, the symptoms of the disease, the treatment given and the name of the vet.

If samples are not being sent to determine the cause of death, in Germany the carcasses should be buried whole (according to the regulations governing animal burial).

When it comes to healthy feeding, a knowledgeable choice of feeding stuffs should be made and a hygienic feeding regime followed. Quantity, quality, nutritive value and suitability of the ration's contents are all important. All foodstuffs should be regularly examined from the standpoints of appearance, smell, cleanliness, foreign bodies (plastic, binder twine, wire, etc.) and freshness. Analysis of the basic forage (i.e. hay and silage) by agricultural laboratories will give valuable information and enable the correct supplements to be given in the form of minerals, trace elements and vitamins. Food should never be offered on the ground, but in sturdy, roomy racks, troughs or on feed tables (concrete ones for silage). These should be easy to clean and kept clear of any possibility of contamination with faeces. The clearing away of waste food and animal waste must be done carefully, and there must be an adequate supply of clean water.

Removal of the antler base in male calves and the antlers in stags is a measure which should be taken to avoid injuries, both to humans and to protect the other animals on the farm. It is an essential part of any health care programme.

Visitors should be kept out of the pastures as a rule, and they should certainly not be allowed to take other animals with them into the fields.

The authorities should be informed at once if disease breaks out among the deer, or among other animals on the farm. Veterinary regulations must be strictly adhered to.

The condition of the animals' housing and its suitability for their needs is another hygiene factor to take into account, and it must also satisfy the requirements of the workforce and any other technical and economic considerations. Planning and upkeep of the right sort of shelter, bedding, grazing and handling areas as well as maintenance of the buildings and equipment are all essential factors in animal health and safety.

A planned programme of preventive measures should include the following:

1. Taking faeces samples every quarter or at least twice a year and then treating any internal parasites found, after veterinary examination.
2. Ensuring pregnant females have adequate minerals and vitamins.
3. Marking newborn calves on their first day, and checking and disinfecting the navel.
4. Removing the antler base on male deer calves at about four months of age.
5. If there have been external parasites, treating the animals at least once a year with contact insecticide (spray or powder) as a precautionary measure.

Decisions about hygiene must always be taken with regard to their suitability to local conditions. The type of site, the number of animals and other external circumstances have a bearing on what should be done, and measures should only be planned and carried out in detail in collaboration with an experienced vet, taking into account all the relevant circumstances.

8.6 Immobilisation Methods

It is necessary to sedate or tranquillise deer when catching, transporting or treating them with preventive or curative medicines, or removing antlers etc. This involves immobilising them by clinical methods, and/or sedating them for capture or handling without danger, but it is not the same as anaesthetising them, which means rendering them unconscious and insensitive to pain (Fritsch).

There are many different drugs available for immobilising animals. However, with deer, as with other wild animals, it is not possible to use those injected intravenously as employed by vets. In deer farming it is necessary to use a tranquilliser gun, so the drug must be suitable for giving as an intra-muscular or a subcutaneous injection. Specific drugs and the necessary equipment for immobilising deer are now available, but they must be handled by someone with knowledge and experience, and also in accordance with legal regulations.

There is no drug from the group of peripheral muscle relaxants which can be fully recommended for deer. Such drugs work by blocking the connection between the motor nervous system and the muscle fibres and so cause paralysis of the limbs and diaphragm (a similar effect to that of curare, used by the Indians for poison arrows). The main reservation about these drugs is

Figure 8.4 Body sites suitable for injecting with tranquillising drugs (shaded).

their narrow dosage band, which could mean that a dose might be fatal in certain circumstances, if it affected the respiratory muscles, or it could lead to circulatory troubles and damage to the heart muscles. Also, for ethical reasons, it must be borne in mind that immobilising the musculature and rendering the animal unconscious can lead to an intolerable psychogenic effect, possibly leading to panic or shock reactions.

Among the peripheral muscle relaxants for use as immobilisation inducers, the Succincholin preparations have been the subject of particular concern. They have a narrow band of tolerance, and there is the aforementioned danger of death from asphyxia or heart failure. Ethical concerns also militate against the use of such a drug, as the animal being treated cannot move or escape, although it is still conscious.

There is now only historic interest in the intra-muscular use of Nicotine-Salicylate, which was of epoch-making importance in its time for immobilising wild animals under the name of Cap-Chur©. Its pharmacological effects are similar to those of the muscular relaxants. However, as it enters the system quickly, it causes panic symptoms such as muscle twitching and cramp, the heartbeat and blood flow increase and breathing may be affected before the desired paralysis occurs. Centrally acting sedatives and narcotics can be added, which can reduce the undesirable side-effects, but since this drug was first used more suitable preparations have come on to the market.

Today there are two proven groups of drugs which can be recommended for sedating deer. These are described as centrally acting muscle relaxants, and they bring about slackness of the muscles by working on the movement centres in the brain or on the reflex centres in the spinal marrow.

Neuroleptica causes a dulling of the mind to a sleepy state and incapacitates the animal by slackening the muscles leading from the central nervous system and dulling the autonomic, vegetative nervous system. The effect it has is similar to that of sleep. With a small dose it has a soothing effect; with larger doses the treated animal will lie still. It should be given without previously disturbing the animals by driving them or otherwise upsetting them.

Xylazin, trade-name Rompun© (Bayer), has been used successfully for deer. It has a sedative-hypnotic effect, relaxes the central muscles and dulls pain. These reactions occur quickly and simultaneously and fulfil the requirements for ideal immobilisation conditions, to enable the required handling and treatment to be carried out. The treated animal will, according to dosage, be put in a sleepy state with general slackness of the muscles and lowering of pain. When given as an intra-muscular dose, the first effects will be apparent after about two–five minutes: the animal's movements will become slower, its alertness less sharp, and its head and neck will drop lower; after this unsteadiness of movement there is an obvious weakness of the rear quarters and the animal will lower itself repeatedly until, about ten–fifteen minutes after dosing, it will be lying down calmly, usually with its head and neck to one side. There may be purring or snoring noises, a light salival flow and the tip of the tongue may hang out; breathing and pulse rate will be slower. If the treated animal is left before the sedative and muscle-relaxing effects of the drug have worn off, ensure that it is in the prone position (or at least on its right side), otherwise the interference with the rumen's working may lead to bloat. Use of Rompun©

should be avoided with heavily pregnant hinds, as it has been known to affect the womb in cattle and there may be danger of abortion.

Rompun© is supplied as a ready-to-use 2 per cent liquid solution (1 ml = 20 mg) in 25 ml bottles for intra-muscular injection. For intravenous or intra-muscular application, the dry form is available in 500 mg bottles (with separately packed, self-sterilising solvent). When using the dry product, the contents of the 500 mg bottle in 10 ml of solvents will give a 5 per cent concentration, in 5 ml of solvent a 10 per cent concentration.

Dosage details available from the manufacturers are mainly for use with wild animals, or wild deer in herds on estates or parks.

The dosage needed for a completely satisfactory effect is very largely dependent on the tameness of the animals to be immobilised. The maker's recommended dosage can vary widely for different animals according to degree of tameness and the conditions under which they are kept. These levels also cover the use of the drug with zoo animals. As a rule, bucks which need to be immobilised in a park or in the wild, require a higher dosage whereas tamer (farmed) animals will require less (Klös and Lang).

From our experience, to immobilise a tame deer of 30–40 kg live weight (a yearling or pricket) will require a dose of 2–2.5 ml of 2 per cent ready-to-use Rompun© solution (used in a short 2.6 m blow-pipe). For deer calves 2 ml of 2 per cent solution is usually enough.

The use of Rompun© has many advantages: multiple effects; high concentration without damaging the tissue; no intra-narcotic or post-narcotic side-effects; long shelf life; it is relatively safe to handle; quickly passes through the body as it breaks down easily and so there is only a short waiting period; and it can be mixed with analeptics. The undesirable effect, which has been described, of animals becoming over-excited by the drug, is not important when the drug is given to farmed deer, as they are relatively tame.

As well as Xylazin, Azaperon is another of the neuroleptic drugs, with the trade name Stresnil© (Janssen). This is said to have a calming effect although the animal remains fully conscious, and is only used with tame or partly tamed animals. There are, however, no reports of its use with fallow deer.

Analgesics act by raising the pain barrier (analgesia = loss of pain) in the brain while at the same time having a sedative effect, producing immobility of the stretched muscle, while the level of consciousness is lowered or completely lost. As with neuroleptics there is no narcotic effect. If the incorrect dose is given it could lead to excitement or cramp and sometimes to breathing difficulties.

The best known drugs in this group are morphine and the like but they come under the heading of dangerous drugs (in the legal definition), as sedatives subject to legal regulations. For this reason, the main drugs used today to give similar results to morphine, but without the risks of side-effects, are the dissociative anaesthetics (anaesthesia = lack of feeling). Ketamin has been developed for this purpose. It goes under the trade names Ketanest© 1 per cent or 5 per cent and Vetalar© 10 per cent (Parke-Davis). It acts quickly, within one–three minutes, has a long-lasting effect – thirty–sixty minutes – and has a large range of therapeutic uses.

Vetalar© (Ketamin hydrochloride) is available in 10 ml bottles as a 10 per cent, ready-to-use solution for intra-muscular and/or intravenous use. It brings about stillness, anaesthesia and painlessness together with unconsciousness, and has no sedative or hypnotic effects. It has a slight effect on the heart's functioning, but respiration is only very slightly affected. Its safety level is high.

A combination of Rompun© and Vetalar©, called 'Hellabrunner Mixture' (Wiesner) has been found successful for immobilising wild animals, because it gives an acceptable immobilisation without harming circulation or causing agitation, and it works quickly and safely at a low dosage. The mixture is made by dissolving the contents of a packet of Rompun powder (= 500 mg Xylazin) in 4 ml Vetalar© (= 400 mg Ketamin). This corresponds to a concentration of 125 mg Xylazin and 100 mg Ketamin per litre. The dose Wiesner suggests for deer is 1–2 ml intra-muscular. Its use fulfils the optimum requirements for an immobilisation method: it is safe to use; widely compatible; quick and safe-acting, giving sufficient muscular slackening; has few side-effects; a relatively short recovery phase; and it is easy to give in low-level doses.

One disadvantage of using this product lies in the rather troublesome method of preparing the solution. Another is its price. As a rule, it is unnecessary to use the 'Hellabrunner Mixture' for farmed deer, as Neuroleptics are very effective for use with tame or semi-tame animals.

After the dose has been given, the immobilised animal should be approached and handled quietly and calmly. The effectiveness of the dose should be checked; the limbs should be tied so as to avoid injury through being kicked or trampled on. The animal should, if possible, be lying prone on soft, level ground, to avoid distension of the rumen and swallowing of saliva and/or food. The head should be lying low, so that saliva can flow away. If unconsciousness seems too deep, the air passages, breathing and pulse should be examined. If necessary, in extreme cases, a suitable antidote prescribed by the vet can be used.

If the animal has to be moved, this must be done as carefully as possible; the animal must never be turned on its back, but always on its front. If the effects are prolonged, e.g. after over-dosing, the eyes must be carefully protected, as they could be damaged by sunlight, by becoming dry, by dust, sand or other foreign bodies, or they could be injured while the animal is being handled. If the dart has not fallen out, it should be carefully removed so that the entry point can be treated. Complications with large wounds and resultant infections do not usually follow when darts are used.

Avoid all unnecessary disturbance while the animal is under the influence of the drug or in the 'recovery phase'. With some of the drugs mentioned there is a subsequent 'sleepy' phase, which is quite normal; the animal should not be disturbed during this stage.

As with other forms of wild animal handling, deer farmers need some type of weapon for applying the immunising drug, to enable an intra-muscular injection to be given at a distance. This distance is not so great on a deer farm as it would be in the wild or on estates or parks, so that the choice of a suitable weapon is made easier.

Sporting guns, particularly the high velocity modern ones, are not suitable. A projectile shot from one of these hits its target with such force that an

Plate 8.5   Blow-tube.

animal would be seriously wounded, suffer broken bones, or even be killed.
The right type of weapon for injection purposes must therefore have low
velocity and the lowest possible weight of projectile. The noise of the report is
a not unimportant consideration, too: if it is too loud it could have undesirable
side-effects. For all these reasons, a purpose-made weapon, specially designed
for the injection of drugs from a distance, is obviously a necessity. There are
many proven versions of such injection weapons and projectiles available.

For distant injections of liquids there are special gas pressure guns and air
guns (narcotic guns) available, and cross-bows, bows and arrows, blow-pipes
and spears are also suitable.

While the use of the so-called narcotic guns for injection may be unavoidable
in the wild and on larger estates, there is a method suitable for farmed deer
called the 'Telinject' system, developed in recent years as an acceptable
alternative, in which special darts are blown through polished blow-pipes. The
system is particularly good for use with domesticated animals, and enables safe
treatment from a shorter distance without causing entry wounds, and without
disturbing the beast to be treated or the rest of the herd. The following advantages can be mentioned: the animals are not frightened more than necessary;
the weapon is easy to handle; and it is cheap and safe to use.

Blow-pipes are made from a special light alloy with low flexibility; long
tubes are then slightly bent to give the correct curvature. Blow-pipe shooting
is easy to learn but needs a lot of practice. Take aim with both eyes open; for a
practised shot it is possible to make a safe hit on a deer from about 10–15 m.

As the blow-pipe is silent, the animals are not panicked into flight after they

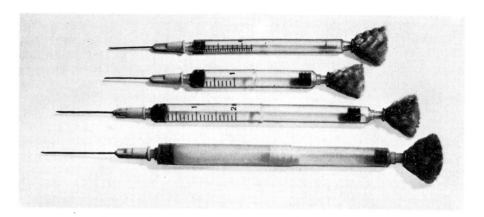

Plate 8.6 'Telinject' darts are reusable, with easily fitted components.

are hit. They often do not react at all to the jab, or just display a short twitching, and they do not show signs of disturbance. It is thus possible, if necessary, to shoot several animals out of a group before the drugs start to take effect and the rest of the animals are disturbed by this.

One model (Application Tube 2) is for use with darts holding 2 ml fluid; it is polished and comes complete with special mouth piece, sight, cleaning kit and carrying strap, and it has been recommended for use with deer. It comes in lengths (according to range required) of 2 m, 1.25 m and 1 m, and there are special types of projectile available for use with it. Another model (Application Tube 3) is for use with syringes holding 2 or 3 ml fluid, the larger size needing an adaptation ring. This tube also comes in 2 m, 1.25 m and 1 m lengths. Specially marked flights are also used on the projectiles with this tube.

Once the blow-pipe method was established in veterinary practice, the idea came of adding to its advantages by extending the range and so making it of more varied practical use. For this purpose a blow-pipe gun was brought onto the market, which also enables better control of the propulsion energy that previously was more or less non-existent. The important features of a blow-pipe gun are an air container shaped like a pistol, a pump (the simplest being a footpump), a 1 m-long tube and a shaft assembled from three pieces with straps. With these weapons shooting can be done at a range of from 1 metre to as much as 30 or 40 metres and it is equally safe for the animals. The pressure can be set or changed to the correct setting for the desired range in a matter of seconds. (It is important to have a manometer, so that propulsion pressure can be measured precisely.)

The dart syringes should contain as much liquid as possible, but still be light and strong. When contact is made with the animal the liquid should be promptly and completely released into the body. The syringes should be easy and safe to fill and carry, but also quick to load into the gun. They should also, of course, be reusable so as to make them cheap and economical.

The syringes are made of light, durable, almost unbreakable plastic. After

Plate 8.7   First effects of intra-muscular injection of tranquilliser (hind quarters relaxing).

filling the syringe with the liquid, the special cannula with its sealed side opening is fitted on. For safety reasons, a cap should be put over the point, so that
the filled (but still unpressurised) syringes can be safely inserted in the gun. Just
before use – and not before – they should be primed to the required pressure
by a simple air-filling device at the back. Then, after the flight has been fitted
and the safety cap removed, the darts are ready for firing. Unused drugs can be
transferred to the bottle provided by emptying the syringe through the rubber
seal. The syringe can be loosened by using the plunger. The tip of the cannula
is blind, and the injection is through a side opening, which is sealed before
shooting with a movable closure device. On entering the muscle this device
is pushed backwards and the pressurised liquid is injected. There are special
cannulas for use with blow-pipes which have plastic sockets, while those for
blow-pipe guns are all metal.

When using such injection systems, the surroundings must be considered
carefully. It is very important to remember whether one is dealing with small
or large deer, relatively tame or timid deer or ones moving over large or small
areas. Sex, age, condition and temperament all have to be taken into account
when determining the dose of the tranquillising drug. There are, therefore,
only a few rules which apply in all situations, of which the most important will
be briefly dealt with in the list below.

The most important recommendation is to ensure that the means of
tranquillising are suitable to the time, place, special circumstances, personnel,
feeding, noise, scent and other habits which determine the life rhythm of the

Plate 8.8   Full effect of tranquilliser (lying still with relaxed muscles).

animals and to which they are accustomed. When deer are to be injected, choose the habitual feeding time, with the usual keeper present; any strangers, such as the vet or the injector, should then take up their appropriate positions. To be on the safe side, several prepared syringes should be kept ready in case of failure of a shot; a second shot may sometimes be needed.

The person responsible for the tranquillising measures must take note of the following:

1. The surroundings and the routine at the time of the injection should be those to which the animals are accustomed. They should be carefully supervised beforehand. During the tranquillising and the subsequent treatment or handling a time schedule should be followed. In West Germany these drugs can only be used by or under the supervision of a vet.
2. The drug and the dosage should be accurately and carefully chosen in consultation with the vet.
3. Spare syringes – about double the number required – should be filled, prepared and kept on hand. The special cannulas and their closures should be tested for leaks and then firmly fixed, with safety caps over the point.
4. Air-fill syringes, fittings and flights should be tested. Damaged flights should be replaced with new ones.
5. Several practice shots should be made at the range which is likely to be used. Make it a habit to practise before shooting!
6. The syringe should not be pressurised with the compressed air until just before approaching the animal. For empty 2 ml and 3 ml syringes, 13 ml air

should be used. If the liquid does not flow, more air should be pumped in. Make sure it is tight and not leaking! Then put on the flight, take off the safety cap and load the dart.

7. Approach the animal as calmly and unobtrusively as possible, always pointing the blow-tube or gun at the animal.

8. If several animals are to be stunned, it is often difficult to keep an eye on those which have been injected first. It is therefore advisable always to inject the beasts from one side only – left or right – so as to avoid the danger of injecting the same animal twice. Also the marksman should choose an animal standing separate from the rest as his target, so that others are not shot by accident (in case of his missing the target, animals moving, gusts of wind, etc.).

9. The point of entry of the dart affects the length of time taken for the drug to take effect. Injections near the head and in the shoulder, for example act more quickly as a rule than those in the hind quarters. If animals are shot there, the defensive reactions are sharper. Shots in the neck or shoulder muscles must always be made at close range and with very careful aim, to avoid at all costs the risk of hitting vulnerable areas of the head.

10. A note should be made of the time immediately after the injection shot. Tranquillised animals should be left to lie quietly on their sides or in the prone position. According to the type of animal, the drug used, the dosage and other circumstances, the full effect will be reached after five–twenty minutes or more. Approach the prone animal slowly and quietly from the rear. It is best to tie the legs: helpers must be close at hand to hold the animal and restrain it if necessary. If possible, notes should be made of the age and weight of the animal, drugs and dosage used, time to take effect, depth of unconsciousness and other remarks. Such notes can be very helpful in similar situations in the future.

11. Used darts should be carefully collected up. Never put unused injection solution into a cannula which has just been used! The syringes should have the air withdrawn by a pump and only after this has been done can the new cannulas be fitted and the syringes filled.

   Defective, bent or broken syringes and cannulas should be emptied, made unusable and put carefully aside. Those syringes and cannulas which can be used again should be washed well and sterilised. When sterilising the syringes, they should be lightly filled with air. The moving parts can be lubricated with a drop of silicone oil. The flights should be removed from the dry syringes and stored with these in the protective case; flights damaged by faulty storage can lead to poor shooting later.

12. The whole apparatus and all its parts should be checked after use, cleaned, put tidily away and kept ready for the next occasion.

When using tranquillising drugs, there is a list of regulations to be adhered to. These are governed by laws on drugs and anaesthetics as well as those on animal welfare and the use of weapons (see page 262).

In Germany all the drugs in question are subject to veterinary prescription rules, according to the regulations of the drugs laws, tranquilliser regulations and the decrees concerning these. Certain conditions must be met in the acquisition, use and disposal of these tranquillising drugs, which must be prescribed and obtained through a vet who will have special information and experience regarding their supply and disposal. With his authority, the drugs can be administered by someone other than a vet; this person then assumes the role of executive assistant.

The carrying of a narcotics gun comes under the German firearms regulations, while blow-pipes and blow-pipe darts do not come under the weapon laws.

8.7   Removal of the Antlers

When keeping herds of deer for agricultural purposes it is only sensible to remove the antlers of the male deer. This not only serves to avoid direct and indirect damage to farm equipment, but also protects the animals and prevents accidents when handling them. This last point is very important in the rutting season. Unless the antlers are removed, there is no way of avoiding injuries when keeping the deer close together, for example in densely stocked pastures, in small paddocks, in cattle-sheds or when transporting, driving, catching or enclosing them.

Injuries could be internal or external, causing bleeding, skin defects, spontaneous abortion, etc. Along with the more or less inevitable damage caused

Plate 8.9   First year's antlers are dangerous to the other deer and to humans.

Plate 8.10 Burning the antler base.

by pushing against each other, the injuries inflicted in pecking order fights, particularly during the rut, are significant. Butting behaviour, which is especially energetic during the rut, often ends in considerable injuries, which are sometimes fatal. Occasionally females are also butted. Even man is in special danger from aggressive bucks at this time, and mention must also be made of the damage which can be caused to fences, trees and hedges by rubbing behaviour to remove antler velvet in late summer.

The removal of the antlers at the correct time and in the right way must therefore be regarded as an essential part of the management of farmed deer. It might also be necessary to remove the antlers of a buck purchased from a hunting estate, a show farm or from the wild. (It is self-evident that an antlered buck cannot be run with other, antlerless, deer until his antlers have been removed.) If the antlers of several bucks are to be removed at the same session, start with the youngest and work through to the oldest animals.

A sensible preparation for the removal of antlers is to tranquillise the animal with drugs. This should be done under the supervision and care of a vet, as described above. As the supply of the drugs is restricted to him, he should also carry out, supervise or lead the operation. He will be able to use the same type of de-horning equipment as used on cattle, adapted for use on deer.

The usual practice with cattle up to three months of age is to destroy or remove the bare base of the horns on the skin by cauterising, burning or gouging out. These methods, however, are not sufficient to prevent the antler development of a deer calf effectively and permanently. This is because the development and growth of a deer's antlers begins not on the outer skin, but on the bone itself (the periost or coronet), so removal of this area is necessary.

The cauterising of the antler base with cauterising sticks, or with liquid or paste applications containing various acids or chloride, has no far-reaching effect. It leads, at its most effective, and even with vigorous use, to the development of malformed antlers.

Burning off the area of the antler base has proved to be the most effective and lasting method with deer calves, in our experience. The method was adapted from the one developed for use on calves by Rosenberger and his colleagues. The calves should be about four months old; with younger calves the technique does not always have a completely satisfactory effect. To carry out the process a branding tool (electro-thermo-cauteriser) is needed, with a hollow at the tip about the size of the antler base, with a sharply angled circular cutting edge. Suitable tools are the de-horners used for calves.

The heated end of the tool, which must be red-hot, should be applied to the skin using light pressure and turned slowly. An angled circular section of skin can then be cut away from the bone and removed. The area underneath should be thoroughly treated, with the periosteum at the antler base being completely removed, down to the skull. Bleeding or other complications have not been reported.

The operation is rather like a combination of simple burning with a cauterising tool and the surgical removal of horns with a de-horning tool, according to Roberts. If it is carried out quickly by an experienced operator, there is, as with calves, no need for general anaesthetics so long as the animal has been sedated when being immobilised.

What is necessary for an efficient and correct operation is to hold the tranquillised animal still. This needs two assistants to hold its head, neck and legs while it is lying on its side. The operator has one hand holding the animal's neck and the other holding the tool, using this so that its heated end can easily cover the antler base.

When about sixty fallow deer calves were cauterised in this way, none showed any sign of antler development in either the first or the second year after treatment. Once the area had healed there were usually no scars or other damage to be seen or felt.

The surgical method of de-horning cattle would need to be modified if used for deer. This is because it is necessary to cut out the periost from the growth point of the coronet, to ensure the permanent removal and prevention of antler growth in the future. This method has been used in experimental conditions but not yet in practice (Breustedt).

For antler removal in bucks which are to be introduced to a farm from a wild herd, a show farm, hunting estate or the like, cutting with a band saw has proved effective. Tranquillising the animal is necessary to facilitate this operation too, but sedation is sufficient. There is no need for anaesthetics, as is the case with cattle, because there is no nervous system in the bare antlers and so no pain is caused. The animal should be firmly held on its side by two assistants. The saw used is the one which helps large animals give birth, according to Liess. The blade must always be used above the coronet, at right angles to the antler stem, and operated with firm strokes through the stem parallel to the coronet. No post-operative complications were reported when this method was used after the velvet had dried and been rubbed off (i.e. from late summer). If there is still some of the blood-suffused velvet remaining, then it is recommended that a cauterising tool is used immediately to staunch any bleeding.

9 Selection and Breeding

Once the deer farm has been set up, the best animals should be selected for a breeding programme. This is the only way to improve your animals and make the herd a viable alternative to farming cattle or sheep.

9.1 Selection Points

The animals should be selected according to the following critera: their resistance to disease, tameness, colour, fertility, temperament, good food conversion efficiency, early maturity, size, good conformation and high killing-out percentage. All these characteristics have an important influence on the success, and above all on the economics of the enterprise.

Pemberton and Smith undertook research on 794 animals at thirty-seven sites in England and Wales, and found no genetic variations. They suggest that these herds had been set up with a small stock of imported beasts, which had then expanded by in-breeding over many generations. They also point to the many colour variations which are a typical feature of domesticated animals.

With a wide sex ratio, the sire is of paramount importance, but in-breeding should be avoided if possible. A change of sire every two years is desirable, especially if the female calves are kept to build up the herd. Bucks can be used successfully for breeding purposes for eight–ten years, so it is a good idea to do an exchange with other deer farmers. (Of course one should first be satisfied about a buck's credentials, particularly as regards his offspring.)

When breeding selectively it is vital to mark each individual animal, and to keep a record of this, and any special colours and characteristics. Only by noting down exact details can an animal's valuable features be perpetuated in the herd and passed down to future generations – and this applies particularly to breeding bucks.

9.2 The Herd Book

A herd book plays an important part in the breeding programme. Used for many years with other farm animals, the herd book has more than proved its worth in improving breed characteristics. The basic details to note down include the marking and description of the animal, plus an assessment of its quality. The hereditability of these characteristics can then be established, and thus important, dominant qualities can be established in the breeding.

Livestock breeding methods are constantly being improved. Performance testing, artificial insemination, embryo transplants and the regulation of the rutting season have been introduced with farmed animals, and some of these techniques are relevant for deer farming.

Performance testing plays an important part in the breeding strategy for deer farming, as an extensive branch of grassland usage. The parents' performance can be judged by that of the offspring as regards a good food conversion ratio, early maturity, health, killing-out percentage and carcass quality.

To ensure the success of a breeding line, every live calf should be marked by the breeder within seven days of its birth, and correctly identified. As the parents must be definitely known there should be only one buck in the herd, and the group should be small enough for the correct mother to be picked out. It is also necessary to pinpoint the aims one is seeking to achieve in the breeding programme. Keep notes in the register of the bodily features of each animal – its weight at certain ages, frame, musculature, colour – and on the sex, the details of the manner of death, carcass scoring, etc. Performance ratings should be followed through, and the entry for each animal should also give its number, year of birth, and details and address of the farm.

These measures are especially important when one is breeding for a tame line, which can have various advantages: lower fences can be employed and handling the animals when feeding and also at slaughter-time is made much easier. It is advantageous, too, for fallow deer farmers to have antlerless bucks. The development of antlers can be prevented by burning them out at the base. With red deer, antlerless stags or polled stags have developed by mutation, so it should be possible to aim for this with fallow deer as well.

In 1977 a breeding herd was set up at the Teaching and Research Centre at Riswick House, consisting of animals which had borne twins and their offspring, with the object of attempting to increase twin births. However, no twin births were recorded over a period of several years, and the trial was abandoned.

Unfortunately, little is known about the genetic characteristics of the fallow deer. Much scientific work needs to be done to obtain the information necessary to achieve the breeder's aims.

9.3   Cross-breeding

Cross-breeding is one method by which certain characteristics may be quickly improved. Breeds are crossed once or several times with others which will inter-breed, a practice which is especially common today with cattle, sheep and pigs to improve their performance, fertility, meat quality and health. With sheep, the crossing of Finnish, lowland and upland breeds has been tried. With cattle, Highland breeds, bison and zebus have been used alone or after crossing to improve the extensive grazing of problem areas. In the past, man has also taken advantage of the infertility of the offspring of a cross-bred animal, for example with the mule.

There have been cases in the wild of crosses between red deer (*Cervus elaphus*) and sika deer (*Cervus nippon*) or wapiti (Lowe and Gardiner). Red deer will also inter-breed with Père David's deer (*Elaphurus davidianus*) (Hösli and Lang). There were crosses of fallow deer with axis deer at the Bloemfontain

Plate 9.1 Sika deer — stag and hind.

Plate 9.2 White-tailed deer — stag and hinds.

Zoo, and a cross between European fallow and the Persian strain at the Georg von Opel open farm in Kronburg and at the animal park in Hellabrun.

It would be advantageous to find a cross with fallow deer which would enable greater body weight and earlier maturity to be passed on to the offspring. Fallow deer have a diploid chromosome count of sixty-eight. Red deer and Père David's deer have very similar chromosomes in number and shape. It is interesting to note that these two types of deer are capable of inter-breeding. The sika deer has several sub-species. The Manchurian type (*Cervus nippon hortulorum*) has, according to research by Gustavsson and Sundt, between sixty-four and sixty-eight diploid chromosomes. When the sika deer were crossed with red deer in Finland, the species used was the *Cervus nippon temminck*, which was imported from Japan in 1860. A type we kept, *Cervus nippon dybowskii*, was kindly researched for us by the Institute of Animal Breeding at the Veterinary College, Hanover. They found sixty-six chromosomes in a male deer. Crossing of this type with fallow deer was not successful, however.

9.4 Other Types

The desired features might be incorporated by choosing other types of deer for cross-breeding, but these must be selected not only for the characteristics which we would wish to introduce into the breed, but also for compatibility as regards region and habits.

Between 1976 and 1978 we carried out trials with white-tailed deer (*Odocoileus virginianus borealis*) which are known as producers of twins and even quadruplets. Mr J. S. Lindzey, of the Wildlife Research Unit at Pennsylvania State University, kindly supplied us with a stag and five hinds. (The white-tailed deer has various sub-species, and is found from Canada to Florida. There have also been wild white-tailed deer in Finland since 1950.)

At the Teaching and Research Institute at Riswick House, Cleves, however, where the site is all grassland, these deer suffered stomach and intestinal inflammation. We could find no single cause, parasitic or otherwise. The two surviving animals were fed mainly on maize silage, but no improvement was apparent. According to Kellogg's report, white-tailed deer in the wild feed mainly on the branches and twigs of trees and shrubs, and only to a lesser extent on grass and weeds. More recent trials have shown that it is possible to feed white-tailed deer mainly on grass and concentrates, but the Lower Rhine site experiment on farming them must be regarded as a failure.

We found that fallow deer have similar characteristics to sika and Dybowski deer. These two types have been successfully enclosed on free range land in Westphalia and southern Germany, and husbandry trials at the Teaching and Research Centre at Riswick House have also been successful.

The species *Cervus nippon nippon* and *Cervus nippon hortulorum* were introduced into Great Britain in 1860. Since then, cross-breeding has occurred in parkland herds (Lowe and Gardiner). The venison from sika deer is said to be even tastier than that from fallow deer.

There is still a gap when it comes to selecting animals to graze on wetter sites, for there is the danger of liver fluke causing disease and fatalities among fallow deer. Marsh deer were considered for this reason, but they need to be examined carefully for their suitability under German conditions.

10 Red Deer Farming

The red deer is the most important deer in the world from an agricultural point of view. They have been known in the wild in England, Scotland, Ireland and Scandinavia for hundreds of years, and can be found on a considerable number of estates in Britain. They were introduced to Australia and New Zealand during the nineteenth century.

Red deer farming began in New Zealand in 1968 and in Scotland in 1969, at a hill farm, Glensaugh, run jointly by the Hill Farming Research Organisation and the Rowett Research Institute. It then spread to Australia and Sweden. A comprehensive literature published on the subject includes *Recommendations on Farming Red Deer* (Anderson, Drew and McDonald, North of Scotland College of Agriculture), and work by Yerex, Young and Wollstädter.

Many of these countries have exported wild venison for decades, particularly to West Germany. The economic situation of the farmers, and particularly the low prices being paid for lamb and mutton, led them to consider alternative uses for their grassland. In New Zealand it was realised that very high prices would be paid in the Far East for some of the by-products of deer farming – pantocrin (antler velvet), tails and pizzles, etc. – for use as traditional remedies. This obviously increased the profitability of red deer farming, when compared with just producing venison alone.

The red deer differs from the fallow deer in only a few respects. Red deer hinds are about twice as heavy as fallow deer, the adults weighing between 95 and 150 kg, with a height of 120–150 cm at the shoulders and a length of about 200 cm. The hide is usually mid to dark brown, and there are few colour variations. The rutting period is from the beginning of October to December, while calving time is June – earlier than for fallow deer. Calves weigh 7–13 kg at birth. There are hardly any twin births. The first of these was observed on the Isle of Rhum in 1971 (Guiness and Fletcher), and the calves were by a naturally polled stag. Cross-breeding with sika, Père David's deer and wapiti has been successful and resulted in fertile offspring.

Red deer are calmer in behaviour than fallow deer and are not panicked so easily, but they seem to be somewhat more susceptible to illness. However, they are sometimes kept in very severe habitat and weather conditions, for example in Scotland, where the rainfall is very high. The stags can be very aggressive, particularly during the rutting season, and they appear to be more aggressive towards hinds which have been hand-reared or which are tamer with humans. (Several injuries and fatalities have been noted.) The loss of antlers during rutting fights seems to be less frequent than with fallow deer.

There has been a lot more research into red deer farming than into farming fallow deer and the following subjects have been studied: the breeding of red deer in farmed conditions; development of the calves; behaviour; nutrition and feeding; slaughtering; meat quality; marketing; and economics.

The important differences between red and fallow deer farming are:

1. Fence height — 1.80–2.00 m.
2. Stocking density — three red deer (and their offspring), per ha on medium fertility land or four per ha on high fertility land.
3. Live weight of the prickets: about 110 kg at fifteen months old.
4. In Germany, the price of venison is lower than that from fallow deer, and the future outlook for venison sales is poorer because of its inferior taste. There is a considerable amount of wild red deer venison available in Germany, for instance, in addition to which imports are high and still increasing.

The main drawback found from several years' research into red deer farming in both Scotland and New Zealand lay in the economics of the enterprise. In 1979 Young gave the total capital costs in Scotland as £11,500 for one hundred head, stocked at one per 2.5 ha; £6,200 stocked at 2.5 per ha; and £3,600 if the stocking rate was ten per ha. The main difference was in the fencing costs. Young estimated, with intensive farming, annual proceeds of £5,536, with variable costs at £1,720, so a net margin of £3,816. With extensive farming the net margin shown was £1,796. The rents and interest paid on the capital costs of the farm are not included in these figures, and they are important considerations for a farmer in Scotland, when he is thinking of the economics of keeping red deer. However, the main consideration is the stocking density on steep and unproductive moorland, where the price of fencing is very high in relation to the other costs of the enterprise.

It is interesting to note that the price of red deer venison in New Zealand (based on carcass price) rose from 0.26 New Zealand dollars per kg in 1962 to 3.2 dollars per kg in 1980 (1 dollar = £0.65). There are also various figures on the economics of deer farming given by Pinney, Wallis, Clouston and Anderson. In these the fencing costs per mile were put at 1,946–3,947 dollars, according to method used, and labour costs at between 1,200 and 1,600 dollars. Clouston in 1976 estimated a gross margin per beast of 10.6 dollars, compared with 14 dollars from sheep or cattle. This was on a price basis of 0.88 dollars per kg for venison compared with 1.21 dollars for lamb or beef. He points out that deer farming is increasingly attractive because venison prices are rising. More recent calculations of income put the gross output from hinds at 229 dollars (including sale of meat, hide, tail, tendons and teeth) compared with 125 dollars in the previous year. For stags this was 668 dollars (389 for meat, 379 for pantocrin, hide, tail, tendons, teeth and penis) compared with 376 dollars in the previous year. The output rises reflected an increase in venison price, but mainly a rise in the price of pantocrin, which cost 180 dollars per kg in 1980.

Baigent and Jarratt came to the conclusion, from their 1977 calculations, that in New Zealand red deer and sheep have the same fixed costs and labour costs. With a meat price of 1.50 dollars per kg dressed weight the gross margin from red deer is double that from sheep, while the price of pantocrin has a big effect on the profitability of a red deer enterprise. Anderson, after a thorough examination of the figures, reckoned that at the present high prices the output per hectare from deer breeding and the production of pantocrin could be 548 dollars and the return on capital 24.5 per cent. Other production methods, aimed at the venison market, still gave outputs of between 169 and 188 dollars per ha. Pinney puts the return on capital at between 14 and 17 per cent.

To increase profitability even further the following possibilities can be looked at: the use of better quality, more productive land; better management; more intensive fertiliser usage; higher stocking rates; lower mortality; more valuable meat, pantocrin and by-products; and cross-breeding (with the wapiti). There is even the improvement of land fertility, brought about by the animal manure deposited, to be added to the list. In his book *Gold On Four Feet*, Anderson states that, at 1978 prices, red deer have 'the potential to be the pot of gold at the end of the rainbow' for those farmers and investors who recognise their potential and have enough cash available to buy in the necessary stock to start red deer farming early enough. If they also have an understanding of the intelligent creatures with which they are dealing, they should be able to reap the benefits of their initiative.

In contrast to the German attitude to red deer, mentioned at the beginning of this book, it must be pointed out that people in New Zealand have a very different view of the animal – much more natural and much less mystical. In addition, the proximity of the Far Eastern market for by-products such as pantocrin offers good opportunities for New Zealand's farmers. We must wait and see how long it is before the production of venison ceases to be a subsidiary aim of red deer farms there.

When looking critically at both fallow and red deer as regards their suitability for western European farmers, and for the utilisation of grassland, the somewhat easier handling of red deer would seem to have favoured this type up to now. Against this, however, the cost of fencing is greater, and profitability not so high on account of the lower prices received for red deer venison. The heavier carcasses or sides are not so easy to butcher as are those of fallow deer, and the venison does not taste as good. The market competition between wild venison and the venison from farmed deer is greater with red deer meat than with fallow deer.

11 Marketing

Deer may be sold on the hoof or as carcasses – but in either case they need to be rounded up first.

11.1 Rounding up the Stock

It is easier to catch deer for selling during the winter than in summer, as they will then be receiving supplementary feed, and this can be offered in a building or in a handling race. There is little problem with adults or animals which are used to being handled – they can be tempted with feed – but more patience is needed with calves and yearlings.

Usually one keeper on his own would not be able to catch the animals. They need to be tempted by food into a more restricted catchment area, and the keeper will then need help from one or two other handlers who are trusted by the deer. Moving the animals should never be a hurried operation, and they must *never* be driven. The evening is the best time for carrying out such work.

Plate 11.1   Encourage the animals – do not drive them.

In summer it is more difficult. The beasts should first be moved to a handling paddock, where suitable arrangements can be made for dealing with them. According to the tameness of the animals, they can be moved gradually towards the handling area by means of tempting food, together with calling and gentle encouragement.

When the animals are to be slaughtered, there must again be no driving, waving, shouting or use of nets for gathering them in. These methods can cause stress in the deer, which is slow to dissipate, and can lead to the taste and keeping quality of the venison being spoiled.

Several trials using feed flavoured with aniseed caused no adverse reactions in the animals. From observations of their behaviour, it was noted that they reacted more to visual stimuli (the keeper and his bucket) and to noise (rattling the bucket, whistling) than to scent.

11.2 Selling on the Hoof

When selling deer live, the same points are to be borne in mind as when buying them. Especially important are: a health check (worming measures should be taken); passing on identification details to the buyer; giving him details of current feeding; careful rounding up of the animals; transferring them as smoothly and calmly as possible to the truck or crate for transporting; and adequate provision of water. When selling males which were not de-horned by the burning method as calves, they should be separated from the females, tranquillised and their antlers sawn off. Handling the animals also gives an opportunity to examine the hooves and check for external parasites. The handler should wear suitable clothing and strong footwear and, if possible, avoid wearing white clothing, which deer react against.

If individual animals are to be caught, we have found that a good method is to hold them firmly and then quickly lift up the hind legs, holding these together if possible. This action restricts the animal's movements, but it is necessary to be on one's guard against its hooves or any quick jerking. It is easier to handle deer in twilight or in the dark, using torches, than in the day time.

Our attempts to introduce a sedative into the food have not proved successful up to now, so the only other alternative is to immobilise the animals. This can only be done when selling live beasts, however, and never if they are to be slaughtered as the drugs may taint the flesh.

11.3 Slaughtering

The aim of the deer farmer is to produce venison which is of a superior quality to the flesh of wild deer. This is only possible when the meat comes from animals of a particular age, being lean and tasty, and is produced according to the stringent rules governing the slaughtering of farm animals.

As the deer farmer is striving to sell a product of as high a quality as possible, at a competitive price, he should be fully aware of the stipulations in force as regards meat production. The legal position in Germany is explained in Appendix 1. It should be noted that, under the meat quality regulations governing cattle, pigs, horses, etc., kept as farm animals, and also animals kept for fur, which are killed other than by shooting, there should be an official inspection before and after slaughtering (by the abattoir or meat control officers), if the meat is to be used for human consumption. The killing of an animal by blood-letting is included in the slaughtering methods. It should be noted that fresh meat from fur-bearing animals can only be imported into Germany if it comes from permitted, supervised, recognised and recommended exporters of wild game, and only if the beasts showed a clean bill of health before slaughter. Meat must be inspected by a vet immediately after skinning, and before and after butchering, passed as acceptable and marked appropriately. At present, only German wild game is exempt from such meat inspection.

The customer also has the right to demand that the venison has been produced according to the most modern standards of hygiene, nutrition and quality.

When animals are shot, it must be pointed out that hunting practice under Section 1 of the German laws on hunting only applies to animals running wild and not privately owned. They are only defined as such if they are truly running wild, not when they are in zoos or animal parks. Hunting can only be allowed in open, unrestricted areas. In large enclosed areas, wild parks or estates, hunting can only take place if the conditions on freedom of living and ownership are met. Thus, according to the hunting laws of the State of North Rhine Westphalia, wild parks and estates must be at least 75 ha in size. Capturing or killing the animals must depend on chance, as in traditional hunting practice. At other parks, farms or enclosures where animals range free, hunting is not allowed, as the animals are not truly living wild, and as they are 'kept', they are not ownerless. In these cases there should be no need for hunting or close seasons, and no appropriation rights for the people allowed to hunt. The animal protection laws are also important. Under these, a vertebrate may only be killed after sedation or as painlessly as possible, as circumstances allow. They note that, apart from the practice of killing an animal by bolt or a quick and humane shot (in the head), the capture and stunning of the animals is often not possible without upsetting the animal to be slaughtered or the other animals. The weapon must be fired from the closest range possible, and by someone skilled and experienced in its use.

Even when animals are released from an enclosure or hunted on the estate, they are not regarded as 'ownerless' and the hunting rules do not apply.

Points against the use of sporting guns for shooting animals are that even when firing from close range there are dangers in built-up areas and when close to populated property. Valuable meat can be damaged by the shot, as can the hide, which will lower the sales value.

In 1981, the Agriculture Office of the Rhineland, together with the German Trials and Testing Centre for Hunting and Sporting Weapons at Altenbeken, carried out trials on the killing of deer with small calibre guns (Kruiper). It was clear that the majority of deer farms were not so isolated that there was no danger in using the traditional sporting guns, from stray bullets, ricochets, etc. Therefore weapons and ammunition were tried which used the minimum amount of force to ensure the required effect. The line of fire must always be chosen to avoid endangering the surrounding human and animal population, and the noise of the report should be kept as low as possible to avoid disturbances. The process should be screened from the sight of neighbours and casual passers-by who might be upset.

For the trials, the German Trials and Testing Centre for Hunting and Sporting Weapons developed the idea of using low-energy small calibre ammunition at short range in a .22 rifle (illegal in the UK). The direction of fire should be from above the animal, as the ground would be a safe background and the animal's head would provide a sufficiently large and vulnerable target.

For ammunition (low shell .22 1r 'hush power'), the German Trials and Testing Centre looked at research by the ballistics expert Professor Dr Sellier. When shooting from above, the only danger to the environment would come from a chance shot which had missed its target and ricocheted from a stone. Trials at different angles of entry on a concrete surface showed that with an angle of more than 45° the shots almost always killed on impact. With a smaller angle, the deflection as it enters the body must be taken into account. If the angle of entry is 30° the deflection is in the line of fire in every case. However, the shots were still capable of penetrating wood 2 cm thick in 70–80 per cent of cases. They did not penetrate a second board partition 2 m away. From these trials, Kruiper deduced that the shot must be chosen so that there is no angle of entry lower than 45°. The best angle was arrived at by ensuring that the height of the muzzle was equal to the distance from the stand (see Figure 4.15), measured along the ground, from the deer itself.

The ground within the shooting area should be as soft as possible and free of stones; sand, ash or loam will all do. The partitions should be of board covered with rubber or sheeting. They should be smooth, solid and at least 2 m high. All the usual precautions must, of course, be taken when handling firearms.

The trials were carried out on three different sites, with thirty-one beasts of varying ages, different heights of the stand and varying sizes of shooting area. On one holding there were problems when killing the animals in an area which was fenced round. When a boarded area was used, however, the animals behaved calmly during the shooting and following the killing of other animals. It was found advisable to bring not more than three beasts into the area at one time; if the area is too small, there is the danger of prickets butting, even against a slaughtered beast. If the marksman on the stand moved or spoke to the beasts there seemed to be no reaction. The animals apparently did not regard the man on the stand as a threat.

The shots were aimed at the skull from either side, and also from the rear. Examination of all the skulls revealed that, in every case, sections of the brain were hit. Exit points were only noticeable in a few cases. Death was instantaneous, some beasts displaying reflex movements, usually of the hind limbs.

Using the .22 1r 'hush power' ammunition, the shots, even without a silencer being used, were hardly audible at about 100 m. The use of a telescopic sight is unnecessary, and a disadvantage at short distances.

The platform of the stand need be no more than 2–3 m high, depending on the size of the slaughtering area. A seat is not needed, as the marksman can move more easily in a standing position. A sight screen in front of the animals is not necessary, but the sides and rear should be screened if possible, to avoid the silhouette of the marksman being visible against the sky, and to prevent onlookers watching the shooting.

The safety and effectiveness of the slaughter weapon is mainly dependent on the skill of the marksman. He must be sufficiently responsible, skilled, sensible and experienced to carry out his work. If he has not had shooting experience, this can be gained on a course run by the German Trials and Testing Centre for Hunting and Sporting Weapons at Altenbeken. The marksman should know something of the anatomy and behaviour of deer so as to be able to aim at the correct angle, as vertically as possible, at the skull of the beast. Even more important than accurate shooting is the patience needed while waiting for the right moment to fire.

The weapon favoured is the .22 small calibre rifle. It does not need to be self-loading, but a repeater is an advantage. Its noise does not disturb the beasts. The necessary gun licence must be held, available through the police according to regulations. The holding of a hunting licence is sufficient.

Another method of slaughtering, which is particularly useful for those farmers with larger numbers of animals, is by stunning with a captive bolt. This method was developed at the Teaching and Research Centre of the Rhineland, Riswick House and is the usual method on some UK farms and in abattoirs. In

Plate 11.2   Handling the head and stunning with a bolt.

Plates 11.3 and 11.4   Holding the head and stunning with a bolt.

this, a crush is used (Plates 11.2, 11.3 and 11.4), at the end of which is a yoke
for holding the animal's head.

Anything leading to stress should be avoided prior to slaughtering. It is a
good idea to move the animals the evening before to a small paddock next to
the slaughtering area. Research at the Rowett Research Institute, Aberdeen,
showed that in a few cases with red deer the pH value of the meat rose from
5.6–5.8 to 6.0–6.2 and a difference was found in the taste and keeping quality
of the meat. However, Douglas and others found that in young red deer of
both sexes, and with castrated stags, under three levels of stress – low, middle
and high – there was no influence on the pH value or the microbiological
composition of the fresh meat. Trials by Kay and others showed that keeping
young red deer in a small enclosure the night before slaughtering led to a rise
in pH value in the muscles, but keeping them in a nearby pasture the night
before slaughtering had no adverse effects.

After killing, the animal can be butchered on the farm in a purpose-built
area, or taken to a butcher nearby. We have used the front-loader of a tractor
for holding the carcass, hanging by the legs, so that the head is at least 20 cm
above ground level, over a plastic container. The carcass can then be bled by
cutting the throat. The paunch can be slit and the stomach, intestines and lungs
removed. These can also be put in the container, which is best lidded to avoid
spillage when carried. The disposal of the offal should be organised in advance
through the proper channels.

Bleeding is important for the final meat quality, as also are the time lapse
between killing and bleeding and the position of the animal (whether hanging

Plates 11.5 and 11.6 Bleeding, and catching the blood and entrails.

up or lying down). In our trials we compared results from different times and positions by measuring the quantity of blood and examining the organs. It was clear that more blood flowed from the hanging than from the prone animal. According to results to date, there was no significant difference if the time lapse was under thirty minutes after killing. If bleeding was delayed for an hour or even two, the heart, liver and chest cavity were suffused with blood; the amount of blood collected was correspondingly less. The butchering methods used were the same. The meat from the animals bled after a time lapse had a more gamey taste than when they were bled immediately. Keeping quality and smoking potential were generally rather worse. In Germany, butchered animals undergo bacteriological tests if there is a lapse of more than thirty minutes between killing and completing the slaughtering operation. Tests on both types of meat showed no significant differences as regards dry matter, inorganic matter, crude protein, total fat content, potash, calcium, phosphorus, magnesium, sodium and iron. This is shown in Table 11.1, which also includes the fatty acids. There were only small differences when deer were compared with lamb.

The cuts for both bleeding and the removal of offal must be carefully made, to avoid staining the carcass and to simplify the collection of blood and offal. Care should be taken to screen the slaughtering operations from spectators, particularly children.

If there are no premises suitable for butchering available on the farm, the carcasses should be taken to a butcher's. During transport, care should be taken to avoid dirtying the carcass, i.e. the truck should have clean containers or be lined with clean, strong plastic sheeting. The maximum time allowed

Table 11.1   Minerals and fatty acids in venison and lamb (in 100 g)

	Unit	Deer bled immediately	Deer bled after 1 hour	Lamb bled immediately
Dry matter	g	30.1	30.1	32.0
Inorganic substances	g	1.14	1.15	1.26
Potash	g	0.36	0.35	0.37
Calcium	g	Traces	Traces	0
Phosphorus	g	0.20	0.19	0.21
Magnesium	mg	23	23	24
Sodium	g	0.07	0.08	0.08
Iron	mg	2.9	2.8	3.0
Crude protein	g	22.1	20.9	22.6
Total fat	g	6.9	8.2	8.3
Myristic acid (C_{14})	% of	3.54	3.65	3.66
Pentadecan acid (C_{15})	the	1.75	1.82	1.97
Palmitic acid (C_{16})		26.07	26.97	23.38
Margarine acid (C_{17})	fat	1.70	1.69	1.80
Stearic acid (C_{18})		33.08	28.76	36.82
Oleic acid ($C_{18:1}$)		20.03	20.60	17.50
Linoleic acid ($C_{18:2}$)		2.11	2.83	1.98
Linolenic acid ($_{18:3}$)		1.20	1.30	1.21
Energy (estimated)	kJ	650	678	711

between killing and skinning is thirty minutes, as laid down in the regulations for farm animals. (Transporting live deer to the abattoir, as happens with farm animals, is not so feasible on animal welfare grounds.)

To have hygienic, acceptable meat, the carcass should be cooled as quickly as possible. The interior temperature should fall quickly to +7°. It should be hung, so that cold air can circulate all round it, so there must be an efficient cooling system available. Of course, storage is not necessary when the customer has agreed to take the carcass away immediately after slaughter. The regulations of all the main game exporting countries are constantly becoming stricter about hygiene.

We have found, over several years of experiments, along with specialists in various fields, that the methods described above – rounding up the animals on familiar ground; skinning and butchering in the slaughter-house – are acceptable and fulfil the necessary requirements of the German meat quality regulations.

By checking the heart, lungs and liver it can be established whether there is parasitic infection present which has not previously been detected in faeces samples, and the appropriate measures can be taken for the herd as a whole.

11.4   Carcasses

Live weights recorded in our trials over eleven years ranged from 39.4–53.8 kg, with an average of 48.2 kg. The deer were weighed between the

Table 11.2 Live weight and carcass weight of fallow bucks (in kg)

Slaughter date	Number of stags	Live weight	Carcass		Killing-out percentage	
			warm	cold	warm	cold
1975 15. 4.	3	32.0		18.0		56.1
2. 7.	3	52.7	31.1	29.1	59.0	55.3
2. 9.	4	48.0		28.3		58.2
1976 8. 7.	4	49.3	38.0	27.5	56.9	55.7
28. 7.	6	51.4		29.7		57.6
23. 9.	5	53.8		29.8		55.3
1977 4. 8.	3	40.3		24.1		59.9
29. 8.	7	43.2	26.4	25.9	61.9	60.0
28. 9.	6	49.8		29.5		59.3
1978 9. 8.	6	41.5	23.9	23.2	57.5	56.4
27. 9.	4	39.4	21.9	21.4	55.6	54.3
7.10.	5	39.4	21.7	21.0	55.7	53.2
1979 26. 9.	3	51.3	30.6	30.1	59.6	58.7
27.10.	10	44.3	26.7	25.7	60.3	58.0
1981 24. 9.	9	47.6	29.6	28.9	62.2	69.7
1982 13. 8.	4	49.9		28.6		57.3
8.10.	4	53.1		31.8		59.9
1983 25. 8.	18	48.7		27.1		55.6
1984 20. 9.	12	50.9	31.1	30.5	61.1	59.9
1985 24. 7.	9	45.7		27.7		60.6
8. 8.	10	44.4		27.3		61.5
1975/85		48.2	29.4	28.5	60.5	59.0

beginning of July and the beginning of October.

The details of slaughter weights for male fallow deer are given in Table 11.2 (killing out weight = live weight including head, skin, innards with intestine and stomach contents, blood, hooves). The average killing-out percentage (cold carcass weight as a percentage of live weight) over the eleven years was 59 per cent. Comparable figures are: 70–75 per cent for pigs; 52 per cent for cattle; 55–60 per cent for calves; sheep 48 per cent; and lambs 48–50 per cent. Möhlenbruch gives an average figure of 53 per cent for four male fallow deer calves slaughtered on 29 September 1976.

The figures from the trials at Romenthal (Schick) were: live weight between 24.2 and 60 kg; carcass weight between 11.7 and 32.8 kg; killing-out percentage between 48.4 and 54.7 per cent. Asher found in his trials with sixty one- to four-year-old male deer that there were only small variations in the killing-out percentage as the animals grew older. However, the proportion of neck and rib meat rose with the greater body weight, while that of rump, back and legs fell. Also important was the increasing fat cover. The best carcasses were from animals aged between one and two years.

Gregson and Purchas achieved similar results with male deer of thirteen, seventeen and twenty-five months of age. The proportion of fat rose with the

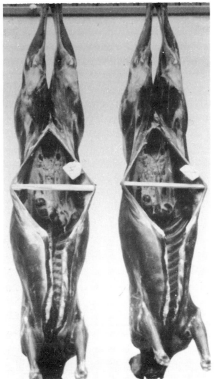
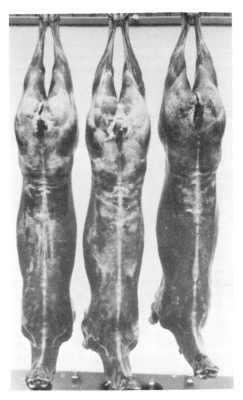

Plate 11.7   Uniform, lean carcasses.   Plate 11.8   Good flesh cover, particularly at the hind quarters.

carcass weight, while the proportion of muscle to bone fell in a similar way. They stated that the proportion of fat and the muscle:bone ratio in fallow deer was much better than that in sheep, cattle or pigs. The carcasses from animals up to two years old were best.

Figures from Buchmann and Schoch in Switzerland, reporting on twelve beasts with an average slaughter weight of 28.6 kg, gave the weight of meat without bones as 18.8 kg. The proportion of rump with bone was 37 per cent of the carcass weight, the back 16.3 per cent and the legs 15.7 per cent – a total of 69 per cent valuable meat joints.

Ledger, Sachs and Smith compared figures for wild deer breeds with those for the African buffalo, and found that deer gave better results. For the buffalo the killing-out percentages were 52.2 per cent with males and 46.4 per cent with females. For eland the figures were 66.5 per cent and 60.3 per cent, and for the Thomson's gazelle 58.6 per cent and 57.1 per cent.

Weighing the various parts of the carcass gave the figures shown in Table 11.3. Carcass analysis of twelve prickets on 20 September 1984: hide 2.9 kg; head 2.6 kg; legs 1.3 kg; blood 2.3 kg; intestines 2.5 kg; heart 0.4 kg; lungs 0.6 kg; liver 0.9 kg; and stomach 3.7 kg.

Table 11.3 Carcass analysis of twelve fallow prickets on 20 September 1984 (in kg)

	Average	Range
Live weight	50.92	46.1–56.3
Slaughter weight, warm	31.06	27.3–34.3
Slaughter weight, cold	30.45	26.8–33.8
Killing-out percentage	61.1	59.2–63.2
Bones	5.07	4.7– 5.3
Hide	2.85	2.4– 3.5
Blood	2.28	1.4– 2.8
Head	2.62	2.4– 3.0
Feet	1.26	1.1– 1.4
Intestines	2.49	2.1– 3.0
Rumen	3.66	3.3– 4.2
Lungs	0.58	0.5– 0.8
Heart	0.38	0.3– 0.4
Liver	0.90	0.8– 1.1
Kidneys with fat	0.59	0.4– 0.8
Neck with bones	2.32	2.0– 2.8
Ribs, neck, with bones	5.16	4.4– 6.2
Legs, with bones	4.75	4.4– 5.3
Saddle, with bones	6.32	5.4– 7.0
Haunch, with bones	11.26	10.1–12.0
Total	47.43	42.7–52.8

The difference from the live weight is because of 2 per cent losses on butchering, approximately 2.5 kg covering fat, blood, bronchial and feeding tubes, and other body fluids.

The economic value of the fallow deer for the farmer lies not only in the live weight gains and the killing-out percentage, but also in the conformity and quality of the carcass. In our experiments, over several years, the male deer carcasses were butchered and the joints evaluated: the figures given in Table 11.4 clearly show that the carcasses had a high proportion of rump meat, averaging 37.6 per cent over five years with a range of 33.6–42.1 per cent. This is 1–2 per cent higher than with calves, almost 10 per cent higher than lambs, and 8–10 per cent higher than pigs. According to Berg, the proportion of rump as a percentage of the whole carcass was 17 per cent higher in the elk than in cattle, while in wild red deer it was 11 per cent higher and in bison 8 per cent higher than in cattle. Ledger's trials with various African wild animals showed the proportion of hind quarter as a percentage of the carcass was 41.5 per cent with buffalo; 44.2 per cent with eland; and 52.7–59.8 per cent with the Thomson's gazelle, the figures being higher for females than for males. Ledger also found that the proportion of muscle as a percentage of live weight was higher in wild animals than in domestic animals.

The proportion of fillet was 2.5 per cent (ranging from 1.7–3.1 per cent). Best neck and back were also high, averaging 17.1 per cent with a range of 13.4–19.5 per cent. The proportion of valuable joints – best neck, back, fillet and rump – was 57.2 per cent on average. The comparable figure for calves is 55–60 per cent; for lamb 45–50 per cent; and for pigs 45–50 per cent. Male deer calves gave a carcass with very little fat, with the exception of the drought

Table 11.4 Results of carcass analysis of fallow bucks (in kg)

Slaughter date	No. of deer	Haunch	Saddle	Fillet	Shoulder leg	Breast flank	Best neck	Neck
Ave 1975/79		9.5	2.6	0.6	3.7	4.0	1.9	2.0
1975 15. 4.	3	7.6	2.2	0.5	2.7	2.4	1.4	1.5
2. 7.	3	10.9	2.6	0.6	4.9	5.3	2.0	2.4
2. 9.	4	10.7	3.0	0.7	4.1	4.5	1.9	2.3
1976 8. 7.	6	10.0	2.6	0.6	3.8	4.3	1.9	1.8
23. 9.	5	11.0	2.8	0.5	4.0	4.3	2.2	2.3
1977 4. 8.	3	9.1	2.5	0.6	3.1	3.5	1.5	2.0
29. 8.	7	9.6	3.2	0.6	3.6	4.2	1.4	2.2
1978 9. 8.	6	8.6	2.4	0.6	3.4	3.6	1.7	1.9
27. 9.	4	8.2	2.1	0.6	3.1	3.4	1.7	1.8
7.10.	5	8.2	2.1	0.6	3.1	3.4	1.7	1.8
1979 26. 9.	3	10.6	2.7	0.7	4.2	4.6	2.3	2.5
17.10.	10	9.8	2.5	0.7	4.1	4.2	2.6	1.8

Slaughter date	No. of deer	Fat Surface	Fat Pelvis, kidneys	Proportion % Haunch	Fillet	Best neck, saddle	Haunch, fillet, best neck, saddle
Ave 1975/79		0.5	0.4	37.6	2.5	17.1	57.2
1975 15. 4.	3	0	0.1	42.1	2.7	19.5	64.3
2. 7.	3	0	0.2	37.8	2.2	17.7	55.7
2. 9.	4	0	0.4	37.9	2.4	17.4	57.6
1976 8. 7.	6	1.7	0.5	33.6	2.0	15.2	50.8
23. 9.	5	2.5	0	36.9	1.7	13.4	52.0
1977 4. 8.	3	0	0.1	37.8	2.5	16.6	56.9
29. 8.	7	0	0.5	37.1	2.3	17.8	57.2
1978 9. 8.	6	0.3	0.4	37.1	2.6	17.7	57.4
27. 9.	4	0.2	0.4	38.3	3.0	17.8	59.1
7.10.	5	0.2	0.3	39.0	3.1	18.1	60.2
1979 26. 9.	3	1.1	0.7	35.2	2.3	16.6	54.1
17.10.	10	0	0.7	38.1	2.7	19.8	60.6

year in 1976, which gave the top figure of 1.8 kg. It must be noted, however, that when the beasts are above sixteen months of age, they lay down fat more quickly. The fat content is low when compared with lambs, calves and beef cattle. Robbins, Moen and Reid reported that with white-tailed deer the females had higher fat and energy levels than the males. It has also been established that with domestic animals, the males produce less fat and more lean meat than do females or castrates on the same level of feeding. In 1976, when there was little grass and only poor quality, there was a bigger build-up of fat cover, the weight rising to 2.5 kg. When the date of slaughter was delayed, it increased further.

The carcass evaluations, kindly carried out for us by Professor Dr Finke of Bonn University's Institute for Animal Breeding and Nutrition, showed good results, which are set out in Table 11.5. Of the one hundred targets to aim for, seventy-six were reached, averaged over five years at various dates of slaughter. As a rule, the September figures were better than those for earlier months. The evaluation of meat characteristics was very satisfactory, with the maximum ten being scored on almost every date. There was a high mark for the lean content of the rump. The valuer praised the uniformity of the carcasses, as compared with those from other farmed animals. Möhlenbruch reported similar results from four carcasses.

Table 11.5 Carcass scoring (100 possible points)

Slaughter date	Number of beasts	Neck, best neck, shoulder, breast	Saddle	Haunch	Surface fat	Pelvis, kidneys	Meat quality	Total
Ave 1975/79		7	15	37	4	3	10	76
1975 15. 4.	3	7	16	33	5	5	10	76
2. 7.	3	9	17	43	3	4	10	86
2. 9.	4	10	19	43	3	3	10	88
1976 28. 7.	6	6	14	38	2	2	9	71
23. 9.	5	5	15	36	2	1	10	69
1977 29. 8.	7	7	14	27	4	4	8	64
28. 9.	6	6	11	33	4	4	10	69
1978 9. 8.	6	7	15	35	4	4	10	75
27. 9.	4	6	15	38	4	4	10	76
7.10.	5	6	15	38	4	4	10	77
1979 26. 9.	3	8	16	43	4	3	10	84
17.10.	10	6	16	39	4	3	10	79

Flesh cover spans the columns: Neck, best neck, shoulder, breast / Saddle / Haunch. *Fat* spans: Surface fat / Pelvis, kidneys.

11.5 Meat Quality

Quality marks, such as content of water, crude protein and fat, inorganic matter, pH value, colour and texture were given for six male carcasses by the Institute for Animal Breeding and Nutrition. As Table 11.6 shows, the water content of venison is similar to that of veal calves with a live weight of 160–170 kg, but rather greater than that of pigs, with a live weight of 100 kg. The crude protein content is higher than the calf's, and similar to that of the pig. The fat content is somewhat greater than that of the calf, but compares with the lower level of the pig. The inorganic matter and the pH value are similar with all three animals. There are differences in colour and texture, with venison being much darker and less firm than pork or veal.

Table 11.6 Meat quality markings (from trials by Finke)

	Deer Average males	Range	Calf (160–170 kg live weight)	Pig 100 kg live weight
Water %	75.5	75–76	75–76	73–75
Crude protein %	22.5	22–24	21–22	22–23
Fat %	1.3	1.1–1.4	0.7–1.0	1.1–1.9
Inorganic substances %	1.1	1.1–1.2	1.1–1.2	1.1–1.2
pH value	5.6	5.6–5.7	5.5–5.7	5.5–5.6
Light colour yE	7.2	6.5–8.2	22–24	22–26
Transmission %	13	11–19		25–45

The chemical composition and the energy content are important considerations for the consumer. In Table 11.7 the results from our trials for venison and lamb are compared with those of other main farm-produced meats. It is clear from these that, given similar situations and feeding conditions, fallow deer venison and lamb are similar in their content of minerals and protein, although venison is leaner. Mineral content is also similar in the other meats. Compared with the meat from other farmed animals, the venison is higher in protein content, lower in fat. The potash and sodium contents of the venison are quite high, while phosphorus and iron levels are the same as those of the

Table 11.7 Composition of various types of meat (g/100 g original matter)

Type of meat	Energy kJ	Albumen	Fat	Minerals	Sodium	Potash
Haunch – fallow deer	650	22.1	6.9	1.1	0.077	0.36
Haunch – lamb	711	22.6	8.3	1.3	0.080	0.37
Haunch – roe deer	443	17.6	1.0	0.8	0.049	0.25
Haunch – red deer	494	16.2	2.6	0.8	0.048	0.26
Rump – veal	431	16.1	1.3	1.0	0.067	0.27
Rump – beef	643	17.4	5.9	0.8	0.066	0.30
Ham – pork	1166	15.2	20.6	0.8	0.065	0.16
Rabbit	669	16.4	6.0	0.9	0.037	0.30
Leg – chicken	485	15.5	2.3	0.8	0.071	0.19

Type of meat	Magnesium	Calcium	Phosphorus	Iron	
Haunch – fallow deer	0.023		0.203	0.003	3 animals
Haunch – lamb	0.024		0.210	0.003	1 animal
Haunch – roe deer		0.004	0.180	0.002	×
Haunch – red deer	0.023	0.005	0.197		×
Rump – veal	0.012	0.010	0.154	0.002	×
Rump – beef	0.017	0.011	0.161	0.002	×
Ham – pork	0.018	0.08	0.154	0.001	×
Rabbit	0.022	0.011	0.176	0.003	×
Leg – chicken		0.011	0.141	0.001	×

Source: × Souci, Fachmann and Kraut.

other animals. At 650 kilojoules the venison's energy level equals that of very lean beef and is above that of veal or poultry.

Tests on the fatty acids present showed that with saturated fatty acids, the palmitic acid level of venison was similar to that of the other meats (Table 11.8). Content of stearic acid was generally equal to that in beef, goat or lamb, higher than that in pork or poultry, and much higher than that found in horsemeat or rabbit. The level of unsaturated fatty acids in the venison was higher than in lamb, but it was lower than that in the other meats. Linoleic acid content was generally the same in the venison as in lamb, while the level of linoleic acid was lower than in pork, horsemeat, rabbit and poultry.

To sum up, it can be stated that venison, with its dark red meat, tenderness, lack of fat, high protein, average energy level and good mineral content is an excellent product and especially good for a healthy diet.

Table 11.8 Content of fatty acid in fat of various animals (% ex fat)

Type of fat	Saturated fatty acids		Unsaturated fatty acids			
	Palmitic	Stearic	Oleic	Linoleic	Linolenic	
Deer	27	29	20	3	1	1
Lamb	23	37	18	2	1	1
Cattle	28	19	44	2	—	2
Pig	21	9	48	9	—	2
Goat	26	24	33	2	—	2
Horse	24	5	30	6	13	2
Rabbit	28	4	35	11	2	2
Chicken	24	7	28	20	2	2

Sources: [1] Own trials; [2] USDA: Home Economics Research Report No. 7.

11.6 Taste

The opinion has often been expressed that the farming of deer leads to a deterioration in the taste of the venison. We therefore held a tasting session in 1975 at which eight people compared numbered portions of venison from a wild deer with that from our farmed deer, which had been slaughtered and bled after one hour. The various criteria on which they were judged are given in the following report. The samples were taken from the same joints (rump), cut in the same way and presented at random.

Table 11.9 Characteristics of venison from various sources (1 = very good, 9 = below standard)

	Taste	Succulence	Fibre	Tenderness	Overall quality
Wild deer	1.71	3.29	1.43	2.00	2.11
Farmed deer bled immediately	1.86	2.71	2.57	2.29	2.36
Farmed deer bled after 1 hour	1.86	3.00	1.43	1.86	2.04

The wild venison was judged to have a slightly better, but not significantly better, taste. However, the succulence of the farmed venison was superior to that of the wild meat. There were no significant differences between the two as regards fibre and tenderness, and this also applies to the overall quality of the meat.

Tests on the possible influence of farming red deer on the taste of the venison have been carried out in Scotland, at the Rowett Research Institute, and in New Zealand, at the Invermay Research Station. Here, too, no significant differences were found. Trials in New Zealand comparing grazing with intensive feeding of red deer showed that swifter growth is linked with higher fat levels in the carcass (Table 11.10). The level of saturated fatty acids was increased at the same time, while that of unsaturated fats was less.

Table 11.10 Influence of husbandry on the carcass quality of 18-month-old red deer

	Carcass weight	Fat content (% of carcass)	Protein content (% of carcass)
Wild deer	36.3	3.0	21.0
Grass-fed deer	51.9	6.0	21.5
Intensively fed deer	58.4	8.6	20.9

Source: Ann. Rep. Res. Div. New Zealand 1975–6.

These seem to point to the influence which feeding has on the taste of meat, a fact which is known with the meat of other farmed animals. If the feeding is similar to the grazing which the wild deer favour, then there should be little difference in the taste of the venison. Rhodes found there was no difference in the taste of beef from cattle fed on grass or on barley, or in the taste of lamb from animals fed on red clover or on barley concentrate. However, in Australia they found the taste was affected by oats, rape, lucerne or white clover. According to Behr, wild venison is tastier in winter than in summer, based on the different forage available and on the hormone activity. It is known that almost all wild game has a stronger smell and taste than normal during the mating season. In deer farming this would only affect the slaughtering date of a few stags, which in any case would not normally be killed during the mating season. This is a more important consideration in the wild, where the sex ratio is about 1:1, and stags are hunted and shot during the rut.

From experience with both farmed and wild animals, it would appear that the behaviour of an animal prior to slaughter has a big influence on the taste, quality and keeping quality of the meat. Disturbance of the animals, particularly if they are put under stress, leads to a build-up of adrenalin which lowers the blood sugar level. This spoils the quality, and particularly the keeping quality, of the meat. Attention must therefore be paid to ensuring calm behaviour in the animals prior to slaughter.

With wild game there is often a longer gap between killing the animal and bleeding it, especially when the shot beast has to be located. The maturing of the meat takes longer in wild venison because of the close texture of the muscles. If the meat is left too long the surface may become slimy, and it will smell strong and 'high'. Several trials and taste samplings were carried out to compare the effects of immediate bleeding with a delay in carrying this out. The results are given in Table 11.11. They show that with the first slaughtering (3 July 1975), the appearance, juiciness, fibre quality and tenderness of the meat, and thus the overall quality, were much improved by immediate bleeding. There were no differences detected in the taste. On the second occasion (3 September 1975), the juiciness of the meat was only slightly better after immediate bleeding, but there were poorer results for the other qualities, with the exception of taste. The results on the third occasion (30 September 1976) show better values given to the taste and appearance after immediate bleeding. On average it would appear that there is no significant difference in the venison between immediate and delayed bleeding, with the exception of the colour of the meat which is darker when bleeding is delayed. It must be noted, however, that with too much delay between slaughter and bleeding, the keeping quality and the bacteriological condition of the meat deteriorates. For this reason, the farmed fallow deer should be bled immediately after slaughter.

Also important when considering meat quality is the question of whether fresh or deep-frozen venison is the better. To try to answer this, two tastings

Table 11.11   Influence of blood-letting on the quality of farmed fallow deer venison (male calves 13–15 months old: 1 = very good, 9 = below standard)

| | 3 July 1975 | | 3 September 1975 | | 30 September 1976 | |
	imm.	after 1 hr	imm.	after 1 hr	imm.	after 1 hr
Taste	3.44	3.44	1.86	1.86	3.20	3.30
Appearance	2.22	3.22	—	—	3.20	3.40
Succulence	3.67	4.11	2.71	3.00	4.50	4.00
Fibre	2.78	3.44	2.57	1.43	4.80	4.20
Tenderness	2.33	3.00	2.29	1.86	3.40	3.30
Overall quality	2.89	3.44	2.36	2.04	3.71	3.70

Table 11.12   Quality comparison of fresh and frozen farmed fallow deer venison (1 = very good, 9 = below standard)

| | 1st date | | | 2nd date | | |
| | Fallow venison | | Lamb | Fallow venison | | Venison from |
	frozen	fresh	frozen	fresh	frozen 1 year	5-year-old buck
Taste	2.11	3.44	3.44	3.20	3.80	4.50
Appearance	1.89	2.33	3.00	3.20	3.30	3.80
Succulence	3.22	4.78	3.89	4.50	2.90	3.40
Fibre	3.00	4.11	4.71	4.80	3.40	3.80
Tenderness	1.44	3.44	3.44	3.40	2.80	3.70
Overall quality	2.33	3.58	3.67	3.71	3.50	3.97

were held and the results are given in Table 11.12. They show that at the first tasting session the frozen meat was given better ratings overall, while at the second, the fresh venison scored well on taste. Thus we were not able to establish any significant differences. However, frozen lamb and fresh venison from a five-year-old buck were marked lower than the fallow deer venison on grounds of poorer taste, appearance and tenderness.

Farmed fallow deer venison is of a definite age and of high quality, and should be suitably recognised as such. Venison is not often produced from the older (breeding) hinds because of the age which they reach.

An interesting list of the commonest 'causes of unsatisfactory quality' has been drawn up by Behr and Greuel. In it they point to the following as causes of poor quality, sliminess, bad taste or smell, or even unusability of wild venison:

- Chasing the wild deer before shooting.
- Shots which wound but do not kill immediately.
- Shots by huntsmen which do not kill immediately, but cause internal injuries.
- Shots which damage the best muscled areas such as the rump.
- Unsuitable surroundings.
- Staining of the venison with internal organ contents.
- Contamination of the chest and stomach cavities with leaves, grass, straw or water.
- Insufficient cooling of the carcass.
- Insufficient bleeding.
- Insufficient protection of the carcass from attacks by vermin, poachers, marauding wild animals or dogs.
- Carrying the carcass in a rucksack, car boot or plastic bag.
- Careless piling up of carcasses during a hunt.
- Long journeys in warm temperatures.
- Leaving carcasses lying in the sun.
- Storing too long, perhaps on the shop shelf.

These faults can all be avoided when venison comes from farmed deer, if slaughtering is carried out in the way recommended earlier.

11.7 Consumer Testing

In order to obtain more detailed information on consumer attitudes to venison, questionnaires were filled in by thirty-eight people from various walks of life at a tasting session. The results are given in Table 11.13.

Those questioned consumed mostly hare and rabbit, because of their taste and availability. Wild ungulates were not eaten so often, but were preferred for taste. Those people who rarely ate game gave high prices and unavailability as their reasons. The results show that to promote farmed deer venison there is a need to make it more easily available, and it would be advantageous if it

Table 11.13   Consumer opinion on buying wild and farmed venison

		%
Do you often eat game?	Yes	75
	No	25
What sort mainly?	Hare, rabbit, etc.	78
	Wild red, roe or fallow venison	41
On what grounds?	Taste	77
	Good availability	49
Why do you not eat game so often?	Do not like the taste	11
	No supply available	67
	Too expensivce	89
	No experience/knowledge of cooking it	11
Main reasons for more frequent purchase	Good availability	84
	Lower price	76
How often would you like to eat farmed venison?	Often	8
	About once a week	5
	About once or twice a week	55
	On special occasions	32
Where would you buy farmed venison?	From producer	61
	From delicatessen	13
	From specialist butcher	34
	From supermarket	18
How would you like to buy farmed venison?	Fresh	100
	Frozen	16
	Oven-ready – frozen	8
	Ready-to-serve	0
What information should be made available?	Recipes	68
	Figures on nutritional value	58

could be offered direct from the farm and as fresh venison. It is also necessary to educate the consumer on suitable cookery methods and the nutritional value of the meat.

The customer's opinion of cooked venison is obviously very important. We conducted several tasting sessions using grilled or stewed meat, with a very varied range of consumers on the tasting panels. On four consumer questionnaires venison was given scores ranging from good to very good in all sections. Particularly favourable markings were given for appearance, texture, tenderness, general taste and mild gamey taste. The results showed that the panels, consisting of journalists, housewives, farmers and students, could also detect differences in taste from the different sex and ages of the beasts.

Fuller questionnaires completed by girl students at a technical college showed that the farmed venison scored very well on its individual taste and on healthy eating grounds; 58 per cent would prepare venison like veal, 89 per cent would serve it on special occasions. The low fat content was valued highly. The label 'farmed venison' was linked with highly prized meat. With the exception of its gamey taste, the grilled venison scored more highly than the stewed.

Among German huntsmen, fallow deer venison in general, but that from calves in particular, is regarded as the best game meat. In other European countries, too, venison from fallow deer is preferred to that from red or roe deer or elk.

If our consumer questionnaire on farmed venison is compared with research by the Central Marketing Company of the German Agriculture Industry on consumer attitudes to various types of meat, there appear to be important advantages for farmed venison. The following attributes were assigned to the various meats:

Pork — tastes particularly good, is succulent, tasty, has a variety of uses, is economical but fatty and does not store well.
Poultry — lean, healthy, light-coloured, economical, but dry, close-textured, much waste, fiddly to eat.
Veal — healthy, lean, tender, light-coloured, keeps well, but too bland, lacking in flavour, variable in quality, can be something quite special, but expensive. Two-thirds of the consumers preferred a pinky-coloured veal.

Individual questioning of consumers showed that their reasons for preferring pink meat were that it tasted better, looked more appetising, was more natural, meatier and tastier, also more succulent and not dry. In the order of preference, beef was first, pork second, veal third and poultry fourth. An interesting point was the prejudice against pale meat, with pork and poultry. The various consumers of veal — whether they ate it often, seldom, or just when eating in restaurants — gave good reports for its leanness and easy availability, and its tenderness. It is often chosen for special occasion dining, particularly by men.

If farmed venison were to be included in the list of meats, and the results of the questionnaires taken into account, it would surely be placed high in the order.

11.8 Supply and Demand

The food buying habits of consumers are important when considering the outlets for farmed venison in Germany. A survey commissioned by the Central Marketing Company of the German Agriculture Industry carried out in 1984 showed that 72 per cent of consumers expressed great pleasure in eating well, and that good taste and enjoyment are of increasing importance. Eighty-eight per cent were of the opinion that quality was the deciding factor when making a purchase.

The overall consumption of meat in the countries of the EEC was constantly rising from 1969 to 1982.

Research by the Central Marketing Group of the German Agriculture Industry also showed an increasing and unsatisfied demand for game meats. The use made of game meat and wildfowl in private households depends on the social status of the household. The consumption of game meat is high among farmers, self-employed persons and businessmen, the first two groups using highly priced game. This is interesting as they are the groups holding the largest numbers of hunting permits (33–37 per cent) in Germany. The eating of game depends, therefore, on both social status and familiarity with game, which are closely connected. It is also known that expenditure on meat in a household rises as the income rises.

A further deciding factor against choosing fallow deer venison is its price. We discovered from our consumer research that the majority of people were prepared to spend between 18 and 22 DM per kilo for saddle of venison. Girls at an agricultural college were questioned, and only 8 per cent of them were prepared to pay more for saddle of venison than for fillet steak. A price of 35–50 DM per kg was put on the meat; 42 per cent of the girls would pay the same price for a good joint of venison as for fillet steak. Thus income levels must be taken into consideration when evaluating the results of the questionnaire.

Graphs showing the price fluctuations (net prices without VAT) of imported game packed for retailing and graded Class A, for the period between 1979 and 1985, are given in Figure 11.1. From this it is clear that roe deer venison is at the top, followed by red deer venison and wild boar. While the saddle of the roe deer was valued more highly than the rump and shoulders, up to 1981, the values were put as equal for the same joints of red deer, and only after that date did the saddle gain higher marks. Interestingly, up until the end of 1985 the shoulder and casserole joints of red deer were marked equally, in contrast to the marking of these joints of roe deer.

The price of roe deer venison rose sharply up to the middle of 1982, when the price for back joints was 29 DM and for rump about 23 DM. In contrast, with red deer the price rose steadily to about 19 DM for back joints and about 17 DM for rump. The price for wild boar reached a low level of about 16 DM for back joints in 1982, followed by a rise up to 1984 and another drop to about 17 DM at the end of 1985.

There are no figures given for fallow deer venison in these graphs. There are considerable price variations according to region, which do not show up in the graphs, because only average prices are given. It is a fact that higher prices are obtained nearer to large cities than in the country, and for the private consumer than for the trade or landowners.

In 1983–84 the prices received by huntsmen for wild deer were 10 DM per kg for red deer, 11 DM per kg for roe and 12 DM per kg for fallow deer. In the same season the price for wild sika deer was 12 DM, for mouflon 9 DM and for black wild deer 10 DM. When looking at these prices it should be understood that they are for the whole undressed carcass, including hide, head and hooves. The weight lost when dressing a carcass comes to about 45 per cent, so the prices must be increased to take this into account and to obtain the price for the meat alone.

Schulz found that wild roe and fallow deer venison were valued equally by the retail trade in general. He puts this down to the fact that whereas with fallow deer demand exceeds supply, with roe deer the supply is about equal to demand. Red deer venison is less highly valued both in the retail and the wholesale market.

When evaluating the future market for farmed fallow deer venison, it should be noted that the meat is of guaranteed quality, whereas the quality of wild venison, whether home-produced or imported, can be vary variable.

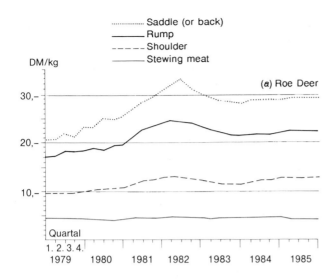

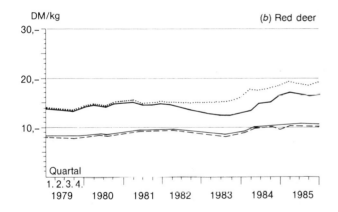

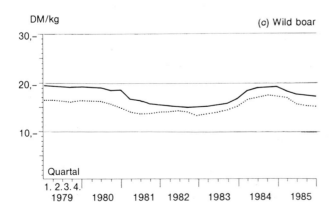

Figure 11.1 Price
levels for various
types of wild game
meat.

The supply of wild game and wild fallow deer venison comes either from hunting circles at home or from abroad. The fallow deer cull in West Germany rose continuously from 1968 up to 1976–7, when a level of 11,465 was reached; in recent years it has remained fairly steady. Recently the heaviest cull has been in Schleswig-Holstein and Lower Saxony, followed by North Rhine Westphalia, Hessen, Baden-Würtemberg and Bavaria.

The supply of wild fallow deer in Germany is therefore very low, and of varying availability according to region and season, the hunting season being limited to a maximum of 1 July to 28 February (restricted between these dates in separate states and according to the variety of game).

Over the last ten years imports of wild game into West Germany have averaged about 20,000 tonnes. Imports of fur and feather game, not including wild boar, fresh, chilled and frozen, were 17,445 tonnes in 1984, most coming from Argentina, Poland and Great Britain. These figures have changed little over the last decade. Most imports arrive between August and December.

The import figures for fresh meat are particularly interesting. From the statistics for 1984 for West Germany it can be seen that fresh meat imports of game from wild furred animals were 17,616 tonnes (Table 11.14), mainly from Argentina and Poland. These were mainly in the form of joints, only about a quarter of the total being in the form of whole, half or quarter carcasses. About 1,100 tonnes were from slaughtered, not shot, beasts. There will probably be an increase in this proportion over the next few years, and the better quality meat will be competitive with the farmed fallow deer venison in Germany. There are a number of abattoirs being set up in both Great Britain and New Zealand, where game meat is processed to health and hygiene levels acceptable to West German authorities (Middleton).

The amount of fallow deer venison imported, according to Schulz's estimates, is about 120 tonnes, that is less than 1 per cent of the total. Included among the imports are meats from antelope, gazelle, bear and kangaroo. Experience in recent years has shown that there is an increasing number of cases of these meats being declared as wild roe or red deer, and passed off as such to the consumer.

Identification is especially difficult with joints of meat. The German Meat and Slaughtering Authorities must, however, undertake testing of meat, including imported wild game. The immunological testing methods used in the past were costly, and the more recently introduced 'electro-phoric' method does not always give an exact identification of the meat, especially when it comes as dressed joints. Pohlmeyer has recently undertaken research on the comparative anatomy of fallow deer, sheep and goats, which shows that the deer skeleton is unique in the formation of the small nostrils and the lack of forehead cavity. The structure of the middle bones of the foot is also different from that of the other two animals. Dondorf and Hofmann were able to show that there is a first carpal bone on the front legs of red and fallow deer which is missing in the roe deer, and the shape of the middle styloid bone is more curved in the fallow than in the red deer. These details help with the identification and checking of whole or half carcasses, but not of joints.

Important aids for the classification of meat and quality guarantees are the German trade grading systems, used for example with veal, beef, pork, lamb

Table 11.14 Imported fresh game meat (hare, rabbit, red deer, fallow deer, roe deer, chamois, elk, antelope, gazelle, bear, kangaroo) in 1984 (in tonnes), according to meat inspectorate

Country	Carcasses; halves; quarters slaughtered	killed	Joints slaughtered	killed	Total (tonnes)
Belgium	—	—	1	4	5
Denmark	—	32	—	—	32
France	24	2	64	151	241
Great Britain	—	511	—	956	1,467
Ireland	—	—	—	5	5
Italy	3	—	—	—	3
Netherlands	8	—	39	24	71
Spain	—	67	—	983	1,050
Austria	—	81	—	398	479
Sweden	—	—	—	274	274
Bulgaria	15	82	41	130	268
Yugoslavia	30	802	—	33	865
Poland	517	537	68	2,023	3,145
Rumania	1	43	—	322	366
Czechoslovakia	205	773	—	545	1,523
Hungary	91	904	1	456	1,452
South Africa	—	—	—	588	588
Argentina	—	350	—	3,200	3,550
Uruguay	—	—	—	295	295
Australia	—	—	—	1,251	1,251
New Zealand	—	—	—	686	686
	894	4,184	214	12,324	17,616

Source: BML.

and mutton. The grades are given according to the age of the animal and the fat and flesh cover of the more important body areas. It would be desirable to have a similar system of grades for venison, to satisfy both producer and consumer, and also to improve the market image for this valuable product.

When looking at the possibilities for marketing farmed venison it must surely be capable of taking over from imported venison. Hardly any meat can compete with farmed venison for quality, with its guarantee of age, taste and freshness, and especially when compared with most imported game venison.

It is quite possible that with a further increase in meat consumption, and with rising awareness of the need for quality and healthy eating, the consumption of a meat as tasty and nutritious as farmed venison will increase, to the detriment of other types of meat. Of course this means that the supply will need to be sufficient, and should be accompanied by thoughtful advertising.

11.9 Finishing and Preparation of the Venison

The finishing needed for farmed deer also gives it an advantage over wild venison, which was usually cured for three to four days, a method originally used to tone down the high flavour of game which had been hung for a long time. Larding with fatty, smoked bacon can make the farmed meat more succulent and tasty, which suits certain palates, but our tests have shown that most people prefer a milder game taste. Venison can also be smoked. Long smoking of the larger joints, such as the haunches, is recommended, as they will then store well. The common practice today in West Germany of short periods of smoking followed by storing in deep freeze has the disadvantage with larger joints that they soon go off after defrosting. Smoked fallow deer haunches are deepish red to brown in colour, finely textured, tender and of superb flavour, and can even be compared with well-known types of ham such as Parma or Black Forest.

Plate 11.9 The saddle is the most valued meat.

Cooked venison haunches are a useful product. Shoulder joints, belly, leg and neck are suitable constituents for sausages, salami, corned venison and pies. When using venison in this way, care should be taken not to mix too much other meat or seasoning with the venison, or its unique flavour will be masked or altered. When making liver pâté or sausage, pork liver should be added, as deer liver is rather strong tasting. Brawn can be made from a mixture of the tongue, heart, liver, head and other meat of the deer. Almost all the offal – heart, liver, lungs, blood and head – can be used to make black pudding or pies. (Care must be taken to make sure the blood has been hygienically collected, however, and is not tainted.) It is obviously necessary to test the blend of meat and spices before retailing, and this is best done in collaboration with a butcher, who will also have the necessary tools and equipment. It is thus possible to make use of all parts of the deer carcass, as with other farmed animals. The product should be identified and suitably labelled, of course, as venison salami, venison sausage or brawn, venison pâté, etc.

It is important for all consumers to know the various cuts of venison, and their quality and uses. These are shown in Figure 11.2.

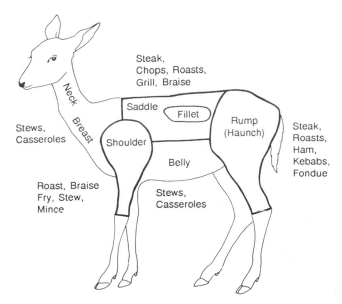

Figure 11.2 Cuts of meat and their uses.

The German trade prefers to handle joints such as saddle, rump, shoulder, fillet, rolled joints or brisket. These oven-ready joints and the smaller cuts are suitable for the smaller households of today when the trend is to buy easy-to-cook products. When looking to the future, we should remember that in Germany a third of all households are single-person households, and about a further third are two-person households. Hotels, restaurants and families with a deep freeze can purchase whole, half or quarter carcasses. This cutting can be done on the farm. Any further butchering or preparation is a skilled job and is covered by regulations of the law, tax and health authorities, which must be strictly observed. Of course this job can be sub-contracted to a local butcher or other skilled tradesman.

Good hygiene control in the production of farmed venison means that it can be sold raw as mince or steaks.

In Germany, the products of a deer farm can be sold through the local outlets, which may include selling direct to the local market, selling to restaurants and delicatessens, or through individual butchers or co-operatives, depending on local circumstances. Of course, when choosing customers, bear in mind the quantity of meat available and the time of year when it is ready for sale. In our experience, most customers need to be informed of the high quality of farmed venison, basing details on meat sampling and tasting. In their turn these people will pass on to the consumer information about the quality of the goods on offer. Delivery dates should be fixed well in advance, to be sure of them being mutually convenient for both producer and wholesaler.

Passing on information to the customer is very necessary and can take several forms. Apart from supplying details about the quality and nutritional value of the goods, publishing suitable recipes is a good idea when trying to sway people towards trying a new product. Advice on preparation and cooking can be given in leaflets or on cards, which can also give details of how farmed venison is produced and its unique qualities.

11.10 Hide and By-products

The animal should be skinned very carefully, as damage to the pelt will lower the quality and affect the selling price. The pelt should be scraped free of flesh, completely covered with curing salts and rolled up.

Many producers have the hides dressed, as there is a ready market, particularly for the porcelain-coloured pelts. Dressing costs are about 40–60

Plate 11.10 A dressed hide.

DM (approx. £15) per hide, according to size and quantity to be dressed.

As early as 1806, Bechstein commented on the quality of the fallow deer's hide: 'The pelts are not too hard, but provide fine leather for leggings and gloves.' Trials at the West German Tanning College in Reutlingen, which is the teaching, testing and research centre for the leather industry and which is financially supported by the North Rhine Westphalia group of fallow deer farmers, showed that working with fallow deer hides presents no problems. When the finished leather was tested, it showed a breaking point of DIN 53 329 307 N/cm^2, the norm being 1,200 N/cm^2. It is therefore hard-wearing enough to be used for the uppers of shoes, provided it is suitably lined. The grain of the leather was not affected before breaking-point was reached. The thickness of the leather tested was 0.9 mm.

Under the microscope, the grain shows a similar pattern to that of goatskin (Plate 11.11). There are fewer curly hairs round the individual pores in the fallow deer than in the goat or red deer skins.

To the touch, fallow deer leather is softer than goatskin, where the grain is often rather coarse. The West German Tanning College speaks of goatskin as being more a 'leather for men's wear', whereas lambskin is softer and more suitable for ladies' wear. Fallow deer skin comes between the two. Keeping deer on farms ensures a better quality skin than that of wild deer, which can be damaged by tearing on hedges or by warble fly. To sum up, the nice soft leather with its attractive, smooth grain is suitable for clothing, handbags or fine-quality shoes.

The price of fallow deer skins has risen in recent years. It is an advantage to collect together skins from a group of farms and offer them for sale to a wholesaler. They can then be dressed, dyed and prepared professionally, ready for the clothing trade.

By-products to be mentioned include the teeth and the horns, which can be used for buttons, ear-rings, brooches, bracelets, cufflinks and other jewellery. Up to now they have had only a limited market in Germany. The Far Eastern market imports pantocrin (antlers in velvet), tails and penises for use in traditional medicines, particularly from the red deer farmers of New Zealand and Australia. The main customers are in South Korea and Hong Kong, but the market has been static for a few years. There are also producers in the USSR and China. The production of pantocrin is a skilled job and in Germany is prohibited under the animal protection laws. The other by-products are prepared according to Asiatic recipes, fermented in wines or liqueurs, ground to powder or mixed with other liquids. They are said to be effective against anaemia, lassitude, high blood pressure, loss of appetite, insomnia, wounds which do not heal and infertility (Wallis and Faulks).

11.11 Selling

When selling venison from the farm gate, the various legal and tax regulations, which are referred to in the appropriate chapters of this book, must be complied with. In more isolated areas of the Federal Republic, on small farms and those with fewer opportunities for farm gate sales, there may be special

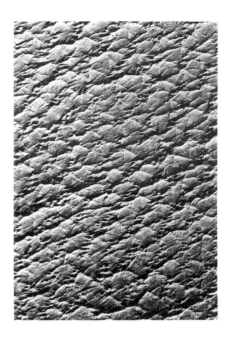

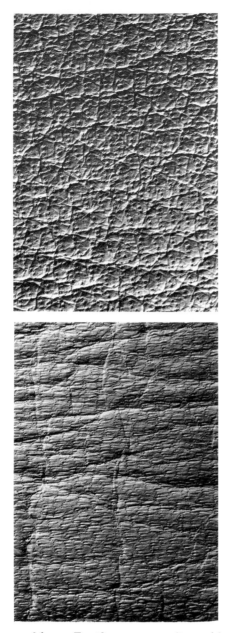

Plate 11.11 Various grains in leather:
(a) *top left* – red deer;
(b) *top right* – goat skin;
(c) *bottom left* – fallow deer.

problems. For these reasons it would seem advisable to follow similar practices when selling venison as with other types of meat. Thus one could sell or buy beasts or carcasses through the channels which have already been tried and tested.

Venison could also be sold through the meat wholesaler, who would deliver the venison, particularly the quality joints, along with other types of meat to speciality restaurants, hotels, etc. In this case, arrangements would have to be made for the VAT payments to be settled between the various suppliers, and a group or co-operative of producers could be formed to help with this.

It is up to the deer farmer to promote his product, stressing the attractiveness of the meat, and its uniqueness and superiority compared with other meats. This can be done in many ways, such as tastings, cookery demonstrations, circulation of recipes, and advertising. Once the product has been developed, the next step is the planning and establishment of the market, its welfare and its growth. This new product has a powerful ally in today's trend towards increasing awareness of health and environmental matters, of natural foods, and the enjoyment of good eating – eating as an expression of high living standards.

12 The Economics of German Deer Farming*

In his *Handbook of Hunting Knowledge* of 1809, Stein set out the first calculations of the economics of a 'deer garden'. Given an area of eighty acres with eighty beasts, he gave an income of 142 imperial dollars, costs of forty-eight dollars and therefore a net profit of ninety-four dollars. It is even more important today, when considering starting a deer farm, to work out a detailed budget. This must include: the farm as a whole; the fields available; any alternative possibilities for using the grassland, such as grazing cattle, sheep or horses; cutting grass for hay; the farmer's own interests and inclinations; and the capital available. In most cases starting a deer farm will be for the purpose of making a living, and so the basic premise for an economical assessment of labour and farming possibilities must be to utilise to the maximum the income, production and marketing factors while paying attention, of course, to prevailing circumstances.

12.1 Labour Requirements

The yearly labour requirement is five working hours per beast with deer farming, compared with between seven and twenty-eight hours with sheep farming and twenty with dairy farming (see Table 12.1). Reckoned on hours per hectare, with medium fertility land grazing at about 70,000 MJ ME, this comes to fifty hours yearly with deer farming, sixty hours with paddock-grazed sheep and thirty to forty-five with dairy cows.

Table 12.1 Labour requirements for various methods of grassland use

Type of animal	Hours per beast animal-related	Hours per beast grassland-related	total	Hours per hectare at 70,000 MJ ME (medium fertility)
Dairy cow	22–50	10–20	32–70	60–140
Grazing bullock	14–20	10–20	24–31	40– 60
Suckler cow	10–15	10–15	20–33	30– 45
Sheep	2– 7.5	2– 8	7–28	50– 70
Deer	2– 3	1– 2	5	40– 60

It should be remembered that the herd also needs looking over once, twice or three times a day, and drinking facilities need checking constantly (see

* I am grateful to Professor Dr G. Steffen of Bonn, for his comments and editing.

Table 12.2). Fences should be checked weekly. At intervals of about three months, faeces samples should be taken and, if necessary, worming treatment given with the feed.

The first peak period of the working year is at calving time, i.e. from the

Table 12.2 Yearly diary for the deer farmer

	I	II	III	IV	V	VI	VII
Breeding hinds	Gestation ——————————————→ Calving						
Stags	Rut ————————————⊣						
Yearlings m							
f							
Calves m						Birth——————————→	
f							
Checking animals	Every day – every 3 days						
Feeding hinds	Concentrates———————————⊣						
yearlings	Concentrates—————————→						
calves							
Faeces sampling	Every quarter ——→						
Worming	As necessary						
Gathering forage						Mowing	
Checking fences	Weekly ——→						
and water							
Fertilising	Soil samples			Potash, Phosphates ————→			
	every other year			Calcium, Nitrogen			

	VII	VIII	IX	X	XI	XII
Breeding hinds	Suckling ——————————→				Breeding —→ Gestation	
Stags	Selection		Removal of antlers		Rut ——————→	
Yearlings m			Slaughter			
f			Sale slaughter			
Calves m			Burning out of antlers			
f						
Checking animals						
Feeding hinds			Concentrates ————————————→			
yearlings						
calves	Concentrates —————————————————⊣					
Faeces sampling						
Worming						
Gathering forage						
Checking fences						
and water						
Fertilising	Potash, Phosphates ——————→					
	Calcium, Nitrogen					

middle of June until the beginning of July. At this time there should be a daily check of the whole herd, and newborn calves should be marked. In the middle of July – according to the state of growth of the grass – the meadows can be partly or completely mown and given a nitrogen dressing. Hay and silage making can be carried out by farm labour or contracted out. From July to September the male deer which are not being sold as live animals are slaughtered. According to market demands the slaughtering dates can be staggered or it can be done as one operation. From July the supplementary feeding of concentrates to the calves can begin, if possible combining this with the daily checking routine. During the second half of September another moderate dressing with nitrogen may be given. In October the calves can be weaned and the antler base of male calves burned out. This is also the time when a new stag may be introduced and matched to the group of hinds. After the rut, in December, the sale of any surplus animals can begin. Also hay, silage and concentrates will need to be fed to supplement the sparse grass growth. Concentrates can be fed during the daily checking of the herd. Hay, straw and silage should be taken out of storage and fed every few days.

It is especially important in periods of frost and snow to check food and water supplies and also check on the animals. At the end of the winter, say in the first half of March, the pastures can be treated with a complete fertiliser, containing potash, phosphates and calcium, and with nitrogen, following soil testing.

The total amount of labour required is therefore quite small, and there are no very heavy jobs to be done. The main peaks of activity are: calving time, in June and July; hay and silage making in July; and weaning the calves in October–November, together with the antler base removal. Weekends and holidays, apart from the daily check, can be kept free. There is no need to take on extra seasonal workers. Even on a large deer farm occupying about 50 ha, or where the deer herd forms part of a general farm, all the jobs can be done by one worker. Certain jobs, such as checking the animals, fences or water troughs, or taking faeces samples, are less intense as the size of the farm and the number of animals increase. The monthly work schedule for an area of 4 ha is given in Figure 12.1.

As the research by Göbbel, Schick and Werner has shown, expenditure on labour depends on the experience of the farmer, on the size and situation of the deer farm, and on his love of animals. The cost per animal decreases with increased stocking density, the cost per hectare with the total size.

It is also important to remember that on a deer farm working hours are not restricted to certain times, as in dairy farming, or with the daily feeding needs of other livestock.

Large machinery is only needed for the bigger transport work (carrying fodder, transporting of animals). If the pastures are partly or completely cut for hay, or silage in very productive areas, this can be done with a small mowing machine or by a contractor, if the farm does not have its own tractor. Buying a new tractor for the purpose is not recommended, as it is not economically sound. Fertilisers can be carried in a pick-up or car.

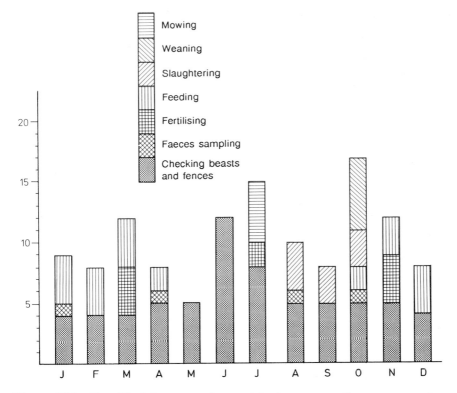

Figure 12.1 Monthly labour requirement in hours over the year on a farm of 4 ha.

12.2 Capital Requirements

The capital required can be divided between the cost of the land (if purchasing or renting); fixed equipment (fencing, water troughs, feed troughs, handling facilities, silos, feed stores); and the stock. It depends on the size of the herd and on the fertility of the land. Total capital expenditure can be spread over several years.

The first thing to do is to obtain the land (if one is not already a landowner), fence it round, and purchase the animals and feeding equipment. Handling equipment such as funnel races, and silos or storage sheds for winter feed, if not already on the site, can be added in the second or third year. This is particularly recommended if the herd numbers are to be built up gradually.

In Germany the costs of buying or renting land are relatively low if one is considering extensive grassland areas, and they have not been taken into account in the following observations and calculations. It must be noted, however, that with a lower stocking rate per hectare, the costs per animal of fencing and equipment are higher than with the higher stocking rate which is possible on more fertile land.

The costs of the deer are taken at 1986 levels – 400 DM (£150) for calves, 500 DM (£190) for yearlings (one-and-a-half year olds), 800 DM (£300) for hinds, possibly in calf. It is not likely that these prices will fall in the future. A downturn in prices for livestock will only occur if market demands are completely satisfied.

The prices for equipment and consumables are given in Tables 12.3 and 12.4. These are, of course, average figures, and prices will depend on regional

Table 12.3 Costs of equipment at 1986 prices in DM (and sterling equivalents) including VAT

	DM	(£ sterling)*
Fencing 100 m, 1.8 m high	450–600	(170–225)
1.65 m medium	300–450	(112.5–170)
1.50 m low	250–300	(94–112.5)
Gate, double	1,100–1,400	(414–526)
single	320–590	(120–222)
Door	120–160	(45–60)
Handling set-up (70–80 sq m)	8,000–10,000	(3,008–3,760)
Handling funnel race (30–50 sq m)	1,500–3,000	(564–1,128)
Shelter	2,000–5,000	(752–1,886)
Feed troughs/racks	500–800	(188–300)
Silo per sq m	25–30	(9.40–11.25)
Water trough excluding piping	80	(30)

* Calculated at the rate of 2.66 DM to £1.

Table 12.4 Cost of goods at 1986 prices in DM (£ sterling)* including VAT

	DM	(£ sterling)*
Ear tag	0.50	(0.20)
Collar	7.0–9.50	(2.60–3.57)
Blow-pipe, long	120.0	(45.00)
short	81.0	(30.00)
Darts	9.50	(3.57)
Small bore gun	620.0–1,560.0	(233.00–586.00)
Carrying crate	250.0–400.0	(94.00–150.00)
Captive bolt apparatus	200.0	(75.00)
Dressing one hide	45.0–60.0	(17.00–22.50)
Soil sampling – extraction	6.0	(2.25)
testing	12.0	(4.50)
Bought-in fertilisers/deciton		
Nitrogen	36.0–72.0	(13.50–27.00)
Potash	10.0–36.0	(3.75–13.50)
Phosphates	17.0–39.0	(6.40–14.60)
Calcium	7.0–17.0	(2.60–6.40)
Complete fertiliser	44.0–60.0	(16.54–22.50)
Concentrates/deciton 100 kg	50.0–60.0	(18.80–22.50)
Hay/deciton	25.0–30.0	(9.40–11.25)
Straw/deciton	9.0–15.0	(3.38–5.67)

* DM:£ sterling at 2.66:1.

variations and on differences in the quantity and quality of the product, and may be subject to change in the future.

Before buying anything it is wise to obtain several estimates, giving clear requirements as regards quantity and quality. There are wide variations in the quality of the various types of posts and wires, for instance. It pays in the long run to buy the best quality one can afford.

Table 12.5 shows the capital requirement (not including land) for a minimum sized plot of 4 ha. This is the minimum requirement for the first two years, and so gives no costs for handling or feed store facilities. There are three levels of stocking given, to correspond with the three levels of fertility of the area (low, medium or high).

Table 12.5 Capital expenditure for setting up deer farming on 4 hectares, 1986 prices in DM (£ sterling)*

	Fertility in MJ ME per ha		
	40,000 5.6 beasts per ha	60,000 8.3 beasts per ha	80,000 11.1 beasts per ha
Animals	13,440 (5,053)	19,920 (7,489)	26,690 (10,034)
Fencing, gates	2,700 (1,015)	2,700 (1,015)	2,700 (1,015)
Feeding and handling equipment	3,000 (1,128)	3,000 (1,128)	3,000 (1,128)
Drinking troughs etc.	180 (68)	180 (68)	180 (68)
Total	19,320 (7,264)	25,800 (9,700)	32,570 (12,545)

* DM:£ sterling at 2.66:1.

12.3 Comparison with Other Animals

When calculating the capital needed, it is helpful to start by looking at comparable livestock enterprises. In Table 12.6 the figures are based on an area of 4 ha of medium-quality grassland, with a fertility rating of 70,000 MJ ME per hectare per year, and costs of shelter and other buildings.

The number of animals ranges from 6.8 to 40, from dairy cows, through the suckler herd, to fallow deer. Because of its higher live weight, the price of a dairy cow is much higher than that of sheep or deer. The total cost for 4 ha of grassland is lowest for grazing bullocks, about the same fairly high level for suckler cows as for sheep, and very low for fallow deer. The money needed for fencing and gates, presupposing own labour, is somewhat higher for deer than for the other types of animals. Against this, dairy cows have the highest costs for sheds and other facilities. These are lower with suckler cows and sheep, and much lower with deer. A similarly favourable picture is shown in the costs of storing fodder.

12.4 Output

The calving and rearing figures given in Table 12.8 are carefully worked out, and compare deer with sheep and cattle. The killing-out percentage of deer is

(text continued on page 247)

Table 12.6 Capital requirements in DM (£ sterling)* for various livestock units on 4 ha grassland of medium fertility (70,000 MJ ME)

Type	Dairy cows	Grazing bullocks	Suckler cows
Number of animals	6.8	8.2	7.2
	DM (£)	DM (£)	DM (£)
Price per beast	2,500 (940)	700 (236)	2,200 (311)
Costs			
Beasts	17,000 (6,390)	5,740 (2,158)	15,840 (5,955)
Fencing, gates (own erection)	1,610 (605)	1,610 (605)	1,610 (605)
Drinking troughs	180 (68)	180 (68)	180 (68)
Sheds and pens	48,360 (18,180)	22,190 (8,342)	23,760 (8,932)
Feeding equipment	10,200 (3,835)	7,380 (2,774)	10,800 (4,060)
Total	77,350 (29,079)	37,100 (13,947)	52,130 (19,598)

Type	Sheep	Deer
Number of animals	31.2	40
	DM (£)	DM (£)
Price per beast	350 (131.58)	600 (226)
Costs		
Beasts	10,920 (4,105)	24,000 (9,023)
Fencing, gates (own erection)	1,610 (605)	2,700 (1,015)
Drinking troughs	180 (68)	180 (68)
Sheds and pens	31,200 (11,729)	8,000 (3,008)
Feeding equipment	15,600 (5,865)	2,400 (902)
Total	59,510 (22,372)	37,280 (14,015)

* DM:£ at 2.66:1.

Table 12.7 Output in DM (£ sterling)* per ha from different types of grassland use (4 ha grassland of 70,000 MJ ME)

Type and stocking rate	Meat and milk production I and II	Meat production and breeding animals	
		deer 600 DM (£225) lamb 400 DM (£150) calf 700 DM (£265) IIa	deer 1,000 DM (£376) IIb
	DM (£)	DM (£)	DM (£)
Deer 10 per ha	3,676 (1,382)	5,816 (2,186)	7,430 (2,793)
Sheep 7.8 per ha	2,073 (779)	3,308 (1,244)	
Suckler cows 1.8 per ha	1,965 (739)	1,707 (642)	
Dairy cows 1.7 per ha	5,950 (2,237)		

* DM:£ at 2.66:1.

Table 12.8 Output from various grassland enterprises (area of 4 ha grassland, of 70,000 MJ ME per ha)

Criteria	FALLOW DEER	SHEEP
Calving (lambing) date	June	February
Calving (lambing) rate %	90	150
Animals reared %	85	140
Weaning	October	July
Finished weight:		
young stock male kg	52	54
young stock female kg	34	54
Killing out: young stock %	57	48
Meat price: adult DM per kg	12 ($4.50)	6 ($2.25)
young DM per kg	16 ($6.00)	8 ($3.00)

	FALLOW DEER					SHEEP				
Output	Number	Size (unit)	DM per kg or head ($)	DM per adult deer ($)	DM per ha ($)	Number	Size	DM per kg or head ($)	DM per ewe ($)	DM per ha ($)
Meat Production										
Carcasses:										
adult	0.07	2 kg	12 (5)	24 (9)	240 (90)	0.2	6.7 kg	6 (2)	40 (15)	315 (118)
young stock male	0.425	12.6 kg	16 (6)	201 (76)	2,016 (758)	0.7	26.0 kg	8 (3)	208 (78)	1,622 (610)
young stock female	0.425	8.3 kg	16 (6)	133 (50)	1,328 (499)	0.7	5 kg	3.5 (1)	18 (7)	137 (51)
Hide or wool	0.92	Piece	60 (23)	9 (3)	92 (35)					
Total				367 (138)	3,676 (1,382)				266 (100)	2,073 (779)
Sale of breeding stock and meat										
Carcasses:										
adult	0.07	2 kg	12 (5)	24 (9)	240 (90)	0.2	6.7 kg	6 (2)	40 (15)	314 (118)
young stock	0.11	3.1 kg	16 (6)	50 (19)	496 (186)	0.76	13 kg	8 (3)	104 (39)	811 (305)
Breeding stock male	0.32	head	800 (301)	256 (96)	2,560 (962)	0.35	head	400 (150)	140 (150)	1,092 (411)
female	0.42	head	600 (226)	252 (95)	2,520 (947)	0.35	head	400 (150)	140 (150)	1,092 (411)
Total				581 (218)	5,816 (2,186)				424 (159)	3,309 (1,244)

(Continued on next page)

Criteria	SUCKLER CATTLE	DAIRY CATTLE
Calving date	January	Autumn
Calving rate (%)	90	95
Animals reared (%)	85	90
Weaning	October	Immediately
Fattened weight:		
young stock male per kg	275	—
young stock female per kg	230	—
Killing out percentages (young stock) %	60	—
Meat price:	DM/kg ($/kg)	DM/kg ($/kg)
adult	5 (1.88)	5 (1.88)
young stock	6.50 (2.44)	600 calf (226)

SUCKLER CATTLE

Output	Number	Size (unit)	DM per kg or head ($)	DM per suckler cow ($)	DM per ha ($)
Meat Production					
Carcasses:					
adult	0.170	51.5 kg	6 (2)	255 (96)	459 (173)
young stock male	0.425	70.1 kg	7 (3)	456 (17)	820 (308)
young stock female	0.425	58.7 kg	7 (3)	382 (14)	687 (258)
Milk					
Total				1,093 (411)	1,966 (739)
Sale of breeding stock and meat					
Carcasses:					
adult	0.17	51.0 kg	6 (2)	255 (96)	459 (173)
young stock	0.55	74.4 kg	7 (3)	484 (182)	870 (327)
Breeding stock:					
male	0.1	head	700 (263)	70 (26)	126 (47)
female	0.2	head	700 (263)	140 (53)	252 (95)
Total				949 (357)	1,707 (642)

DAIRY CATTLE

Output	Number	Size (unit)	DM per kg or head ($)	DM per dairy cow ($)	DM per ha ($)
Meat Production					
Carcasses:					
adult	0.25	70 kg	@ 5 (2)	350 (132)	595 (224)
young stock male	0.45			180 (68)	306 (115)
young stock female	0.45			180 (68)	306 (115)
Milk		4,500 kg	@ 0.62 (0.23)	2,790 (1,049)	4,743 (1,783)
Total				3,430 (1,289)	5,950 (2,237)

DM:$ at 2.66:1.

more favourable, particularly compared with sheep. The price of the venison was set fairly low, based on our experience at the time, at 12 DM (£4.50) per kg for the adults and 16 DM (£6) for the yearlings, as it seemed best to base it on long-term expectations. The prices given for lambs and beef cattle are the average prices then being paid for carcasses in the Rhineland.

The output figures for the various animals are given in the top section of Table 12.8 for meat production only, and in the lower section for both meat and breeding stock. In both cases there is a clear lead for deer farming over sheep and the suckler herd, but it comes below milk production. At the same time, it would appear a better return to sell a fifteen-month-old deer at a price of 600 DM (£225) than to take the slaughter price. Of course, the output rises if the price of breeding animals rises.

Similar trends are shown in the sale of breeding animals from sheep flocks or suckler herds, but it must be taken into account, of course, that the possibilities for the sale of these are not so favourable as for deer.

12.5 Variable Costs

A comparison of the various types of animal, as regards their usefulness for extensive pasture, clearly shows the advantages of deer, in their lower feeding requirements, low live weight and their longer productive life, which can be up to fifteen years.

The main expenditure required is for the replacement of the herd; again, this is lower for deer because of their longer life compared with cows. Marketing costs are quite high for deer, but this is not the case when selling live animals. For sheep, the costs of flock replacements, marketing and fodder are favourably low, while they are high for cattle, caused by high replacement and food costs. The comparison also shows that fencing costs for deer farming, which are only slightly higher, can be kept down by using farm labour. Feeding and storage facilities are included with the costs of buildings for sheep and cattle.

The variable costs of forage for deer are lower than for sheep or cattle. This is because they can graze outdoors throughout the year and the costs of winter feeding are lower. In Table 12.9 variable costs are indicated for different regimes. This makes clear the high costs of dairy farming and the advantages of deer farming, if the conversion of existing buildings or the provision of new ones should be necessary.

12.6 Gross Margin

As a measure of performance for a given farming enterprise, the gross margin may be worked out and compared with that of the various alternatives. The gross margin is reached by the subtraction of the variable costs from the output. When defining the size of the enterprise, we set such factors as acreage and personnel at a minimum.

In Table 12.11 the gross margins are worked out for different deer farms,

Table 12.9 Variable costs in DM per ha (£ per ha)* for various grassland enterprises (area of 4 ha grassland, 70,000 MJ ME per ha)

Type and stocking rate	Without forage		With forage	
	Without buildings I	Without buildings II	Rebuilding old sheds III	Newly built sheds IV
	DM/ha (£/ha)	DM/ha (£/ha)	DM/ha (£/ha)	DM/ha (£/ha)
Fallow deer 10 per ha	1,051 (395)	1,449 (432)	1,449 (545)	1,449 (545)
Sheep 7.8 per ha	993 (373)	1,591 (598)	1,669 (627)	2,176 (818)
Suckler cattle 1.8 per ha	1,166 (438)	1,771 (666)	1,834 (689)	2,203 (828)
Dairy cattle 1.7 per ha	2,927 (1,100)	3,554 (1,336)	3,894 (1,464)	4,404 (1,656)

* DM:£ at 2.66:1.

and these are compared with sheep, suckler herds and dairy herds, on a per hectare basis. In column I the costs of buildings and forage are excluded. There is a clear advantage for deer farming compared with sheep or suckler herds. Deer farming appears even better if the basic forage costs of the three types of husbandry are included. The gross margin is higher from dairy farming.

An outstanding result is achieved by selling breeding stock, as can be seen in column II (a). The income can be increased again if some of the bucks are sold off as breeding stock. Of course, the gross margin per animal and per hectare in sheep farming also rises if sales of stock are made for breeding, but it should be realised that the possibilities are not so favourable as they are with deer farming.

The need for buildings is an important point to consider when making a change in an agricultural enterprise. This may come about when extending the acreage or expanding the stock of animals, or perhaps when changing from dairying to pig farming. The figures given in columns III and IV refer to the conversion of an existing building or the necessity of building a new one. Both measures lead to a considerable reduction in the net margin with either sheep farming, dairying or with the suckler enterprise. With deer farming, on the other hand, the net margin stays intact, as such building measures are unnecessary except in cases of very exposed situations, where cheap shelters may have to be erected.

Together with staffing requirements, the number of hours to be worked is to be considered for the various types of management. The return per working hour (Table 12.12) is higher with deer farming than with all other types of stock farming, especially if the conversion of an old building has to be undertaken. If new buildings are needed, sheep and suckler herds come out on the negative side. When selling breeding stock, obviously the return per working hour will rise according to the price achieved for each animal.

The gross margin will also be influenced by the situation, stocking density, prices obtained and above all by the skill of the person in charge of the enterprise.

(text continued on page 252)

Table 12.10 Variable costs per hectare for various grassland enterprises (area of 4 ha grassland, of 70,000 MJ ME per ha)

		FALLOW DEER					SHEEP				
		Number	Unit size or DM	DM per kg or head	DM per adult	DM per ha	Number	Unit size or head	DM per kg or head	DM per ewe	DM per ha
Food requirements per year											
for adult	MJ ME	4,200					6,400				
for young stock	MJ ME	3,000					3,000				
concentrates ration	MJ ME	300					400				
Liveweight (adult)	kg	50					54				
Productive life	years	15					5				
Stocking density (adults + young stock)	animals per ha	10					7.8				
Variable costs without forage I											
Stock replacement		0.07	head	600	42.00	420.00	0.2	head	240.00	48.00	374.40
Concentrates, minerals		0.25	300 MJ ME	50.00	12.50	125.00	0.33	400 MJ ME	50.00	16.50	128.70
Water, electricity					1.00	10.00				2.00	15.60
Drugs, veterinary costs					3.00	30.00				7.00	54.60
Insurance					8.00	80.00				10.00	78.00
Insemination, keeping sire, etc.		1,000 m			4.50	45.00	1,000 m			6.00	46.80
Fence (self-erected)		1	3.0	13% pa	7.00	70.00	1	1.57	13% pa	6.50	51.00
Gates (self-erected)			400	13% pa	1.30	13.00		50	13% pa	0.20	1.60
Feeding equipment											
Racks (ready-made)		1	1,000	13% pa	3.20	32.00					
Silo (ready-made)		1	400	13% pa	1.30	13.00					
Drinking troughs		1	180	13% pa	0.23	2.30	1	180	13% pa	0.23	2.30
Handling set-up (self-erected)		1	400	13% pa	1.30	13.00	1	100	13% pa	0.40	3.25
Marketing		1	(head)	18.00	16.60	166.00	1	(head)	18.00	28.80	224.60
Other costs (dressing/tanning costs)											
Marking (ear tags, collars)		1	(head)	7.00	3.20	32.00	1	(head)	1.00	1.60	12.50
Total variable costs without forage I (DM)					105.13	1,051.30				127.23	993.30
(£ sterling @ 2.66 DM:£1)					39.52	395.23				47.83	373.42

(Continued on next page)

FALLOW DEER

Variable forage costs	Number	Proportion	Unit size or DM — ha	DM per kg or head	DM/ha	DM per adult (DM/adult deer)
Grassland – grazing		80%	0.078	320.00	256.00	25.60
Grassland – for silage		20%	0.020	710.00	142.00	14.20
Variable costs (without buildings) II (DM)					1,449.30	144.93
(£ sterling)					544.85	54.48
Cost of converting existing sheds						
Variable costs when converting old buildings III (DM)					1,449.30	144.93
(£ sterling)					544.85	54.48
Variable costs when building new sheds IV (DM)					1,449.30	144.93
(£ sterling)					544.85	54.48

SHEEP

	Number	Proportion	Unit size or head — ha	DM per kg or head / DM/ha	DM per ewe	DM per ha
Grassland – grazing		65%	0.083	540.00	44.80	349.60
Grassland – for silage		35%	0.045	710.00	31.90	249.20
Variable costs (without buildings) II					203.93	1,591.20
					76.67	598.20
Cost of converting existing sheds					10.00	78.00
Variable costs when converting old buildings III					213.93	1,669.20
					80.42	627.52
Variable costs when building new sheds IV					278.93	2,176.20
					104.86	818.12

SUCKLER CATTLE / DAIRY CATTLE

Food requirements per year		SUCKLER CATTLE	DAIRY CATTLE
for adult	MJ ME	38,000	53,000
for young stock	MJ ME	8,000	
concentrate ration	MJ ME	4,800	10,000
Live weight (adult)	kg	275	500
Productive life	years	6	4
Stocking density (adults + young stock)	animals per ha	1.8	1.7

	Proportion	Unit	Price	DM/cow	DM/ha	Proportion	Unit	Price	DM/cow	DM/ha
Variable costs without forage I										
Stock replacement	0.17	head	1,700	289.00	520.00	0.25	head	2,400	600.00	1,020.00
Concentrates, minerals	4	4,800 MJ ME	50.00	200.00	360.00	11.6	dt	48.00	556.00	945.20
Water, electricity				29.00	52.20				35.00	59.50
Drugs, veterinary costs				15.00	27.00				70.00	119.00
Insurance				35.00	63.00				100.00	170.00
Inseminating, keeping bull, etc.				25.00	45.00				50.00	85.00
Fence (self-erected)	1,000 m		1.57	28.30	51.00	1,000 m		1.57	30.00	51.00
			13% pa					13% pa		
Gates (self-erected)	1		50	0.90	1.60	1		50	1.00	1.70
			13% pa					13% pa		
Feeding equipment										
Racks (ready-made)	1		45	0.80	1.50					
			13% pa							
Silo (ready-made)	1		200	3.60	6.50					
			13% pa							
Drinking troughs										
Handling set-up (self-erected)	1	head	20.00	20.00	36.00					
Marketing	1	head	120.00			1	head	120.00	120.00	204.00
Other costs									50.00	85.00
						Variable costs of building				
						Variable costs of machinery				
Marking (ear tags, collars)	1	per head	1.00	1.10	2.00	1	per head		110.00	187.00

	DM/cow	DM/ha	DM/cow	DM/ha
Total variable costs without forage I (DM)	647.70	1,165.80	1,722.00	2,927.40
($ sterling)	243.50	438.27	647.37	1,100.53

	Proportion	ha	DM/ha	DM/cow	DM/ha	Proportion	ha	DM/ha	DM/cow	DM/ha
Variable forage costs										
Grassland – grazing	65%	0.36	560.00	201.60	362.80	50%	0.29	560.00	162.40	276.08
Grassland – for silage	35%	0.19	710.00	134.90	242.80	50%	0.29	710.00	205.90	350.03

	DM/cow	DM/ha	DM/cow	DM/ha
Variable costs (without buildings) II (DM)	984.10	1,771.40	2,090.30	3,553.51
($ sterling)	369.96	665.94	785.83	1,335.91
Cost of converting existing sheds	35.00	63.00	200.00	340.00
Variable costs when converting old buildings III (DM)	1,019.10	1,834.40	2,290.30	3,893.51
($ sterling)	383.12	689.62	861.02	1,463.73
Variable costs when building new sheds IV (DM)	1,229.10	2,203.40	2,590.00	4,404.00
($ sterling)	462.07	828.35	973.68	1,655.44

Table 12.11 Gross margin in DM per hectare (£ per hectare)* for various grassland enterprises (area of 4 ha, 70,000 MJ ME per ha)

Type and stocking rate	Without forage	With forage		
	Without buildings	Without buildings		
			Selling breeding stock	Hinds 1,000 DM
	I	II	IIa	IIb
	DM/ha (£/ha)	DM/ha (£/ha)	DM/ha (£/ha)	DM/ha (£/ha)
Fallow deer 10 per ha	2,625 (987)	2,227 (837)	4,367 (1,642)	5,987 (2,251)
Sheep 7.8 per ha	1,073 (403)	483 (182)	1,718 (646)	
Suckler cattle 1.8 per ha	800 (301)	195 (73)	−64 (−24)	
Dairy cattle 1.7 per ha	3,010 (1,132)	2,396 (1,028)		

Type and stocking rate	With forage	
	Converting buildings	New buildings
	III	IV
	DM/ha (£/ha)	DM/ha (£/ha)
Fallow deer 10 per ha	2,227 (837)	2,227 (837)
Sheep 7.8 per ha	404 (152)	−103 (−39)
Suckler cattle 1.8 per ha	−132 (−50)	−237 (−89)
Dairy cattle 1.7 per ha	2,056 (773)	1,546 (581)

* DM:£ at 2.66:1.

Deviations from the average results are given in Table 12.13 by Göbbel. They show clearly that poor output (from sales of breeding stock, sale of carcasses, increasing herd size), low stocking rate and poorer meat price lead to a poorer return per animal per year.

The various influences on the economics of the enterprise are set out in Table 12.14. With returns per animal per year at a level of 100 DM (£38), an improvement in breeding rate from 85 to 90 per cent gives an increase of 24 DM (£9). Increasing the carcass weight at slaughter by 1 kg gives up to 18 DM (£6.75) increase in returns; improving the productive life by two years gives an increase of 8 DM (£3); and a rise in meat price of 1 DM (37p) − above 15 DM (£5.60) per kg − gives an increase of 25–30 DM (£9.40–£11.30) per head. The various influences are clearly shown, therefore.

The figures underline the importance of good husbandry in deer farming,

Table 12.12 Gross margin in DM (£)* per working hour for various grassland enterprises (area of 4 ha, 70,000 MJ ME per ha)

Type and stocking rate	Working hours per ha	Without buildings II DM (£)	With forage Selling breeding stock IIa DM (£)	Converting buildings III DM (£)	New buildings IV DM (£)
Fallow deer 10 per ha	50	4,453 (1,674)	87.33 (33)	44.53 (17)	44.53 (17)
Sheep 7.8 per ha	60	8.05 (3)	28.63 (11)	6.74 (3)	−17.72 (−7)
Suckler cattle 1.8 per ha	45	3.24 (1)	−1.42 (−1)	2.92 (1)	−5.28 (−2)
Dairy cattle 1.7 per ha	100	23.96 (9)		20.56 (8)	15.46 (6)

* DM:£ at 2.66:1.

Table 12.13 Possible fluctuations in the budget

	Average result	Possible fluctuations	± gain in DM per beast per year
Breeding result	85 %	60–90%	overall: −104 to +21
Slaughter weight	27 kg	25–30 kg	− 38 to +25
Replacing herd	15 years	every 5 years	− 70
Bought-in feed (concentrates, hay, forage)	33 DM	⅓ of the requirement	− 37
Stocking density	10 beasts per ha	12–5 beasts per ha	+322 to −800 DM per ha
Meat price	15 DM per kg	12(8)–18(10) DM per kg	− 77 to + 77 overall: −354 to +123

Source: Göbbel.

Table 12.14 Factors influencing the budget

		Increased profit in DM per beast per year
Breeding result average 85%	+ 5%	+ 24 DM = + 20% over average profit
Slaughter weight average 27 kg	+ 1 kg per calf	+ 12 DM to + 18 DM = + 15% over average profit
Productive life average 15 years	+ 2 years − 2 years	+ 8 DM − 10 DM
Meat price Average 15 DM per kg carcass weight	+ 1 DM per kg	+ 25 DM to 30 DM = 22% over average profit

Source: Göbbel.

as with the farming of other livestock. A certain size of farm is also needed in order to achieve good returns in the long term. When farming deer for venison production alone, a minimum of 4 ha with forty to fifty deer is advisable.

At the Teaching and Research Centre for Animal Husbandry at Riswick House, in the Agricultural Region of the Rhineland, work has been carried out for many years on the comparison of various types of stock farming given the same situation and climatic conditions. The results from several years are given in Table 12.15. From these we can see that the highest gross margin per hectare comes from dairy cows with followers, followed by deer with sales of breeding stock. Deer farming aimed at meat production alone shows better returns than suckler herds or sheep farming. When considering gross margin per working hour, deer farming was clearly superior to all the other types.

Table 12.15   Results from Riswick House (Coenen)

Enterprise	Dairy cows and followers	Suckler cattle	Sheep	Does and followers	Deer for meat production
Average of the years	1981–3	1977–83	1981–3	1981–3	
Number of mother animals	218	16	271	60	60
Area of forage used (ha)	116	6.4	22.5	5.4	5.4
Market output DM per beast	5,085	1,580	357	532	442
Variable costs including machinery and rent	2,885	860	210	166	166
Gross margin DM per beast	2,200	720	147	366	276
Grazing area per beast	53.2	40.0	8.3	9.0	9.0
Forage costs DM per ha	1,000	700	700	1,000	1,000
Gross margin DM per ha	3,136	1,100	1,071	3,066	2,066
Working hours per ha	122	45	64	56	56
Gross margin DM per working hour	26	24	17	55	37

12.7   Main, Secondary or Incidental Enterprise?

In Germany, milk quota regulations and the worsening market for beef are creating many problems for the single-enterprise farm. The choice lies between a reduction in output per beast and cutting down the numbers of cattle. For the future, the question arises as to whether any improvement in production from dairy cattle, as a result of scientific progress, should be made use of or not. If it is, the number of beasts kept must be cut. How should the resultant surplus area of grassland be used? Coenen, at the Teaching and Research Centre at Riswick House, worked out some possibilities based on long experience of various types of grazing animals. He showed that, after cutting down the stock on a farm, the best way to obtain an increase in gross margin per hectare from the grassland, equivalent to about 300 litres of milk per cow and a profit of about 12 per cent, is by moving from dairying to deer farming. At the same time the need for labour can be reduced. The gross margin per working hour rises by about 1 DM (37p) from 26 DM (£10) to 27.10 DM (£10.37). Of course there are other possibilities which may be considered, such as using the buildings vacated by the dairy cows for beef cattle or pigs. Here, too, however, the pasture left vacant could be used for deer farming, and this would make sound economic sense.

Lastly there is the question of how much usable land a single enterprise needs if it is to be solely devoted to deer farming, to achieve an income of 30,000 DM (£11,300). At today's prices, the area of medium fertility land for good milk and meat production (excluding sales of breeding stock) would need to be: dairy cows 38 ha; sheep 107 ha; suckler cows 143 ha; and deer 44 ha.

Of course there are also other factors to consider with the various alternatives, such as the number of permanent staff and their adaptability. Work loads in dairy farming and deer farming are very different, as we mentioned at the beginning of this chapter. In most cases it is hard to improve on deer when the area of pasture needed is considered.

There may be other problems with a secondary or incidental enterprise. Often there have been generations of farmers working the land, which could be a more important factor than in a single enterprise. As against this, income often comes from more than one source, and the main occupation could provide a sufficient or satisfactory income. People have always been prepared to put capital into the farming of land which they already own rather than risk it on a single enterprise in which profit is the main aim. For them, deer farming is a strong possibility when compared with dairying, with its constant need for labour, or sheep, which needs a lot of labour at peak periods like lambing time, or even with keeping a suckler herd. This is, of course, provided that the necessary basic conditions as regards situation, acreage and skilled husbandry are fulfilled. In these situations, deer farming could also contribute towards lightening the burden of the specialist dairy farmer who wishes to go out of milk production.

In all the types of farming mentioned, including deer farming, there must be the right conditions if one is to be successful. These include the situation of the farm, the establishment of the herd, the quality of the livestock and, above all, the skill of the farmer and his willingness to listen to advice and to learn from experience. If these conditions are not fulfilled, then, as with all other livestock farming, failure is inevitable.

13　The Outlook for Deer Farming

13.1　Building up a Good Volume of Production

To satisfy demand, there must be a good supply of the product. Wild game meat imports into Germany stood at about 20,000 tonnes during the 1980s.

With production of 250 kg per ha of venison per year one needs 4 ha for one tonne of venison. To compensate for the import of 20,000 tonnes of game meat, there would therefore be a need for 80,000 ha of deer pastures. However, it is also expected that requirements will rise, perhaps by 10 kg per head, by 1995. For Germany, with about 60,000,000 consumers this would mean 600,000 tonnes of meat.

If the demand for venison in Germany were to rise by 1 kg per head per year, a further 2.4 million fallow deer carcasses would be needed.

It would seem, therefore, that as far as one can see, all the female calves will be needed to build up the deer herds. Only when this build-up has been achieved can a larger number of the animals be slaughtered. This statistic is affected by the fact that hinds are long living and so the replacement requirements are low.

Plate 13.1　First showing of farmed deer at the 'Green Week', Berlin 1985.

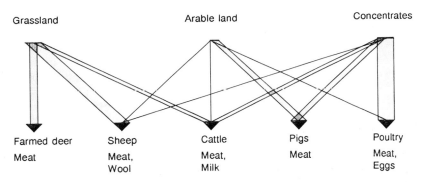

Grassland   Arable land   Concentrates

Farmed deer   Sheep   Cattle   Pigs   Poultry

Meat   Meat,   Meat,   Meat   Meat,

              Wool   Milk   Eggs

Figure 13.1   Feed sources for various types of farm animal.

13.1.1   Meat Production from Grassland in Order of Precedence

Meat production in Germany and in the EEC is increasingly dependent on the importation of feeding stuffs. This is especially true of pigs and poultry, but also increasingly of beef cattle. The production of compound feeding stuffs in the EEC has quadrupled in the last twenty years. The proportion of home-grown feed grains fell in comparison with imported feeding stuffs.

In Figure 13.1 the chart shows the varying dependence of various types of animal on grassland, arable land and bought-in feed. It can clearly be seen that the feeding needs of deer farming are almost entirely satisfied by the conversion of grassland growth. Sheep farming uses a little food from arable land or bought-in feed, mainly for feeding lambs. Farm-produced fodder is used to a moderate extent in pig keeping, but only to a small extent in poultry keeping, in comparison with bought-in concentrates.

If one looks at the situation of the market for cereals, beef and milk in Germany and the European Community, and also considers the overwhelming preference for pork consumption in Germany, then the meat produced by deer farming, which mainly comes from grassland, is seen to be at a great advantage.

13.1.2   Environmentally Acceptable Stock Farming

Environmental demands on agriculture, and the constantly rising demands for quality produce, have had their main effects on livestock husbandry. Buildings must satisfy strict rules on construction, temperature, distances from dwellings, storage and disposal of faeces. The Clean Air Act and, for example, the sewage regulations of North Rhine Westphalia are linked with financial charges for storage of effluent. Added demands are made for protecting water, countryside and nature. The prohibition or limitation of the use of hormones and veterinary drugs reduces the competitive advantage of animals reared by intensive methods. The ruminants, such as cattle, sheep and deer, have considerable advantages over pigs and poultry from the standpoint of smell and noise pollution. Also with deer farming there is no necessity to erect buildings or to store manure. It should therefore gain in importance compared

Plate 13.2   Environmentally acceptable use of grassland for farmed deer.

with other types of livestock farming, especially in areas concerned for the environment. In addition, the end-product, farmed venison, has every chance of improved sales.

To sum up, it can be said that the outlook for deer farming would seem to be very favourable, both as an economical enterprise with low labour requirements, and from the point of view of production, marketing and the environment. Rapid growth in the numbers of enterprises and deer herds should confirm this within a few years.

Appendix 1 German Law, Insurance and Taxation

As it was only in 1974 that the first trials on deer farming were undertaken at the Teaching and Trials Centre at Riswick House, it has not yet been possible to solve fully all the problems which are connected with farming these animals. To answer all the legal questions which arise would need a lengthy compendium of details applicable to each area of the country. Judicial settlements and the drawing up of appropriate laws will only gradually begin to affect this new facet of animal husbandry.

The law as it applies to deer farming has been investigated by Hötzel, Heinen and Recken. They point to the fact that the problem in Germany is that under the law there are only two basic types of animal, wild or tame. This comes under the rules set out in the Code of Civil Law (Section 960). Wild animals include those running free in the wild, captured wild animals and tamed wild animals. There would be fewer problems with making legal decisions about farmed deer if they could be clearly categorised as domestic animals. If, however, they are regarded as being in a transitional stage between wild ranging and domestic animals, many difficulties arise. We believe that the basic problem will soon be solved, following recent research on animal behaviour, the experience of many deer farming enterprises, and the increasing tameness of the animals, which we have already noted. In the following sections we deal with the laws applicable to deer farming under the headings of setting up the enterprise, husbandry, slaughtering and marketing.

Laws and Regulations*

Setting up the Enterprise

Setting up a deer farming enterprise comes under the Laws on Nature Conservancy and Care of the Countryside – Federal Nature Conservancy Act 20 December 1976. In Section 24 it is laid down that the setting up, extension and working of farm enterprises requires the consent of the appropriate office of the local authority. This can only be granted, without prejudice to other regulations, if the animals are kept in suitable conditions and properly looked after. Also any buildings must be such that they do not detract from the environment or the amenities of an area or limit access to the open countryside. The states lay down more detailed regulations; they can for instance make their approval dependent on a sound commercial basis, make exceptions for certain farms, and make stipulations for provisional consent to be given. The appropriate local laws – Nature Conservancy, Countryside Protection and Care of the Countryside Acts – mention free ranging or farmed deer only in Baden-Würtemberg, North Rhine Westphalia and Schleswig-Holstein; in Bavaria and Hessen they are not mentioned. Establishing the farm needs the approval of the Countryside Authority (in Lower Saxony and North Rhine Westphalia); the Nature Protection Authority (in Baden-Würtemberg); the Hunting Authority (Bavaria); or the Higher Countryside Protection Authority (Hessen and Schleswig-Holstein). The exception is the Rhineland-Palatinate, where hunting estates and estates set up for meat production do not need consent (Countryside Protection Laws 5 February 1979). The basic premise, which is laid down in the Federal Nature Protection Laws, is also to be found in the State Rules and Regulations. This is that the rearing of the animals should be in accordance with accepted practice and that farming should leave free access to extensive areas of the countryside.

---

* I am grateful to Dr Hötzel L.D. for his help in checking this chapter.

From experience to date, it does not seem to be thought that a deer farm comes under the heading of an 'animal park'. Recent judgements (in the Bavarian Administrative Court 17 October 1983) stated that deer farming is a type of animal husbandry and as such is linked with land use. The Upper Court in Cologne determined in 1982 that deer farming is an agricultural pursuit with the aim of animal breeding and meat production. The impact on nature and the countryside is less damaging than that of cattle or horse enterprises, as the fence posts for a deer enterprise can be spaced 15 to 20 m apart, instead of 2 to 3 m as with the other two types of animals. There is no need for buildings such as stables or milking parlours. Shelters which may be needed in extreme conditions and any handling sheds can be screened by planting trees or hedges to fit in with the landscape. Deer are very suitable to be kept in areas where water-gathering and conservation are important considerations, as there is no necessity for manure heaps. The argument that they damage the sward is not supported by evidence from several years' research.

When considering the position of a deer farm under the Building Regulations, it is important to discover if the applicant or farmer is the owner of the agricultural enterprise or not. Landowners do not need planning consent for fencing, shelters, and handling buildings which do not exceed a certain height. If these are not used for agricultural purposes, then each case needs to be judged on its merits. It is advisable to clarify the position with the local authorities before work is undertaken, to avoid complications arising.

From experience to date it can be stated that decisions on consent for deer farming depend on the attitude of the local officials. The applicant cannot appeal against their decision, but has the right to make sure that the authorities consider and judge the application from all points of view. If the applicant does not have the necessary skill or knowledge, he should avail himself of the services of the local advisory officers, as in North Rhine Westphalia. It can be stressed that deer farms, like any other properly run farms, do not intrude on the landscape. Access to the countryside is not possible over the pastures themselves, but according to the countryside laws, the only stipulations are that footpaths, moorland or common land and other areas not used for farming should be accessible.

Limitations on use in areas protected for water-gathering or nature conservation are of course applicable to deer farming. If there is sufficient reason, taxes may be levied by local authorities. The refusal of planning consent without adequate reasons or under unfair injunctions is not acceptable. Such a ruling can be fought by putting one's case and arguments before the magistrates. Planning payments should not be necessary, since deer farming is an established practice, as with other farming enterprises.

The Federal Forestry Laws of 2 May 1975 contained no conditions applicable to deer farming. These could however be contained in the State Laws. For example, under the North Rhine Westphalia State Forestry Law of 29 July 1969, the enclosure of woodland is subject to planning dues. Thus, if woodland is to be included in a deer enterprise, permission will be necessary from the local forestry authority. They will decide on whether the small area of woodland is significant enough to matter to the local people seeking recreation. They can also refuse permission if there are sufficient reasons to believe that such enclosure would be of detriment to the general interests of the local community. The best advice to follow is that the enclosure of wooded areas should only be undertaken if it is necessary to provide shelter for the deer in windy areas or those with heavy rainfall. Individual trees will also need to be protected against browsing deer.

The Higher Court of North Rhine Westphalia ruled in a judgement on 7 March 1985 that the enclosing of woodland on a deer farm was damaging to the natural environment and permission should be refused.

Husbandry

The Federal Hunting Act (29 June 1976) does not allow hunting over a deer park or farm if an adequate safe fence has been erected round it, since it then becomes an enclosed area. Controversy can arise if unmarked deer, contrary to all experience to date, were to leave the herd and get out of the estate through a damaged fence or a gate which had been left open. If they are not recaptured by the landowner and they then cause injury to other unmarked beasts, the regulations under the wild animal protection laws – Sections 29 and following – come into force. The ownerless animal reverts to being a wild animal which may be hunted and comes under Hunting Laws. This shows the importance of clearly visible identification of farmed deer. As long as the deer are in the ownership of the farmer, he is responsible for any damage caused by an animal which breaks out of the farm (Federal Laws Section 833). Ownership is only forfeited if insufficient action is taken to recapture an animal, or this action is broken off, or if there is no identification.

According to a ruling of the State Court at Kiel in 1984, attempts to recapture an animal can only be accepted as sufficient if they are carried out thoroughly and carefully and with the obvious intention of recapturing the animal. The hunting authorities in the neighbourhood must also be informed. For this reason also, the use of an identification collar is recommended.

If the recommended guidelines for deer farmers on stocking density, sex ratio, antler removal, feeding, shelter provision and slaughtering are correctly followed, then the demands of the Animal Protection Laws will be fully met.

The Game Laws do not apply to deer farming, as they only affect animals without an owner. Neither do the regulations on close seasons, culling plans and annexation rules apply. The huntsman must inform the deer farmers in advance of the dates of the hunt. The State Court in Münster ruled on 21 January 1983 that the general rules of commerce obliged huntsmen to give notice of the hunt in advance. Huntsmen must recognise the danger they could present to farmed deer. If they failed to give notice, it would be treated as negligence. Following this, the huntsmen must compensate for any damage caused, if the deer were to panic or jump against the fence, and if they were killed or injured.

If the farmer is going to kill deer by shooting, he will need a gun licence (under the Firearms Regulations, Section 28), an ammunition licence (Section 29) and a shooting permit (Section 45). The only exceptions are air guns, dart guns and CO_2 guns.

Shooting equipment does not require a permit. Holders of firearms certificates do not need a licence to buy the ammunition suitable for the weapon covered by the licence. Holders of a hunting permit do not need a gun licence if the gun is only used on the hunting estate, and they are also covered for the transport of the weapons to the hunting area.

Shooting permits are obtained from the local police. It is immaterial whether the shooting is to be done on one enclosed estate or outside this area. The applicant must give his reasons for wanting the permit, must be adult, responsible and able. Holders of hunting permits also need a shooting permit, since they will be shooting on the enclosed area of the deer farm. There is a useful course available for deer farmers at the German Trials and Testing Station for Sporting and Hunting Guns at Altenbeken.

When animals are being transported for sale, the provisions of the Animal Protection Laws must be followed. If possible the animals should be transported singly and untethered. Recommended dimensions for carrying crates for female deer or calves are (internal measurements): 130 cm long, 80 cm wide and 100 cm high. For bucks the measurements should be: 180 cm long, 60 cm wide and 140 cm high. Animals which are still under the effects of immobilising drugs should not be transported or carried away.

When undertaking trading in animals the local authorities should be informed at the start of the operation. This does not apply to farmers dealing in farm animals from their own enterprise, or to breeders who belong to a registered co-operative. When farmed deer are recognised as farm animals, there will be no necessity for consent to be obtained for trading in them.

For the conditions governing ownership and living area, the rules are laid down in the Code of Civil Law (BGB), Sections 958 following. The animal is either in the ownership of a person or ownerless. A mobile object will become ownerless if the owner of it renounces his claim. Hötzel points to the fact that the courts have often upheld the interpretation, that each piece of land which is mainly hedged around, no matter how large it is, means a state of captivity for the animal, and it follows that the animals are in the ownership of the person who has obtained them legally or has taken over ownership. Here again we can see the importance of the identification of the deer, preferably by means of coloured collars.

The responsibility of the stock farmer comes under Section 833 of the Federal Laws. According to this, the owner of an animal has the obligation to compensate for any injuries caused. This liability does not apply if the injury was caused by an animal kept for the purpose of the work, production or livelihood of its owner, provided that the owner has taken proper care to supervise the animal or that the injury would have been caused even if this care had been taken. Farmed deer kept for breeding or slaughtering are there to provide a livelihood for their owner. Hötzel points to the fact that the 'domestic animal ownership' rule does not apply in the case of silver foxes, which have been farmed (for fur) for a long time and over several generations, and which usually return to the farm if they escape. This is also the case with bees, because they are not under the total care and control of the bee keeper. While farmed deer are not regarded as domestic animals, the responsibility of the farmer must be settled according to the reason for the injury being caused. In this case it is immaterial whether the owner has had the animal in his care for his livelihood and well-being or not. It is the farmer's responsibility also if he has relinquished or lost possession of the animal which has escaped. He is responsible for injury to life and limb, or health and damage to possessions.

When selling, the relative provisions of the Federal Civil Laws, in particular the responsibility for loss of property (Section 459), must be observed. Under Section 481 (Animal Sales), special provisions are only relaxed for the sales of horses, donkeys, mules and asses, cattle, sheep and pigs. These are set out in Sections 482–492.

The Federal Laws on Animal Breeding, 20 April 1976, which apply to the males of most species of domestic animals, are at present applicable just as infrequently for deer farming as are the Animal Epidemic Laws of 23 February 1977. This expressly exempts 'wild or captured wild animals'. But it is earnestly recommended that deer are included in the future if they are likely to be affected by an epidemic. By this means the deer farmer would have obligations on his part to pay the animal epidemic dues, but he would also be liable to gain compensation for the loss of animals due to the epidemic. It is also not clear whether farmed deer come under the regulations of Section 24 on the duty to display notices on the outbreak of an epidemic, under the Federal Hunting Laws. Hötzel points out that under Section 1 of the Animal Epidemic Laws, 'Slaughtering Animals', in the meaning of the law, are animals which are meant to be slaughtered so that their meat can be used for human consumption. This would cover all farm animals.

When immobilising deer (see page 187), the Firearms Regulations of 4 March 1976 apply, under which the use and possession of all narcotic guns, with which animals are shot for stunning or marking purposes, is subject to the granting of a licence. No permit is needed for a blow-pipe. For narcotics guns an application must be made for a gun licence to the local or regional police. Holders of a valid hunting permit do not need a gun licence.

The provisions of the Federal Drugs Laws, 24 August 1976, apply when using immobilising drugs. The farmer may, under Section 57, only use those drugs which are not available free of prescription if he obtains them from the vet who is employed by the farm, or from a pharmacist. Vets may supply the farmer with drugs for the animals to be treated by them, and the farmer may keep them in readiness for use. This also applies to the supply of drugs for use in any preventive measures advised and supervised by the vet for farm animals. However, the amount of drugs supplied should not exceed the reasonable amount which would be indicated as necessary by the vet. The local government officer is empowered, under the regulations, to ensure that people, who can only be supplied with drugs through pharmacists, vets or manufacturers, should have access to advice on the supply, storage, use and disposal of surplus of these drugs.

In Section 56 it is stated that feed additive drugs prescribed by a vet may be supplied by the manufacturer to the farmer without conditions. The ready-to-feed mixture must be labelled clearly with the words: 'feed additive preparation'.

Care must be taken, in addition, when animals are kept for meat production, that only those drugs are used which are tested and approved for such purposes, if there are no restrictions on their use, and, where a vet's prescription is required, they should only be used with the necessary approval and advice of the vet. Drugs must of course not be used if they remain active in the meat.

Slaughtering

When killing deer, it is very important to realise that hunting practices of shooting are only permitted, under the Federal Laws on Hunting, for wild, free ranging animals which are not in private ownership. Even wild animals in a zoo are not regarded as 'ownerless'. Therefore, basically, hunting can only be undertaken in open, wild, unenclosed areas; and in large, private estates, wild parks or hunting estates where the provisions for free ranging and on lack of ownership apply. The decisive factor is whether killing the animal by hunting, which is a matter of chance, is necessary. In a writ issued on 14 April 1978, the Minister for Food, Agriculture and Forestry in North Rhine Westphalia gave the decision that hunting should not be permitted in safari parks, because the animals are not living wild and, as they are being kept, they are not 'ownerless'. Safari parks are enclosed estates in which even limited hunting is not permitted. As the animals do not come under the Hunting Laws, there is no obligation to draw up a culling plan. There is no hunting season, no estate tax and no appropriation rights for those with hunting permits.

Under Section 4 of the Animal Protection Laws, animals are to be sedated before slaughter.

Killing with a gun is only allowed in circumstances where restraining equipment can be used which does not cause disturbance to the animals. In these circumstances the gun must only be used from the longest range possible and by a person having the necessary skill and experience in shooting vertebrates. A gun licence is needed under Section 45 of the Firearms Laws, and this also applies to holders of a hunting permit.

The Law on Slaughtering Animals, 21 April 1933, revised in the introductory act in the Penal Code of 2 March 1974, states that warm-blooded creatures should be sedated before the start of bleeding. Exception is made in the case of emergency slaughter. It is laid down in the regulations that by 'slaughter' is meant any killing of an animal where blood-letting takes place. The slaughtering is to take place in a closed-off area; and there must be at least enough provision to ensure that slaughtering is not open to public gaze. One exception to the rule on sedation is in emergency, when there is a possibility that the animal would die before sedation could be given.

Sedation must be undertaken in such a way that all unnecessary disturbance and pain for the animals are avoided. It must be quick and effective. Striking or cutting the throat or breaking the neck of the beasts to be slaughtered are methods which are not permitted, neither is hanging the animal up by its rear legs before sedation. Skinning, butchering, sticking, scalding or hanging up of a slaughtered (i.e. sedated and bled) animal must not be carried out until the animal is completely dead and all movement has stopped.

Finally it must be stated again that the laws have still made no definite rulings as to whether the killing of farmed deer comes under the slaughtering laws or under the provisions of the hunting laws. However, there are advantages in deer being considered on a similar basis to other domestic animals.

Under the meat Supervision Laws of 3 June 1900, last revised in 1981, it is laid down that for cattle, pigs, horses, etc. kept as farm animals, and also for fur animals, which are killed in other ways than shooting, an official inspection (by a meat and livestock inspector) must be carried out before and after slaughter, if the meat is to be used for human consumption. With farmed animals the livestock inspection would take the form of regular health checks on the farm by an official vet. Slaughtering may take place without permit if the animals show no signs of ill-health at the date of slaughter. A distinction is made between private slaughtering, when the meat is to be used privately by the owner, and business slaughtering, where the meat, dressed or not, is destined for sale for profit.

There is the provision that slaughtering may be carried out in a place other than a public abattoir. This comes under the Law on the Building of Public, Compulsory Abattoirs of 18 March 1968, which states that slaughtering is to be carried out in a public abattoir or, if such is not available, and there is no annexe or utility area available, it may be done in some other slaughter-house. If this happens, the many regulations on slaughter-houses, tools, personnel and meat preparation must be followed. If a farmer wishes to plan the erection of such a slaughter-house on his own farm, he is strongly advised to contact the local veterinary authorities in advance. Application must be made to the local authorities before building slaughtering premises. Permission will be granted only if the applicant is responsible, fulfils the minimum requirements laid down and complies with all the regulations. The supervision of a licensed building is done by the official vets, who act under the authority of the meat and hide inspectors.

Marketing

Fresh game meat may only be marketed through licensed butchers if it has been subject to the regulatory veterinary inspection before and after butchering, and if the meat has been passed and labelled accordingly. Even the cutting up of the carcass into halves or quarters may only be done on licensed premises. If the carcasses are to be cut into smaller joints, the butchering authorities must be informed. The meat must be hygienically and properly produced, handled, stored and transported. In addition, it must be pointed out that these same rules apply to fresh game meat which is imported into Germany. For these reasons, deer farmers raising deer for venison production must be prepared to obey the same regulations and maintain the same standards of hygiene in the production and handling of their product.

The hygiene regulations apply also to farmers and other personnel producing meat for profit. They also cover the selling of home-produced or bought-in meat. Under the Food Hygiene Regulations the selling area must be of sound construction, of sufficient size, dry, light and well ventilated. The floor must be solid, impermeable, resistant to fats and acids and easy to clean. The walls should be either painted with washable paint or tiled to a height of at least 2 m. Sales and work tables should also be topped with smooth, splinter-free and easily washed material. There must be hand washing facilities. There should be suitable cold stores to give a storage temperature of not more than 7°C. Packaged meat can only be sold at a temperature up to 6°C. Unpackaged food is to be covered to avoid customers touching it or breathing over it.

Other regulations to be observed are contained in the Food Laws of 17 January 1936, amendment 21 December 1958, by which it is forbidden to treat animals with antibiotics prior to slaughter, and to implant or inject the animals with hormonal products. The Regulation on chemical additives of 3 August 1977 states in particular that food may not be sold which has been produced from animals treated with oestrogen, androgen or steroids to influence the keeping quality, or the quality of the meat and its fat content. Deer farming, which does not use such products, is thus shown to advantage in complying with legal requirements.

When transporting meat, the Hygiene Regulations apply, and these forbid the carrying of unskinned game in the same lorry as unpackaged foods. Whole carcasses of meat can be carried for a journey of up to one hour's duration.

Most food in Germany comes under one or other group heading in the legal trade classification, based on the Trade Classification Laws of 23 November 1972. Goods can be classified in the interests of the producers and the quality and outlets for their produce, and in the interests of the marketing authorities. Grading can be done on grounds of quality, source, type and variety, date of production, picking or harvesting, handling, presentation, cleanliness, conformation, selection and consistency of certain characteristics. Description of contents, sell-by dates, packer and weight must be given. From experience up to date, it would seem that applying the appropriate standards to most agricultural products has led to an increased consumer awareness of quality. There is also the possibility of introducing grading classes for farmed venison.

Of importance in the marketing of farmed venison is a ruling by the European Court (RS 149/73) that the term 'wild' effectively means that it encompasses those animals living freely in the wild, which can be hunted. From this, reindeer meat is classed with meat from farmed animals, while caribou meat is classed as 'wild'. The basic premise of this judgement shows that the similarity of goods does not exclude their different treatment on grounds of other determining factors. This ruling, which applies to the import of meat into the EEC, shows that the type of meat is of less importance when classifying an animal as wild or domestic than the matter of whether it is in the care of humans or not.

It is important that food is not wrongly labelled when put on the market. It is advisable to describe the meat produced from farmed deer as 'farmed venison'. This cannot then be regarded under the law as giving a false impression to the consumer. According to legal interpretation, there are no reservations about the terms 'farmed venison', 'farmed (calf) venison' and 'farmed (fallow) venison'.

When selling from a permanent site (farm shop), the Shop Opening Hours must be observed. This does not apply to farmers who only occasionally sell produce at the farm gate (Reinken, Nies, Roder and Seemann).

Carcass Disposal

The Carcass Disposal Law of 2 September 1975 applies to the carcasses – dead, stillborn, premature foetuses, or slaughtered animals, which are not to be used for human consumption – and parts of the bodies – those from abattoirs including blood and feathers, skins, hides, horns, hooves, bones or wool or other parts of the animal which are not used for human consumption, and animal products, in particular prepared meat. For the individual states the authority is vested in the appropriate laws. Farmed deer come unequivocally under the provisions of the Carcass Disposal Laws. However, the provisions on exemptions from dues and payment do not apply to farmed deer, i.e. payments may be levied.

To sum up, it may be stated that the authoritative law for deer farming is contained in separate Acts. In several areas, however, deer farming is not covered in the very precise details of the Laws and Advice on particular types of animal. Until a suitable revision of the Rules and Regulations is made, deer farmers need to refer to the Laws and Provisions at present in force, and act accordingly.

Insurance

Deer farmers come under Section 833 of the Federal Civil Code on 'Farmers' Liability'. In this it is stated: 'If a man is killed by an animal, or his body or health is injured by the same, or his property damaged, then the owner of the animal is obliged to recompense the injured party for the damages so sustained. This liability does not apply if the animal which has caused the damage is a domestic animal, kept for the purpose of serving the farmer for his use or as a working animal, and if the owner of the animal has exercised all reasonable care and supervision of the animal or if the damage would have been caused even if this care and supervision had been undertaken.' Section 834 states: 'Whoever undertakes the care and supervision of an animal on behalf of its owner is responsible for damage caused by the animal to a third party in the manner stated in Section 833; this responsibility does not apply if he takes all reasonable care or if the damage would have been caused even if this care had been taken.' At present we must state that farmed deer are not recognised as domestic animals under the law. For this reason it is strongly recommended that landowners and tenants in their status as animal owners should be covered by Third Party Compensation Insurance. Most insurance companies are prepared to undertake such insurance for the agricultural enterprise, with a suitable clause in the overall policy to include farmed deer (Farmers' Liability Insurance). For tenants the premium will vary according to the type and nature of the risk. Sometimes there may be supplementary premiums to be added to the private personal insurance policy or the house and landowners' policy. The details could be discussed with the insurer's representative. Damage to land is generally excluded and can only be insured under a special clause. Secure fencing and identification of the deer by marking are important considerations which can help to keep down the level of premiums paid.

In certain cases it may be advisable to take out insurance against loss, from causes such as theft, robbery, rustling, slaughtering by intruders and being struck by lightning. The insurers will take note of the fact that at present this is a new, not yet assessable risk. The premiums will depend on the extent of the compensation, number, purchase price or market value of the animals, position of the deer unit and the state of the fencing. In some cases escaping animals or those lost through goring with the antlers may not be covered. Insurance against theft is therefore recommended to those deer farmers whose units are in isolated situations, if the geography of the area is of advantage to the thief, and if daily supervision of the animals is not possible.

Taxation

As regards the unit valuation of the agriculture and forestry authorities, the Federal Finance Minister in the Regulation of 27 December 1977 laid down that deer breeding and farming should come under Section 51 of the Valuation Act, if they are carried out in connection with utilisation of the land with the aim of meat production. To enable calculations to be made of the deer stock in terms of grazing units of beasts, the following comparisons have been drawn up: stags, adult hinds and deer one year and older: 0.08 units; calves under one year old: 0.04 units. From this, fallow deer are reckoned to be on the same scale as goats (0.08 units) but lower than sheep (0.1 units).

As for income tax, the income from deer farming comes under revenue from agriculture or forestry (Section 13. Income Tax Laws). Under the Profits Tax, when considering turnover from deer farming within an agricultural or forestry enterprise, from living or dead animals and from hides, in conformity with Section 24, an average profit of 7 per cent, plus 1 per cent inflation rate, is to be taken as the norm. According to Section 12 of the Profits Tax Laws, for business enterprises and for opting agricultural or forestry landowners, who pay tax at the standard rate, the lower rate of 6.5 per cent is levied on live animals, meat, skins and hide. The half or quarter carcasses which are included in the sales figures are still regarded as agricultural produce. The further preparation of meat into joints, sausages, etc., is counted as a business activity.

Bibliography

AAFJES, J. H.: Changes in blood volatile fatty acids after their infusion into the rumen of a cow. Brit. vet. J. **120**, 487–489, 1964.

ABRAMS, J. T.: Fundamental approach to the nutrition of the captive wild herbivore. Symp. Zool. Soc. Lond. **21**, 41–62, Academic Press, London 1968.

VAN ACKEN, D.: Zum Tagesrhythmus des Damwildes. Z. f. Jagdwissenschaft **18**, 96–103, 1972.

Agricultural Research Council: The nutrient requirements of ruminant livestock. Commonwealth Agric. Bureaus, London, 221–267, 1980.

ALVAREZ, F., F. BRAZA and A. NORZAGARAY: The use of the rump patch in the fallow deer *(D. dama)*. Behaviour **56**, 298–308, 1976.

ANDERSON, R.: Gold on four feet. Melbourne 1978.

ANDREWS, J. R. H.: A host-parasite checklist of helminths of wild ruminants in New Zealand. New Zealand Veterinary Journal **21 (3)**, 43–47, 1973.

ANTHONY, R. G.: Influence of drought on diets and numbers of desert deer. J. Wildl. Managem. **40 (1)**, 140–144, 1976.

ARC-Agricultural Research Council: The nutrient requirements of ruminants livestock. Farnham Royal, Slough, England, 1980.

ARMAN, P.: A note on parturition and maternal behaviour in captive red deer. J. Repr. Fert. **37**, 87–90, 1974.

– R. N. B. KAY, E. D. GOODALL and G. A. M. SHARMAN: The composition and yield of milk from captive red deer. J. Repr. Fert. **37**, 67–84, 1974.

ARMSTRONG, N., R. E. CHAPLIN, D. I. CHAPMAN and B. SMITH: Observation on the reproduction of female wild and park fallow deer in southern England. J. Zool. **158**, 27–37, 1969.

ASHER, G. W.: Meat production from fallow deer. Royal Soc. New Zealand **22**, 299–301, 1985.

– Oestrous cycle and breeding season of farmed fallow deer, *Dama dama*. Reproduction & Fertility **75**, 521–529, 1985.

– and J. L. ADAM: Reproduction of farmed red and fallow deer in northern New Zealand. Royal of New Zealand **22**, 217–224, 1985.

BACH, P.: Damwild, Alternative zum Milchvieh? dlz, 228–232, 1985.

BAIGENT, P. N. and I. S. JARRATT: The economics of the deer farming industry. New Zeal. Agricultural Science **11**, 206–211, 1977.

BAKER, K.: Reproductive biology of fallow deer *(Dama dama)* in the Blue Mountains of New Zealand. University of Otago, Dunedin N.Z., 1974.

BANNERMANN, M. M. and K. L. BLAXTER: The husbanding of red deer. Proc. Rowett Institute, Aberdeen, 1–79, 1969.

BARTH, D.: 10 Jahre Thibenzole zur Parasitenbekämpfung. Die Pirsch **23**, 576–577, 1971.

BATCHELER, C.: A study of the relation between roe-, red- and fallow deer. J. Anim. Ecol. **29**, 375–384, 1960.

BATTY, A. F.: Gastro-intestinal parasites of wild fallow deer *(Dama dama* L.). J. Helminthology **44 (1)**, 57–61, 1970.

BECHSTEIN, J. M.: Handbuch der Jagdwissenschaft. Verlag J. C. Monath und J. F. Kußlerschen Buchhandlung, Nürnberg und Altdorf 1806.

BEHR, CH.: Lebensmittelhygienische Anforderungen an Wildbret und ihre Berücksichtigung in der in- und ausländischen Gesetzgebung. Diss. Univ. Bonn, S. 1–279, 1976.

– und E. GREUEL: Lebensmittelhygienische Aspekte bei der Wildbretgewinnung. Z. f. Jagdw., **21–23**, 41–50, 1975–1977.

BERNER, O.: Wildbret vom Bauernhof. top agrar **10**, 24–26, 1976.

BIERSCHWAL, C. J., E. C. MATHER, C. E. MARTIN, D. A. MURPHY and L. J. KORSCHGEN: Some characteristics of deer semen collected by electroejaculation. J. Amer. Vet. Med. Ass. **157 (5)**, 627–632, 1970.

BIRD, M.: Deer farming research findings. NZ J. Agr. **X**, 50–53, 1974.

BISSELL, H. D. and W. C. WEIR: The digestibility of interior live oak and chamise by deer and sheep. J. Anim. Sci. **16**, 476–480, 1957.

BLAXTER, K. L.: Symposium on 'The nutrition of new farm animals'. Conventional and unconventional farmed animals. Proc. Nutr. Soc. **34**, 51–56, 1975.

– R. N. B. KAY, G. A. M. SHARMAN, J. M. M. CUNNINGHAM and W. J. HAMILTON: Farming the red deer – The first report of an investigation by the Rowett Research Institute and the Hill Farming Research Organisation –. Her Majesty's Stationery Office: 1–93, 1974.

– Red deer in the UK – farm livestock of the future: historical background to the farming of red deer in Scotland. BVA Congress, Univ. Aberdeen, 9–14 Sept. 1979.

– and W. J. HAMILTON: Reproduction in farm red deer, 2. Calf growth and mortality. J. agric. Sci., Camb. **95**, 275–284, 1980.

BLEICHNER, K. L. and W. C. ELLIS: Effect of source and amount of roughage on size of rumen papillae in cattle. J. Animal Sci. **27**, 1161, 1968.

BLEWETT, D. A., K. M. G. ADAM and G. A. M. SHARMAN: A Babesia sp. in Scottish red deer. J. Protozool. **4 (3)**, 448, 1974.

BOBECK, B.: Hirschbrunft mit dem Dummy. Jäger, 70–71, 1982.

BOCH, J. und R. SUPPERER: Veterinärmedizinische Parasitologie. Verlag Parey, Berlin und Hamburg 1971.

BÖCKELER, W. und R. SEGEBADE: Prüfung der Wirksamkeit vin Panacur gegen Magen-Darm-Nematoden des Damwildes. Tierärztliche Umschau **9**, 473–477, 1977.

BÖKÖNYI, S.: Angaben zum frühholozänen Vorkommen des Damhirsches, *Cervus (Dama) dama* (Linné, 1758) in Europa. Säugetierkundl. Mitt. **19 (3)**, 206–217, 1971.

– Development of early stock rearing in the Near East. Nature **264**, 19–23, 1976.

BOESSNECK, J.: Die Haustiere in Altägypten. Veröffentl. Zool. Staatssammlung **3**, 1–50, München 1953.

BOGNER, H.: Damwild – ein landwirtschaftliches Nutztier? Tierärztl. Praxis, Z. f. Tierarzt **6**, 257–265, 1978.

– Erfahrungen mit Farming von Damwild. Deutscher Wildgehege-Verband e.V., Informationen zur Haltung von Wild **3**, 26–31, 1982.

– und P. MATZKE: Geweihamputation bei Cerviden aus der Sicht der Ethologie und des Tierschutzes. Berl. Münch. Tierärztl. Wschr. **98**, 229–231, 1985.

– B. MITTRACH und K. POPP: Nutztierartige Haltung von Damwild in Gehegen. Arbeitsblatt Landwirtschaftl. Bauwesen, 1983.

BOMMERT, U.: Verhaltensbeobachtungen bei einer Damtierherde 1974/76. Unveröffentlichte Aufzeichnungen.

BOYD, J. M.: Experimental management of wildlife in the Scottish Highlands and Islands. Symp. zool. Soc. Lond. **21**, 311–318, 1968.

V. BRAUNSCHWEIG, A.: Wild als Lebensmittel. Wild und Hund **12**, 519, 1977.

– Altersschätzung beim Damwild. Wild und Hund, 31–33, 1985.

BREUSTEDT, H.: Persönl. Mitt. vom 12. 11. 1976.

BRINK, A. S.: Der Weg zur Warmblütigkeit. In: Grzimeks Tierleben. Ergänzungsband: Entwicklungsgeschichte der Lebewesen. Kindler-Verlag: 252–254, 1972.

BRÜGGEMANN, J., K. WALSER-KÄRST und D. GIESEKE: Untersuchungen über die Parotissekretion bei Schafen. Tierphysiol. Tierern. Futtermittelkd. **20**, 295–305, 1965.

– U. DRESCHER-KADEN und K. WALSER-KÄRST: Die mutterlose Aufzucht von Rotwildkälbern mit unterschiedlicher Rationsgestaltung. Z. Tierphysiol. Tierernähr. Futtermittelkd. **31 (4)**, 182–200, 1973.

– – Die Zusammensetzung der Rotwildmilch: I. Der Rohnährstoffgehalt (Rohfett, Rohprotein, Lactose und Rohasche). Z. Tierphysiolog. Tierernähr. Futtermittelkd. **31 (4)**, 227 238, 1973.

BRYANT, M. P.: Identification of group of anaerobic bacteria active in the rumen. J. Animal Sci. **22**, 801–813, 1963.

BUBENIK, A. B.: Der Feinbau der Geweihe von Cervus (Dama) dama Linné,1758, und mesopotamicus Brooke, 1875, und ihre Entwicklungsstufe. Säugetierkundl. Mitt. **7**, 90–95, 1959.

– Beitrag zur Geburtskunde und zu den Mutter-Kind-Beziehungen des Reh- und Rotwildes. Z. Säugetierkunde **30**, 65–128, 1965.

– Das Geweih (Entwicklung, Aufbau und Ausformung der Geweihe und Gehörne). Paul Parey, Hamburg/Berlin 1966.

BUCKLAND, D. E., W. A. ABLER, R. L. KIRKPATRICK and J. B. WHELAN: Improved husbandry system for rearing fawns in captivity. J. Wildl. Managem. **39 (1)**, 211–214, 1975.

BÜTZLER, W.: Kampf- und Paarungsverhalten, soziale Rangordnung und Aktivitätsperiodik beim Rothirsch (Cervus elaphus L.). Fortschritte der Verhaltensforschung – Beihefte Tierpsychologie **16**, 1–80, Verlag Paul Parey, 1974.

CADMAN, W. A.: The fallow deer. Forestry Comm. Leaflet No. 52, London 1966.

CARNE, P. H.: Roe deer, fallow and sika. Oryx, **2**, 388–391, 1954.

– Roe deer and fallow. Oryx **3**, 104, 1955.

CATAR, G.: Further Toxoplasma isolation from animals. Journ. Parasitology **56**, 408, 1970.

Centrale Marketinggesellschaft der deutschen Agrarwirtschaft, CMA Fleischreport, Heft 6/81, 9/81, 10/85.

CHAPLIN, R. E.: Deer. Poole, Dorset. Blandford Press, 1977.

– and R. W. G. WHITE: The use of tooth eruption and wear, body weight and antler characteristics in the age estimation of male wild and park fallow deer (Dama dama). J. Zool. Lond. **157**, 125, 1969.

– – The influence of age and season on the activity of the testes and epididymes of the fallow deer. J. Repr. Fert. **30**, 361–369, 1972.

CHAPMAN, D. I.: The fallow deer situation in Epping Forest, Essex, England. Biological Conservation **1 (3)**, 252–253, 1969.

– Immobilisation of deer. Vet. Res. **93**, 113–114, 1973.

– Reproductive physiology in relation to deer management. Mammal. Rev. **4 (3)**, 61–74, 1974.

– and N. G. CHAPMAN: Observations on the biology of fallow deer (Dama dama) in Epping Forest, Essex, England. Biol. Conserv. **2 (1)**, 55–62, 1969.

– – Preliminary observations on the reproductive cycle of male fallow deer (Dama dama L.). J. Reprod. Fert. **21 (1)**, 1–8, 1970.

– – Maxillary canine teeth in fallow deer, Dama dama. J. Zoology Proc. Zool. Soc. Lond. **170**, 143–147, 1973.

– and N. CHAPMAN: Fallow deer: their history, distribution and biology. Lavenham, Dalton 1975.

– – Fallow deer. London. The British Deer Soc., 1970.

CLIFT, T. R., J. CHALLACOMBE and P. E. DYCE: Electric fencing for fallow deer. Royal Soc. New Zealand **22**, 363–365, 1985.

CLOUSTON, F. R. S.: Financial returns and export possibilities from venison. In: Deer farming in New Zealand, Progress and prospects. Editorial Services Limited, Wellington, 37–46, 1976.

COENEN, J.: Zehn Jahre Damtierhaltung auf Haus Riswick. Landw. Zeitschrift, 2868–2869, 1984.

– Erfahrungen mit Mutterkühen, Schafen und Damtieren als Alternative zur Milchviehhaltung. Tierärztliche Praxis 12, 1–4, 1984.

COLUMELLA: (AHRENS, K., aus dem Lateinischen übersetzt, eingeführt und erläutert) Über Landwirtschaft – Lehr- und Handbuch der gesamten Acker- und Viehwirtschaft aus dem I. Jahrhundert u. Z.Akademie-Verlag Berlin, 1976.

COPE, A. C. and V. HORSLEY: Reports on the outbreak of rabies among deer in Richmond Park during the years 1886–7. H.M.S.O. London 1888, zit. nach Chapman and Chapman.

CORRIGIAL, W. and W. J. HAMILTON: Reaction of red deer hinds to removal of their suckled calves for hand-rearing. Appl. Anim. Ethol. 3 (1), 47–55, 1977.

COUCHMAN, R. C.: Deer farming – for those who can wait. Journal Agr., 393–395, 1978.

CREMER, H. D., W. AIGN, I. ELMADFA, E. MUSKAT und M. WESTHOFF: Die Große Nährwert-Tabelle. GU-Ratgeber, Inst. f. Ernährungswissenschaften I der Universität Gießen. Gräfe und Unzer Verlag, München 1979.

CRESCENTIIS, P. DE: Von der Jagerey. Franckfurt am Mayn 1583.

CRHA, J.: Rumen ciliates in fallow deer (Dama dama L.) in Namest Preserve. Acta Vet. Brno 41, 355–362, 1972.

CZERKAWSKI, J. W.: Methane production in ruminants and its significance. Wld. Res. Nutr. Diet. 11, 240–282, 1969.

– K. L. BLAXTER and F. W. WAINMAN: The effect of linseed oil and of linseed oil fatty acids marjorated in the diet on the metabolism of sheep. Brit. J. Nutr. 20, 485–494, 1966.

DANIEL, M. J.: A survey of disease in fallow, Virginia and Japanese deer, chamois, tahr, and feral goats and pigs in New Zealand. N. Z. J. Sc. 10, 949–963, 1967.

DANSIE, O.: Observations on the weighing of park deer. Br. Veterinary Journ. 133 (2), 215–218, 1977.

DAVIDSON, W. R., J. M. CRUM, J. L. BLUE, D. W. SHARP and J. H. PHILLIPS: Parasites, diseases, and health status of sympatric populations of fallow deer and white-tailed deer in Kentucky. Wildlife Diseases 21 (2), 153–159, 1985.

DEER ADVISORY COUNCIL OF VICTORIA: Deer in Australia. Fisheries and Wildlife Division, Ministry of Conservation, Melbourne, 1979.

DELAP, P.: Roe deer and fallow. Oryx 3, 38–39, 1955.

– Some notes on the social habits of the British deer. Proc. Zool. Soc. Lond. 128, 608–612, 1957.

DESCH, CHR.: Wege zum Erfolg oder Mißerfolg bei der Damwildhaltung. Landw. Wildgehege 3, 17, 1986.

Deutscher Jagdschutz-Verband e.V. (Bearbeitung WIESE, M.) DJV Handbuch 1979–85. Verl. Dieter Hoffmann, Mainz 1979.

DIJKSTRA, N. D., H. WEIDE und P. VAN ADRICHEM: Vergelijkend onderzoek over de verteerbaarheid van ruwvoeder door hamelns en door melkkoeien Versl. Landbouerk. Onderz., Wageningen 68, 1962.

DISSEN, J.: Untersuchungen über die Verdaulichkeit von Rohnährstoffen verschiedener Futterrationen an Rehwild (Capreolus C. Capreolus L.) und Ziegen (Capra A. Hircus L.) sowie Beobachtungen über das äsungsverhalten von Gehege-Rehen. Diss. Bonn, 1–100, 1983.

DISSEN, J. und W. HARTFIEL: Beobachtungen zum Äsungsverhalten sowie Untersuchungen zur Nährstoffverdaulichkeit von Rehwild. Z. Jagdwiss. 31, 83–91, 1985.

DLG-Futterwerttabelle. für Wiederkäuer. 5. Auflage, DLG-Verlag, Frankfurt 1982.

DLG-Futterwerttabelle, Mineralstoffgehalte in Futtermitteln. DLG-Verlag, Frankfurt, 2. Auflage, 1–199, 1973.

DLG-Futterwerttabelle, Aminosäurengehalte in Futtermitteln. DLG-Verlag, Frankfurt, 1–114, 1976.

DONDORF, W. und W. HOFMANN: Unterschiede in Größe und Form der Griffelbeine (Ossa metacarpalia II und V) und der Vorderfußwurzel (Os carpale primum, Os carpale secundum et tertium) zwischen dem Rothirsch (*Cervus elaphus* Linné 1758) und Damhirsch (*Dama dama* Linné 1758). Jagdw. **30**, 155–164, 1984.

DRESCHER-KADEN, U.: Die mutterlose Aufzucht von Rehkitzen mit verschiedenen Milchaustauschertypen. Tierärztl. Umschau **8**, 396–402, 1972.

– Untersuchungen am Verdauungstrakt von Reh, Damhirsch und Mufflon. Mitteilung 1: Gewichtserhebungen und Kapazitätsmeussungen am Verdauungstrakt, insbesondere am Pansen-Haubenraum von Reh, Damhirsch und Mufflon. Z. Jagdwiss. **22 (4)**, 184–190, 1976.

– U. V. SCHULZ und J. GROPP: Die mutterlose Aufzucht von Rehkitzen mit verschiedenen Milchaustauschfuttertypen. 2. Mitteilung. Tieräeztliche Umschau, 224–236, 1973.

– und E. A. SEIFELNASR: Untersuchungen am Verdauungstraktvon Reh, Damhirsch und Mufflon Mitteilung 2: Rohnährstoffe im Panseninhalt von Reh, Damhirsch und Mufflon. Z. Jagdwiss. **23**, 6–11, 1976.

– – Untersuchungen am Verdauungstrakt von Reh. Damhirsch und Mufflon. Mitteilung 3: Mikroorganismen im Pansen von Reh, Damhirsch und Mufflon. Z. Jagdwiss. **23**, 64–69, 1977.

– – Untersuchungen am Verdauungstrakt von Reh. Damhirsch und Mufflon. Mitteilung 4: Fermentationsprodukte im Pansen von Reh. Damhirsch und Mufflon. Z. Jagdwiss. **23**, 126–131, 1977.

DREW, K. R.: The farming of red deer in New Zealand. Wld. Rev. Animal Prod. **12**, 49–60, 1976.

– and G. J. GREER: Venison production and carcass composition of red deer. New Zealand Agr. Sci. **11**, 187–189, 1977.

– and R. W. KELLY: Handling deer run in confined areas. Proc. New Zealand Soc. Animal Prod. **35**, 213–218, 1975.

– and M. F. McDONALD: Deer farming in New Zealand. Progress and prospects. Editorial Services Limited, Wellington 1976.

DROST, S.: Die Sarkosporidien des Schalenwildes. III. Sarkosporidien beim Rot- und Damwild. Angew. Parasitologie **18 (4)**, 219–225, 1977.

EIBEN, B. und K. FISCHER: Untersuchungen über die Beziehungen der Aktivität der Alkalischen Phosphatase und dem Geweihbildungszyklus beim Damhirsch (*Dama dama* L.). Jagdw. **29**, 244–247, 1983.

– – Untersuchungen verschiedener Blutparameter beim Damhirsch (*Dama dama* L.) im Jahresgang. Jagdw. **30**, 235–242, 1984.

– ST. SCHARLA, K. FISCHER und H. SCHMIDT-GAYK: Seasonal variations of serum 1,25-dihydroxy-vitamin D_3 and alkaline phosphatase in relation to the antler formation in the fallow deer (*Dama dama* L.). Acta Endocrinologica **107**, 141–144, 1984.

ELLIOTT III, H. W. and R. H. BARRETT: Dietary overlap among axis, fallow and blacktailed deer and cattle. Range Management **38 (6)**, 546–550, 1985.

EISFELD, D.: Der Proteinbedarf des Rehes (*Capreolus capreolus* L.) zur Erhaltung. Z. Jagdwiss. **20**, 43–48, 1974.

ENTZEROTH, R.: Floristische Aufnahme von Wildgehegen im Rheinland zur Ermittlung der von wiederkäuenden Schalenwildarten verschmähten Pflanzen. Jagdw. **24**, 187–194, 1978/79.

ENZINGER, W. und W. HARTFIEL: Noch Nicht veröffentlichte Untersuchungsergebnisse.

ERHARDOVA-KOTRLA, B. und A. KORTRLY: Die Dauer des Parasitismus bei manchen Säugetiernematoden. Helminthologia **11**, 1–4, 1970.

ERIKSEN, E.: Indfangning at hjortevildt ved immobilisering med neuroleptika. Nord. Vet.-Med. **22**, 385–400, 1970.

ESPMARK, Y. and W. BRUNNER: Observations on rutting behaviour in fallow deer, *Dama dama* (Linné, 1758). Säugetierkundl. Mitt. **22**, 135–142, 1974.

EVERS, G.: Hinweise zum Zaunbau. Landw. Wildgehege **2**, 67–68, 1985.

EWER, R. F.: Ethologie der Säugetiere. Verlag Paul Parey, Berlin und Hamburg 1977.

FAO: World meat situation and outlook. FAO-Report, Rom, 1980.

FEHR, R.: Der Schutzgedanke in Rechtsverordnungen nach § 13 des Tierschutzgesetzes. Tierzüchter **6**, 254–256, 1981.

FELL, B. F., M. KAY, F. G. WHITLAW and R. BOYNE: Observations on the development of ruminal lesions in calves fed on barley. Res. Vet. Sci. **9**, 458–460, 1968.

FIELD, R. A., O. A. YOUNG, G. W. ASHER and D. M. FOOTE: Characteristics of male fallow deer muscle at a time of sex-related muscle growth. Growth **49**, 190–201, 1985.

FINKE, K.: Erfassung und Bewertung der Schlachtkörperqualität von Damtierkälbern. Pressein-formation der Landwirtschaftskammer Rheinland 1975.

FISCHER, D. v.: Bedarfsgerecht, kostenbewußt, umweltfreundlich. Landw. Z., 902–903, 1985.

– Leistungsfähige Grasnarben gefragt. Landw. Z., 1732–1735, 1985.

FISCHER, K.: Untersuchungen zur Fortpflanzungsfähigkeit von jungem weiblichem und männlichem Damwild (*Dama dama* L.). Jagdw. **29**, 137–142, 1983.

– Provozierte Spätgeburten 1983. Jagdw. **30**, 124–126, 1984.

FLEMING, G.: Animal Plagues: Their History, Nature and Prevention. Chapman & Hall (Vol. 1) 1871, Bailliére, Tindall & Cox (Vol. 2), London 1882: zit. nach Chapman and Chapman.

Food and Agriculture Organization of the United Nations: The world meat economy in figures. FAO Economic and Social Development Paper, Rome 1985.

Föreningen för Svensk Hjortavel: Information om hjortavel i Hägn, 1975.

FOX, M. W.: Influence of domestication upon behaviour of animals. Vet. Rec. **80**, 696–702, 1967.

FREERICKS, A.: Mutterlose Damtieraufzucht. Landw.Wildgehege **2**, 28–30, 1985.

FRITSCH, R.: Rechtliche Grundlagen der Immobilisation. Vortrag 1978.

– Medikamente zur Immobilisation. Vortrag 1978.

FÜRSTENBERG, P., Frhr. v.: Wildtiernutzung und -bewirtschaftung in Afrika südlich der Sahara. Forstarchiv **47**, 153–158, 1976.

GAUTHIER, D. and C. BARRETTE: Suckling and weaning in captive white-tailed and fallow deer. Behavior **94**, 128–149, 1985.

GEIGER, G., R. HOFMANN und R. KÖNIG: Vergleichend-anatomische Untersuchungen an den Vormägen von Damwild, *Cervus dama* (Linné, 1758) und Muffelwild, *Ovis ammon musimon* (Pallas, 1811). Säugetierkundl. Mitt. **25 (1)**, 7–21, 1977.

GEISSLER, B.: Auswirkungen der Brunft auf das Wildbretgewicht beim Damhirsch. Z. f. Jagdw. **17**, 31–33, 1971.

Gesellschaft für Ernährungsphysiologie der Haustiere: Empfehlungen zur Mineralstoffversorgung. Energie- und Nährstoffbedarf landw. Nutztiere Nr. 1, DLG-Verlag, Frankfurt 1978.

GIBBS, E. P. J., A. MCDIARMID and J. J. ROWE: Management of deer for experimental studies with foot-and-mouth disease virus. Vet **96 (23)**, 503–506, 1975.

– K. A. J. HERNIMAN, M. J. P. LAWMAN and R. F. SELLERS: Foot-and-mouth disease in British deer: transmission of virus to cattle, sheep and deer. Vet. Rec. **96 (26)**, 558–563, 1975.

– and M. J. P. LAWMAN: Infection of British deer and farm animals with epizootic haemorrhagic disease of deer virus. J. Comp. Path. **87 (3)**, 335–344, 1977.

GILBERT, B. K.: Development of social behaviour in the fallow deer *(Dama dama)*. Dep. Zoology, Duke University, Durham, N.C., 867–876, 1967.

– The influence of foster rearing on adult social behaviour in fallow deer. I.U.C.N. Symp. Alberta, Canada, 1971. I.U.C.N. Publ. New Series 24, 247–272 Vol. 2, Morges, Schweiz 1974.

GODYNICKI, S.: Tetnice glowy u daniela (*Dama dama* L.). Arteries in the head of fallow deer *Dama dama*. Pol. Arch. Weter. **15 (4)**, 855–868, 1972.

GÖBBEL, T.: Dem Könner bieten Damtiere echte Einkommenschancen. Landwirtschaftskammer Rheinland, 1984.

GÖLTENBOTH, R. und H.-G. KLÖS: Zur Immobilisation von Zootieren mit Vetalar und Rompun. Vortrag 1976.

GOSS, R. J. and R. POWEL: Induction of ectopic antlers by subcutaneous grafts of fallow deer periosteum. Am. Zoologist **23**, 971, 1983.

GOSSOW, H.: Einfluß des Geweihwechsels auf die Rangordnung im Hirschrudel. Umschau **7**, 241–242, 1971.

GRADL-GRAMS, M.: Verhaltensstudien an Damwild (*Cervus dama* L. 1758) in Gefangenschaft. Zool. Garten N.F. Jena **47**, 81–108, 1977.

GRAF, W.: Territorialism in deer. J. Mammalogy **37**, 165–170, 1956.

GREGSON, J. E. and R. W. PURCHAS: The carcass composition of male fallow deer. Royal Soc. New Zealand **22**, 295–298, 1985.

GREUEL, E. und SCHMIDT-SCHOPEN: Wissenswertes über Wild. Verbraucherdienst **20**, 29–35, 1975.

GRZIMEK, B. und L. HECK: Unterfamilie Elche, Unterfamilie Renhirsche, S. 259–272, in Grzimeks Tierleben, 13. Enzyklopädie des Tierreiches. Kindler-Verlag, München 1972.

GÜRTLER, H.: Die Physiologie der Verdauung und Absorption in: KOLB, E.: Lehrbuch der Physiologie der Haustiere, VEB Fischer Verlag, Jena 1980, Teil I, 177–377.

GUINNESS, F. E. and J. FLETCHER: First ever recorded incidence of twins born to a red deer hind in Britain. Deer **2**, 680–682, 1971.

– G. A. LINCOLN and R. V. SHORT: The reproductive cycle of the female red deer. J. Repr. Fert. **27**, 427–438, 1971.

GUSTAVSSON, I. and C. O. SUNDT: Three polymorphic chromosome systems of centric fusion type in a population of manchurian Sika Deer (*Cervus nippon hortulorum* Swinhoe). Chromosoma (Berl.) **28**, 245–254, 1969.

HÄNEL, J.: Wildtiere als Proteinquelle in Afrika. Institut f. Angewandte Zoologie der Univ. Bonn, 1–106, 1981.

HAGEMEISTER, H. und W. KAUFMANN: Hydrogenierung von ungesättigten Fettsäuren im Verdauungstrakt der Milchkuh. Kieler Milchwiss. Forschungsber. **31**, 41–52, 1979.

– – Mikrobielle Synthese nicht flüchtiger Fettsäuren in den Vormägen von Milchkühen. Kieler Milchwiss. Forschungsber. **31**, 11–29, 1979.

– – und A. WIECHEN: Messungen des Resorptionsortes von Fettsäuren im Verdauungstrakt der Milchkuh. Kieler Milchwiss. Forschungsber. **31**, 5–10, 1979.

HAGER, P. und H. ZIMMERMANN: Damhirschhaltung. Landwirtsch. Beratungszentrale Lindau, 1979.

HAIGH, J. C. Fallow deer immobilisation with fentanyl and a neuroleptic. Vet. Rec. **100 (8)**, 386, 1977.

HALTENORTH, TH.: Beitrag zur Kenntnis des Mesopotamischen Damhirsches – Cervus *(Dama) mesopotamicus* Brooke, 1875 – und zur Stammes- und Verbreitungsgeschichte der Damhirsche allgemein. Säugetierkundl. Mitt. **7**, 1–89, 1959.

– Lebensraum, Lebensweise und Vorkommen des Mesopotamischen Damhirsches, *Cervus mesopotamicus* Brooke, 1875. Säugetierkundl. Mitt. **8, 9**, 15–39, 1960–1961.

HAMILTON, W. J. and K. L. BLAXTER: Reproduction in farm red deer, 1. Hind and stag fertility. J. Agric. Sci., Camb. **95**, 261–273, 1980.

– R. J. HARRISON and B. A. YOUNG: Aspects of placentation in certain cervidae. J. Anat. **94**, 1–33, 1960.

HANSEN, P. D. von und K. BÜLOW-LOTZE: Das Ansprechen des Damschauflers. Verlag M. H. Schaper, Hannover 1964.

HANNSON, I. and G. MALMFORS: Meat production from moose, *Alces alces* (L.) (Commission of animal genetics). Europäische Vereinigung für Tierzucht, 29. Jahrestagung Stockholm, 1978

HARTFIEL, W.: Eine Alternative zur Landschaftspflege. Landw. Z. Rheinland **48**, 2273, 1975.

– Reh- und Rotwild wiederkäuergerecht füttern. Grundlagen und praktische Erfahrungen. Die Pirsch **28**, 1167–1171, 2139–2141, 1976.

– Bedingungen für eine pansengerechte Fütterung von wiederkäuendem Schalenwild. Niedersächs. Jäger **24**, 404–410, 1979.

– und G. W. BREDER: 'Wiederkäuergerechte' Wildfütterung. Die Pirsch/Deutscher Jäger **18**, 517–520, 1973.

– Ist der Strohaufschluß mit Ammoniak praxisreif? Der Bayr. Schafhalter **3**, H.6, 2–7, 1979.

– Rundschreiben des Bundesverbandes Deutscher Damtierhalter e.V., Vereinigung Nordrhein-Westfälischer Damtierhalter e.V. Bonn, Nr. 1, 1981.

– Bekämpfung der Nekrobazillose. Landw. Wildehege **2**, 10–13, 1985.

– und N. BAHNERS: Zur Selenversorgung von Wiederkäuern. VDLUFA-Schriftenreihe 16, Kongreßband, 511–518, 1985.

– J. PHEIFFER und J. DISSEN: Energetische Untersuchungen an Reh und Schaf mit Hilfe der quantitativen Thermographie zur Beurteilung des Energiebedarfs im Winter. Zschr. Jagdwiss. **31**, 34–41, 1985.

HASSENBERG, L.: Zum Fortpflanzungsverhalten des mesopotamischen Damhirsches, *Cervus dama mesopotamica* BROOKE, 1875, in Gefangenschaft. Originalarbeiten, S. 161–194, 1977.

HATLAPA, H.: Postnarkotische Behandlung von Wildtieren. Vortrag 1977.

– Tierschutzgerechte Haltung von Damwild in Gehegen zum Zwecke der Fleischproduktion einschließlich der Gewinnung von Nebenprodukten. Gutachten, 1979.

HATLAPA, H. H. M. und H. III. Prinz REUSS: Wild in Gehegen. Verlag Paul Parey, Berlin 1974.

HECK, L.: Unterfamilie Echthirsche. In.: Grzimeks Tierleben **13**, 180–183. Kindler-Verlag, München 1972.

HEIDEMANN, G.: Zur Biologie des Damwildes (*Cervus dama* Linné, 1758). Diss. Kiel, 1971. Verlag Paul Parey, Berlin und Hamburg, 1–93, 1973.

– Zur Einbürgerung von Damwild (*Cervus dama* Linné, 1758) im Raum Schleswig. Z. f. Säugetierkunde **38**, 341–347, 1973.

– Zur Problematik der Haltung von Damhirschen in Gefangenschaft. Information Deutsche Tierfreunde e.V. **15**, H. 33/34, 21–22, 1975.

– und W. KNIEF: Untersuchungen zum Stabilitätsverhalten von Damhirschgeweihen (*Cervus dama* Linnaeus, 1758). Z. f. Säugetierkunde **31**, 126–136, 1976.

HEINEN, E.: Rechtsfragen der Damhirschhaltung. Natur + Recht **4**, 54–63, 1982.

HEMMER, H.: Domestikation. Verarmung der Merkwelt. F. Viehweg, Braunschweig 1983.

– The aptitude and selection of large mammals for game farming and domestication. Acta Zool. Fennica **172**, 233–236, 1984.

HERRE, W.: Zahmes Wildtier – wildes Haustier. Wild und Hund **78**, 201–203, 225–229, 1975.

– Zähmung des Wildtieres. Wild und Hund **81**, 101–105, 133–135, 1978.

HILDEMANN, H. J.: Untersuchungen an Hautdrüsenorganen von Reh und Damwild in Verschiedenen Jahreszeiten. Diss. Universität Kiel, 1975.

HIRNEISS, R.: Raniden gegen Rachenbremsen und Leberegel. Die Pirsch – Der Deutsche Jäger **26**, Heft 4, 1974.

HOBSON, P. N., S. O. MANN, R. SUMMERS and B. W. STAINES: Rumen function in red deer, hill sheep and reindeer in the Scottish Highlands. Proc. Roy. Soc. Edinb. (B) **75**, 181–198, 1976.

HOFMANN, R.: 1 Hirsch = 5 Rehe? – Neue Erkenntnisse über das Äsungsverhalten der Wiederkäuer. Die Pirsch **10**, 539–543, 1975.

– Zur adaptiven Differenzierung der Wiederkäuer: Untersuchungsergebnisse auf der Basis der vergleichenden funktionellen Anatomie des Verdauungstrakts **6**, 351–358, 1976.

HÖSLI, P. und E. M. LANG: Die Chromosomen des Davidhirsches *(Elaphurus davidianus)*. Schweiz. Arch. Tierheilk. **112 (8)**, 395–396, 1970.

HÖTZEL, H.-J.: Vom Wild zum landwirtschaftlichen Nutztier. Agrarrecht **6**, 301–311, 1976.

– Rechtsfragen der Damtierhaltung (I) und (II). Landw. Wildgehege **2**, 45–50, 74–77, 1985.

HOHBERG, W. H. Frhr. v.: Georgica Curiosa oder von dem Adelichen Land- und Feldleben. Nürnberg 1682.

HUBER, S.: Experiment – Haltung von afrikanischen Wildtieren zur Fleischproduktion. Tieräztl. Umschau **24**, 544–546, 1969.

HUNGATE, R. W.: The rumen and its microbes. Academic Press, New York–London 1966.

HUTYRA, J. MAREK, R. MANNINGER und J. MÓCSY: Spezielle Pathologie und Therapie der Haustiere I. VEB Gustav Fischer Verlag, Jena 1959.

Infektionsschutz des Tieres. Kompendium für Veterinärmedizin, 2. Auflage. Verlag Hoffmann, Berlin 1975.

JACKSON, J. E.: The feeding ecology of the fallow deer *(Dama dama* L.) in the New Forest. Diss. Univ. Southampton, März 1974.

JACKSON, J.: The occurrence of certain ectoparasites on fallow deer *(Dama dama)* in the New Forest. J. Zool. Lond. **177 (4)**, 494–496, 1975.

– The annual diet of the fallow deer *(Dama dama)* in the New Forest, Hampshire, as determined by rumen content analysis. J. Zool. Lond. **181**, 465–473, 1977.

– The duration of lactation in New Forest fallow deer *(Dama dama)*. J. Zool. Lond. **183 (4)**, 542–543, 1977.

JACZEWSKI, Z. and W. MICHALAKOWA: Observations on the effect of human chorionic Gonadotrophin on the antler cycle of fallow deer. Experiment. Zoology **190, 191**, 79–87, 1974/5.

JANSEN, J. Jr.: Some problems related to the parasite interrelationship of deer and domestic animals. Int. Congr. Game Biol. **6**, 127–132, 1963.

JEITTELES, L. H.: Über die geographische Verbreitung des Damhirsches in der Vorzeit und Genenwart. Zoologischer Garten **15**, 288–297, 1874.

JENTSCH, W., H. WITTENBURG und R. SCHIEMANN: Die Verwertung der Energie durch wachsende Bullen. 3. Mitt.: Vergleichende Untersuchungen über Verdaulichkeit von 44 Rationen und pansenphysiologische Parameter bei Jungbullen und ausgewachsenen Schafen. Arch. Tierernähr. **26**, 575–585, 1976.

KAUFFOLD, P.: Der Einfluß von Ernährungsfaktoren auf die Pansenschleimhaut. Diss. B, Akademie Landw. Wiss. DDR, 1974.

KAUTZSCH, H.: Die Jägersprache in ihren zumeist vorkommenden der Zusammengehörigkeit nach geordneten Ausdrücken. Verlag J. Neumann-Neudamm, 10–11, 1935.

KAY, R. N. B.: The productive potential of domesticated red deer. Ann. Rep. Studies in Animal Nutrition and Allied Sci. **37**, 125–134, 1981.

KELLY, R. W., and J. A. WHATELEY: Observations on the calving of red deer *(Cervus elaphus)* run in confined areas. Applied Animal Ethology **1**, 193–300, 1975.

KENNAUGH, J. J., D. I. CHAPMAN and N. G. CHAPMAN: Seasonal changes in the prepuce of adult fallow deer *(Dama dama)* and its probable function as a scent organ. J. Zool. Lond. **183**, 301–310, 1977.

KILEY-WORTHINGTON, M.: The tail movements of ungulates, canids and felids with particular reference to their causation and function as displays. Behaviour LVI, 69–115, 1975/76.

KING, H. M. and B. R. HEATH: Game domestication for animal production in Africa. World Animal Review **16**, 23–30, FAO, Rome 1975.

KISTNER, T. P., G. R. JOHNSON and G. A. RILLING: Naturally occurring neurologic disease in a fallow deer infected with meningeal worms. J. Wildl. Dis. **13 (1)**, 55–58, 1977.

KLAPP, E.: Wiesen und Weiden. Verlag Parey. Berlin und Hamburg 1971.

KLOPFER, P. H. and M. S. KLOPFER: Notes on hand-rearing fallow deer. Intern. Zoo. Yearbook **4**, 295–296, 1962.

KLÖS, H. G. und E. M. LANG: Zootierkrankheiten, Krankheiten von Wildtieren im Zoo, Wildpark, Zirkus und in Privathand sowie ihre Therapie. Verlag Paul Parey, Berlin 1976.

KNAUER, N.: Leistungsstand und Leistungsfähigkeit des Grünlandes im schleswig-holsteinischen Küstenbereich. Das wirtschaftseigene Futter **19**, 44–58, 1973.

KOBER, W.: Aktinomykose beim Damwild. II. Mitteilungen. Z. f. Jagdwiss. **11**, 110–111, 1965.

KOCH, E.: Rotwildhaltung als landwirtschaftlicher Betriebszweig? Der Tierzüchter **10**, 464–466, 1976.

KOPSTADT, J. A.: Ueber Cleve. – In Briefen an einen Freund. Aus den Jahren 1811 und 1814. Verlag der Hermannschen Buchhandlung, Frankfurt 1822.

KOSSOW, R.: Die Winterfütterung von Damtieren in Gattern. Dipl.-Arb. Landw.-Fakultät, Bonn 1982.

KRAFT, H.: Der Nasenspiegel der Damhirsche, *Cervus (Dama) mesopotamicus* Brooke, 1975, und *dama* Linné, 1758. Säugetierkundl. Mitt. **7**, 95–98, 1959.

KROSTITZ, W.: The new international market for game meat. FAO. Unasylva **31** (no. 123), 32–36, 1979.

– The new international market for game meat. Unasylva **31**, Nr. 123, 1980.

KRUIPER: Gutachten zur Tötung von Damtieren mit der Schußwaffe. Information zur Haltung von Wild, 24–30, 1/1983.

KRZYWINSKI, A., A. NIEDBALSKA and L. TWARDOWSKI: Growth and development of hand reared fallow deer fawns. Acta Theriologica **29**, 349–356, 1984.

KUNKEL, A. O., E. FEHLIN, J. D. ROBINS and J. H. SINCLAIR: Relationship of development of ruminal mucosa of lambs to feed consumption and feedlot performance. J. Anim. Sci. **18**, 1560–1561, Abstract 1959.

Kuratorium für Technik und Bauwesen in der Landwirtschaft: Datensammlung, Spezielle Betriebszweige in der Tierhaltung.

KURKELA, P.: Prospects for reindeer husbandry based on grass and silage feeding. Acta Vet. Scand. Suppl. **60**, 5–75, 1976.

KURTEN, B.: Pleistocene mammals of Europe. Neidenfeld and Nicolson, London 1968.

KUTZER, E.: Die wichtigsten Parasitosen des heimischen Nutzwildes und ihre Bekämpfung. I. Endoparasiten der wildlebenden Wiederkäuer. Tierärztl. Monatsschr. **58**, 448–453, 1971.

– Wild im Gehege gesund erhalten. Die Pirsch **23**, Heft 13, 1971.

– und H. PROSL: Ranide® – ein geeignetes Mittel zur Bekämpfung des Rachendassel-befalles bei Reh- und Rotwild. Österreichs Weidwerk, Heft 12, 1973.

LABESIUS, H. K. W.: Ertragsorientierte Rehwildzucht. Z. St. Hubertus **64 (4)**, 145–147, 1978.

Landwirtschaftskammer Rheinland: Damkalb – Fleisch mit besonderer Note. 16 S. Bonn 1978.

LANGER, P.: Oberflächenmessungen an der Innenauskleidung des Ruminoreticulums von Rehwild *(Capreolus capreolus)* und Damwild *(Cervus dama)*. Z. Säugetierkunde **39**, 168–190, 1974.

LAWMAN, J. P., D. EVANS, E. P. J. GIBBS, A. MCDIARMID and L. ROWE: A preliminary survey of British deer for antibody to some virus diseases of farm animals. Br. Vet. J. **134**, 85–91, 1978.

LBL: Daten Damhirschhaltung. Landw. Beratungszentrale, 1984.

LEDGER, H. P.: The body and carcass composition of East African ruminants. J. Agric. Sci. **65**, 261–287, 1965.

– Body composition as a basis for a comparative study of some East-African mammals. Symp. Zool. Soc. Lond. no. 21 (Ed: Crawfood, M. A.), New York & London, Acad. Press, 289–310, 1968.

LEMKE, K.: Weidwerk-Lexikon. VEB Deutscher Landwirtschaftsverlag, Berlin 1981.

LEONARDI, G. and C. PETRONIO: The fallow deer of European Pleistocene. Geologica Romana XV, 1–67, 1976.

LEUN, A. A. J. VAN DE: Hertenteelt – een feasibility studie. Instituut voor veeteeltkunding onderzoek. 'Schoonoord'. Rep. 13: 130, 131, 1978.

LINCOLN, G. A.: The role of antlers in the behaviour of red deer. J. Exp. Zool. **182**, 233–250, 1972–1973.

– The effect of the epididymis on the growth of antlers of castrated red deer. J. Reprod. Fert. **42**, 159–161, 1975.

– R. W. YOUNGSON and R. V. SHORT: The social and sexual behaviour of the red deer stag. J. Reprod. Fert., Suppl. **11**, 71–103, 1970.

LISTER, D., D. N. RHODES, V. R. FOWLER and M. F. FULLER: Meat animals, growth and productivity. Nato advanced study institutes series, serie A: Life Sciences, Vol. 8. Plenum Press, New York–London 1976.

LOWE, V. P. W. and A. S. GARDINER: Hybridisation between red deer and sika deer with particular reference to stocks in N.W. England. J. Zool. Lond. **177**, 553–556, 1975.

MACDOUGALL, D. B., B. G. SHAW, G. R. NUTE and D. N. RHODES: Effect of pre-slaughter handling on the quality and microbiology of venison from farmed young red deer. J. Sci. Food Agric. **30**, 1160–1167, 1979.

MALOIY, G.: Pers. Mitteilung, 1977.

– and R. KAY: A comparison of digestion in red deer and sheep under controlled conditions. Quart. J. Exper. Phys. **56**, 257–266, 1971.

– – E. GOODALL and J. TOPPS: Digestion and nitrogen metabolism in sheep and red deer given large and small amounts of water and protein. Brit. J. Nutr. **24**, 843–855, 1970.

MARPMANN, H.: Tabelle der Waidmannssprache. Verlag J. Neumann, Neudamm und Berlin 1942.

MATZKE, P.: Über einige Gesundheitsprobleme bei Damwild in Mastgehegen. Bay. Landw. Jahrb. **59**, 484–495, 1981.

MATZNER, B.: Baitrag zur Nahrungsbiologie des Damwildes (*Dama dama* Linné, 1758). Wissensch. Hausarbeit, Kiel 1976.

MAUTZ, W. W.: Confinement effect on dry matter digestibility coefficients displayed by deer. J. Wildl. Managem. **35 (2)**, 366–368, 1971.

– Control of antler growth in captive deer. J. Wildl. Man. **41**, 594–595, 1977.

MCALLUM, H. J. F.: Some veterinary techniques used in New Zealand deer farming. N. Z. Vet. J. **25 (5)**, 130–131, 1977.

MCDIARMID, A.: Deer more profitable than sheep? The Veterinary Record **96**, 495–496, 1975.

– Some disorders of wild deer in the United Kingdom. Vet. Rec. **97 (1)**, 6–9, 1975.

MEGENBERG, C. V.: Das Buch der Natur. Verlag J. Abel, Greifswald 1897.

MEGENBERG, K. V.: Naturbuch/Von Nutz/eigen schafft/wunderwirckung und Gebrauch aller Geschöpff/Element und Creacurn. Frankfurt am Mayn 1544.

MEHLITZ, S.: Das Damwild (*Cervus dama* L.). In: Buch der Hege, von Stubbe, H., I: 44–69, Deutscher Landwirtschaftsverlag, Berlin 1972.

MEIER, E.: Beiträge zur Geburt des Damwildes (*Cervus dama* L.). Z. f. Säugetierkunde **38**, 348–373, 1973.

MENKE, K.-H.: Neue Nährstoffbedarfsnormen für Schafe. Der Tierzüchter **27**, 502–506, 1976.

– Berechnungen zum Energie- und Proteinbedarf von Schafen. Übers. Tierernähr. **5**, 1–46, 1977.

MERKEL-GOTTLIEB, A.: Nutztierartige Damwildhaltung und rechtliche Ausgestaltung. Diss. Hohenheim, 1979.

MEYER-BRENKEN, H.: Die Farbenvaritäten des Damwildes im Tiergarten Kirchrode. Niedersächsischer Jäger **13**, 289–306, 1967.

MIDDLETON, J.: Marketing Scottish venison. Economics and Management Series, No. 1, Edinburgh 1979.

MILNE, J. A., J. C. McRAE, A. M. SPENCE and S. WILSON: Intake and digestion of hill-land vegetation by the red deer and the sheep. Nature **263**, 763–764, 1976.

MITCHELL, B., D. McCOWAN and I. A. NICHOLSON: Annual cycles of body-weight and condition in Scottish red deer. J. Zool. Lond. **180**, 107–127, 1976.

– B. W. STAINES and D. WELCH: Ecology of red deer. A research review relevant to their management in Scotland. Institute of Terrestrial Ecology, Banchory 1977.

MÖHLENBRUCH, G.: Stoffwechsel- und Feldversuche zur Frage der Nutzung von Damtier-kälbern *(Cervus dama dama)*. Diss. Bonn 1976.

MOEN, A. N.: Wildlife ecology (An analytical approach). W. H. Freeman and Company, San Francisco 1973.

– Energy conservation by white-tailed deer in the winter. Ecology **57**, 192–198, 1976.

MOORE, G.: Deer farming is an art. New Zealand Deer Farming Annual, 38–39, 1978.

MOORE, G. H., G. M. COWIE and A. R. BRAY: Herd management of farmed red deer. Royal Soc. New Zealand **22**, 343–355, 1985.

MUELLER, C. C.: Der mesopotamische Damhirsch – Geschichte und Geschichten. Zeitschr. d. Kölner Zoo **21**, 127–134, 1979.

MÜCKE, F.: Wald und Wild in der Bibel. Verlag J. Neudamm, 1896.

MÜLLER, D.: Erfahrungen mit der Damwildhaltung in landwirtschaftlichen Betrieben. Tierzüchter, 236–237, 1983.

MÜLLER, H.: Über den Einfluß einer künstlichen Veränderung am Geweih eines Damhirsches *(Dama dama)* auf das Verhalten der Artgenossen. Diplomarbeit d. Zoolog. Institut d. Univ. Zürich, S. 1–41, Oktober 1970.

MÜLLER-USING, D. und R. SCHLOETH: Das Verhalten der Hirsche (Cervidae). Handbuch der Zoologie VIII, 10. Teil. Verlag de Gruyter & Co., Berlin 1967.

MULLEY, R. C. and A. W. ENGLISH: The effects of castration of fallow deer *(Dama dama)* on body growth and venison production. Animal Production **41**, 359–361, 1985.

MUNDAY, B. L.: A serological study of some infectious diseases of Tasmanian wildlife. J. Wildlife Diseases **8**, 169–175, 1972.

NACHTSHEIM, H.: Vom Wildtier zum Haustier. Alfred Mezner Verlag. Berlin 1936.

NAGY, J. G. and W. L. REGELIN: Comparison of digestive organ size of 3 deer species. J. Wildl. Managem. **39 (3)**, 621–624, 1975.

NAHLIK, A. J. DE: Deer management. Improved herds for greater profit. David & Charles, New Abott 1974.

NETTLES, V. F., A. K. PRESTWOOD and R. D. SMITH: Cerebrospinal parelaphostrongylosis in fallow deer. J. Wildl. Dis. **13**, 440–444, 1977.

New Zealand Deer Farmers Association: New Zealand Deer Farming Annuals 1975–85. Wellington, Box 11–137.

NIETHAMMER, G.: Die Einbürgerung von Säugetieren und Vögeln in Europa. Verlag Paul Parey, Hamburg und Berlin 1963.

NOCKELS, CH. F., L. D. KINTNER and W. H. PFANDNER: Influence of ration on morphology, histology and trace mineral content of sheep rumen papillae. J. Dairy Sci. **49**, 1068–1074, 1966.

NORDENFLYCHT-LÖDDERITZ, E. G.: Das Damwild. In: Die hohe Jagd. Berlin 1922.

North of Scotland College of Agriculture: Red deer farming. College Bulletin Nr. 4, 1978.

NOTZ, F. W. v.: Damhirsche einstmals und heute. Sankt Hubertus **63**, 65–69, Wien 1977.

NUESSLEIN, F.: Jagdkunde. 8. Auflage, BLV, München 1976.

ODUYE, O. O. and O. A. OKUNAIYA: Haematological studies on the White Fulani and N'Dama Breeds of cattle. Bull. epizoot. Dis. Africa **19**, 213–218, 1971.

278 Deer Farming

ØSTERGAARD, V., A. DANFAER, J. DAUGAARD, J. HINDHEDE og I. THYSEN: Foderfedtets idflydelse på malkekøernes produktion. 508 Ber. Statens Husdyrbrugs Forsøg, København, 1–140, 1981.
PAULI, L.: Eine frühkeltische Prunktrense aus der Donau. Germania 61, 459–486, 1983.
PAV, J., D. ZAJICEK and M. DVORAK: Clinical examination of the blood of roe deer Capreolus-Capreolus and fallow deer Dama dama naturally invaded by parasites. Vet. Med. 20 (4), 215–221, 1975.
PAVLANSKY, R. und A. BUBENIK: Von welchem Gewebe geht der eigentliche Reiz zur Geweihentwicklung aus? I. Mitteilung: Ein Versuch der Transplantation eines Geweihzapfens bei einem Damspießer, Dama dama (Linné, 1758). Säugetierkundl. Mitt. 3, 49–53, 1955.
PECHUEL-LOESCHE: Brehms Tierleben 3, 459–462, Leipzig 1891.
PEMBERTON, J. M. and R. H. SMITH: Lack of biochemical polymorphism in British fallow deer. Heredity 55, 199–207, 1985.
PHILIPPS, J. H., J. P. HARLEY and W. J. RUDERSDORF: New host record for Setaria yehi Disset, 1966, and range extension records for Dictyocaulus viviparus (Bloch, 1782) and Ostertagia mossi Dikmans, 1931, in Fallow Deer (Dama dama L.). Proc. Helminthological Soc. 41 (2), 250, 1974.
PIATKOWSKI, B.: Nährstoffverwertung beim Wiederkäuer. VEB Fischer Verlag, Jena 1975.
PIETROWSKI, R.: Untersuchungen zum Verhalten von Damwild bei nutztierartiger Haltung. Arbeiten aus dem Institut für Tierzuchtwissenschaft der Universität Bonn, Heft 69, 1984.
PINNEY, B.: The economics of farming red deer, New Zealand Agric. Sci. II, 202–205, 1977.
POHLMEYER, K.: Zur vergleichenden Anatomie von Damtier, Schaf und Ziege. Verlag Paul Parey, Berlin u. Hamburg 1985.
PRINS, R. A. and M. J. H. GEELEN: Rumen characteristics of red deer, fallow deer and roe deer. Journ. Wildlife Managem. 35, 673–680, 1971.
PUTMANN, R. J.: Consumption, protein and energy intake of fallow deer fawns on diets of differing nutritional quality. Acta Theriologica 25 (33), 403–413, 1980.
PUTTICK, G.: Analysis of fallow deer population on Groote Schuur Estate. Dissertation, University of Cape Town, South Africa, 1972.
RAZZAQUE, M. A., J. H. TOPPS, E. D. GOODALL and R. N. B. KAY: Metabolism of nucleic acids by sheep and red deer. Proc. Nutr. Soc. 32, 59A–60A, 1973.
RECKEN, J.: Wildtiere in Gehegen. Agrarrecht 15, 157–164, 1985.
REINKEN, G.: Zukünftige Produktion und Absatzentwicklung in der Landwirtschaft. In: Die Zukunft des länDlichen Raumes. 2. Teil: Entwicklungstendenzen der Landwirtschaft. Forschungs- und Sitzungsberichte der Akademie für Raumforschung und Landesplanung, Band 83. Raum und Landwirtschaft 9, S. 45–59, 1972.
– Braucht die Landwirtschaft neue Produkte? Agrarwirtschaft 22, 278–283, 1973.
– Stand und Entwicklungsmöglichkeiten der Fleischproduktion. International conference on meat and pork production, Elmia Jönköping, Schweden, Juni 1974, S. 1–24.
– Grünlandnutzung durch Damtiere. Landw. Z. Rheinland 142, 2274–2276, 1975.
– Damtier-Gehege zur Landschaftspflege – Erste Versuche. Allgem. Forstz. 31, 876–877, 1976.
– Ist Landschaftspflege mit Damtieren möglich? Wild und Hund 79, 231–234, 1976.
– Nutzung von Öd- und Grünland durch Damtiere. Der Tierzüchter 28 (12), 560–563, 1976.
– Zielvorstellungen der Landwirtschaft und deren regionale Konsequenzen. A) Ökologische Zielvorstellungen. In: Die Zukunft des ländlichen Raumes, 3. Teil. Forschungs- und Sitzungsbericht der Akademie für Raumforschung und Landesplanung 106, 77–95, Hermann Schroedel Verlag, Hannover 1976.

– Grün- und Brachlandnutzung durch Damtiere. Anregungen für Produktion und Absatz. Landwirtschaftskammer Rheinland, Heft 10, Bonn 1977.
– Experienze sugli allevamenti di daino. Atti II e III Convegno. Università di Perugia, 1982.
– Zur Problematik des Geweihes bei der Damtierhaltung. Aktuelle Arbeiten zur artgemäßen Tierhaltung 1983. KTBL-Schrift Nr. 299, 217–223, 1984.
– Wirtschaftliche Verwertung von Damtierfellen. Landw. Wildgehege **2**, 33, 1985.
– Damwild oder Damtier – Gegensatz oder Unterschied? Landw. Wildgehege **2**, 72–74, 1985.
– Zum Beitrag von H. BOGNER und P. MATZKE 'Geweihamputation bei Cerviden aus der Sicht der Ethologie und des Tierschutzes'. Berl. Münch. Tierärztl. Wschr. **98**, 1985.
– TH. GÖBBEL, H. J. HÖTZEL, E. KÖRNER und V. POTTHAST: Damtiere. Anregungen für Produktion und Absatz. Rhein. Landw. Verlag, Bonn 1984.
– H. H. NIES, H.-J.RODER und G. SEEMANN: Ab-Hof-Vemarktung. Anregungen für Produktion und Absatz. Rhein. Landw. Verlag, 1985.
Rheinische Landwirtschaftliche Berufsgenossenschaft: Hochsitze für die Damtierhaltung – Bauanleitungen –.
RHODES, D. N.: What do we want from the carcass? Meat animals, growth and productivity. Nato advanced study institutes series, serie A: Life Sciences **8**, 9–26, Plenum Press, New York & London 1978.
RIBEIRO, J. M. C. R., J. C. MACRAE and A. J. F. WEBSTER: An attempt to explain differences in the nutritive value of spring and autumn harvested dried grass. Proc. Nutr. Soc. **40**, 12 A, 1981.
RIEDER, J. B.: Dauergrünland. BLV-Verlagsgesellschaft, München 1983.
RIECK, W.: Die Setzzeit bei Reh- und Rot- und Damwild in Mitteleuropa. Z. f. Jagdw. **1–2**, 69–75, 1955–56.
ROBBINS, CH. T., A. N. MOEN and J. TH. REID: Body composition of white-tailed deer. Journ. Animal Sc. **38 (4)**, 871–876, 1974.
ROBERTS, G. P., A. McDIARMID and F. GLEED: The presence of erythritol in the fetal fluids of fallow deer *(Dama dama)*. Res. Vet. Sc. **20**, 254–256, 1976.
ROHR, K. und M. OKUBO: Über den Einfluß höherer Mengen an Kokos- und Palmkernfett auf die Leistung von Milchkühen. Milchwiss. **23**, 608–614, 1968.
– R. DAENICKE und H. J. OSLAGE: Untersuchungen über den Einfluß verschiedener Fettbeimischungen zum Futter auf Stoffwechsel und Leistung von Milchkühen. Landbauforschung Völkenrode **28**, 139–150, 1978.
RÖHRS, M.: Biologische Anschauungen über Begriff und Wesen Domestikation. Z. Tierz. und Züchtungsbiol. **76**, 1–23, 1961/62.
ROLLE, M. und A. MAYR: Mikrobiologie, Infektions- und Seuchenlehre. 4. Auflage. Ferdinand Enke, Stuttgart 1978.
ROSENBERGER, G.: Die Enthornungsmethoden für Rinder. 2. Auflage. Schaper, Hannover 1964.
– Krankheiten des Rindes. Paul Parey, Berlin and Hamburg 1970.
ROTH, H. H., M. A. KERR and J. POSSELT: Studies on the utilization of semi-domesticated eland (*Taurotragus oryx*) in Rhodesia. 5. Reproduction and herd increase. Z. Tierzüchtg. Züchtgsbiol. **89**, 77–91, 1972.
Rowett Research Institute: Annual reports of studies in animal nutrition and allied sciences. Bucksburn, Aberdeen, Scotland. 1971–1985.
RÜSSMANN, J.: 10 Jahre Erfahrungen mit Damtieren. Landw. Wildgehege **1**, 5–8, 1984.
RUHDEL, H. J.: Gedanken zur Wildfütterung. Kraftfutter **10**, 404–407, 1974.
SAMBRAUS, H. H.: Verhaltensänderung durch Domestikation. Der Tierzüchter **20**, 580–581, 1968.
– Was ist Prägung? Ein Beitrag der Verhaltenskunde zur mutterlosen Aufzucht von Haustieren. Der Tierzüchter **27**, 381–383, 1975.
– Der Bison – eine Alternative zum Mastrind? Tierzüchter, 31–33, 1981.

280 DEER FARMING

SCHAAL, A.: Observations préliminaires sur le cycle sexuel du daim. Mammalia **49**, 288–291, 1985.

SCHAEFFER, K. H.: Praxis der landwirtschaftlichen Haltung von Damwild. Eigenverlag, 1982.

SCHELLNER, H.-P.: Krankheiten des Damwildes (*Cervus dama* L. 1758), Untersuchungsergebnisse von 1977–1982. Berl. Münch. Tierärztl. Wschr. **95**, 293–294, 1982.

SCHICK, R.: Untersuchungen zur Haltungstechnik und Wirtschaftlichkeit der nutztierartigen Haltung von Damwild (*Cervus dama* L. 1758) unter Berücksichtigung bayrischer Standortbedingungen. Diss. Univ. Bodenkultur, Wien 1981.

– H. BOGNER, P. MATZKE, W. BRAUN, G. BURGSTALLER und H. VOLLERT: Untersuchungen zur Haltungstechnik und Wirtschaftlichkeit der nutztierartigen Haltung von Damwild im Vergleich zur Koppelschafhaltung. Bayr. Landw. Jahrb. **60**, 396–455, 1982.

SCHLOETH, R.: Einige Verhaltensweisen im Hirschrudel. Revue Suisse de Zoologie **68**, 241–247, 1961.

SCHMID, E.: Damhirsche im römischen Augst. Ur-Schweiz – Mitteilungen zur Ur- und Frühgeschichte der Schweiz **XXIX**, 4, 53–63, Basel 1965.

SCHMID: Tierische Rohstoffe von Rehen und Hirschen. Fleisch **31 (12)**, 226–227, 1977.

SCHORMÜLLER, J.: Lehrbuch der Lebensmittelchemie. Springer-Verlag, 2. Auflage, S. 313–330, 334–336, 1974.

SCHULZ, M.: Der Markt für Damwildfleisch in der Bundesrepublik Deutschland. Hausarbeit f. Diplomprüfung. Bonn 1978.

SCHUSTER, A.: Wildkälber-Aufzucht.Versuchbericht 1974, unveröffent licht.

SHORT, H. L.: Rumen fermentations and energy relationships in white-tailed deer. J. Wildl. Managem. **27**, 184–195, 1963.

– Effects of cellulose levels on the apparent digestibility of feeds eaten by muldeer. J. Wildl. Managem. **30**, 163–167, 1966.

SICKENBERG, O.: *Dama clactoniana* (Falc.) in der Mittelterrasse der Rhume-Leine bei Edesheim (Landkries Northeim). Geol. Jahrb. **83**, 353–396, 1965.

SEIFKE, A.: Nematodirus roscidus erstmals für Deutschland nachgewiesen. Angew. Parasitologie **9 (1)**, 11–15, 1968.

SIMPSON, A. M., A. J. F. WEBSTER, J. S. SMITH and C. A. SIMPSON: The efficiency of utilization of dietary energy for growth on sheep and red deer. Comp. Bioch. Phys. Part A Comp. Phys. **59A (1)**, 95–99, 1978.

SKINNER, J. D.: An appraisal of the eland as a farm animal in Africa. Afr. Wildlife **20**, 29–40, 1967.

– An appraisal of the status of certain antelope for game farming in South Africa. Z. Tierzüchtg. Züchtgbiol. **90**, 263–277, 1973.

SOUCI, S. W. und H. BOSCH: Lebensmittel-Tabellen für die Nährwertberechnung. Wissenschaftliche Verlagsgesellschaft mbH, 2. Auflage. Stuttgart 1978.

– W. FACHMANN und H. KRAUT: Die Zusammensetzung unserer Lebensmittel. Nährwert-Tabellen. Wiss. Verlagsgesellsch. Stuttgart 1981.

SPIRO, J. M.: Aspects of biology important in the farming management of fallow deer (*Dama dama*) at South Kaipara Head. Master Thesis, University of Auckland, 1979.

SPONECK, C. P., Graf v.: Roth-, Dam- und Rehwild. Heidelberg 1811.

STEEN, E.: Some aspects of the nutrition of semi-domestic reindeer. Symp. Zool. Soc. Lond. **21**, 117–128, 1968.

STEEN, W.: Versicherung von Schalenwild im Rahmen der nutztierartigen Haltung von Wild. Landw. Wildgehege **1**, 12–13, 1984.

STEINAUF, D.: Beobachtungen am Mesopotamischen Damwild, *Cervus (Dama) mesopotamicus* Brooke, 1875, in Gefangenschaft. Säugetierkundl. Mitteilg. **7**, 99–103, 1959.

STERBA, O. and K. KLUSÁK: Reproductive biology of fallow deer, *Dama dama*. Acta Sc. Nat. Brno. **18**, Praha 1984.

STODDART, D. M. (CHAPMAN, D. I. and N. G. CHAPMAN): Maxillary canine teeth in fallow deer, *Dama dama*. J. Zoology Proc. Zoo. Soc. Lond. **170**, 43–162 (2), 1973.

STONEHOUSE, B.: Thermoregulatory function of growing antlers. Nature **218**, 870–872, 1968.

STUBBE, CH.: Schalenwildverluste im Winter 1962/63. Z f. Jagdwiss. **9**, 121–124, 1963.

STUBBE, H. (Hrsg.): Buch der Hege. Haarwild **1**, Berlin 1973.

SULLIVAN, T. P., L. O. NORDSTROM and D. S. SULLIVAN: Use of predator odors as repellents to reduce feeding damage by herbivores. J. Chemical Ecology **11**, 921–936, 1985.

SUTTIE, J. M.: The effect of antler removal on dominance and fighting behaviour in farmed red deer stags. J. Zool. **190**, 217–224, 1980.

TEER, J. G.: Commercial uses of game animals on rangelands of Texas. Journ. Animal Science **40 (5)**, 1000–1008, 1975.

TELINJECT: Die Telinject-Fibel. Ludwigshafen 1978.

THIEDE, G.: Europas grüne Zukunft. Econ Verlag, Düsseldorf–Wien 1975.

TIERSON, W. C.: Controlling deer use of forest vegetation with electric fences. J. Wildlife Managem. **33 (4)**, 922–926, 1969.

TOCKA, I.: Chov pantových jeleňov v ZSSR. Pol'ovnicky Zbornik *(Folia venatoria)* **4**, 265–270, 1974.

TOPS, J. H.: Behavioral and physiological adaptation of wild ruminants and their potential for meat production. Proc. Nutr. Soc. **34**, 85–100, 1975.

TRAUTTMANSDORFF, K. E.: Semiferox auf Brachland. Alternativen zur naturnahen Nutzung von Grenzertragsbhöden. Forschungszentrum Graz, Veröffentlichung 26, 1978.

TREICHLER, J.: Ein Beitrag zur Ernährung des Rehwildes (*Capreolus capreolus* L.) unter besonderer Berücksichtigung der verschiedenen Möglichkeiten der Winterfütterung. Diss. Tierärztl. Hochschule Hannover, 1972.

TREUS, V. and D. KRAVCHENKO: Methods of rearing and economic utilization of eland in the Askaniya-nova Zoological Park. Symp. Zool. Soc. Lond. **21**, 395–411, 1968.

TWIGG, G. I., D. M. HUGHES and A. MCDIARMID: The low incidence of leptospirosis in British deer. Vet. Rec. **93**, 98–100, 1973.

UECKERMANN, E.: Erhebung über die Wildverluste durch den Straßenverkehr und die Verkehrsunfälle durch Wild. Z. f. Jagdwiss. **10**, 142–168, 1964.

– Zur jagdlichen Nutzungsfähigkeit von Rot-, Dam- und Schwarzwildbeständen nach Beobachtungen in einem Jagdgatter. Z. Jagdwiss. **18 (39)**, 24–31, 1972.

– und P. HANSEN: Das Damwild. Paul Parey, Berlin 1968.

ULMENSTEIN, R. V.: Beiträge zur Aufzucht, Jugendentwicklung und Elternbindung handaufgezogener Damwildkälber *(Dama dama)*. Jagdw. **31**, 65–72, 1985.

ULOTH, W.: Vorkommen des Europäischen Damhirsches, Cervus (Dama) dama (Linné, 1758), außerhalb seines natürlichen Verbreitungsgebietes. Säugetierkundl. Mitt. **19 (3)**, 202–205, 1971.

ULRICH, H.: Über das Vorkommen der Rachenbremse beim Damwild (Cephenomyia multispinosa sp. nov.). Zool. Anzeiger **111**, 43–45, 1935.

VERME, L. J. and J. U. OZOGA: Effects of diet on growth and lipogenesis in deer fawns. J. Wildl. Man. **44**, 315–324, 1980.

VIDACS, G. and G. M. WARD: Parakeratosis of rumen epithelium produced by an all concentrate ration. J. Dairy Sci. **43**, 875, 1960.

WAGENBACH, H.: Damtierhaltung als Betriebszweig? Feld und Wald **97**, 16–18, 1978.

WALKER, M. L. and W. W. BECKLUNG: Checklist of the internal and external parasites of deer, Odocoileus hemionus and O. virginianus, in the United States and Canada. USDA-Index-Catalogue 1 (III–V), 1970.

WALLIS, T. and J. FAULKS: Production and marketing of deer byproducts. New Zeal. Agric. Sci., **11**, 195–198, 1977.

WALZ, K. W.: Haltung von Damwild zur Fleischproduktion und Landschaftspflege. Die Pirsch, 648–649, 1978.

WEIERS, C. J.: Betriebswirtschaftliche Beurteilung der Grünlandnutzung durch Damtiere, Mutterkühe und Koppelschafe. Mitt. f. Wirtschaftsberatung der Landwirtschaftskammer Rheinland Nr. 6, 1977.

WEISS, F. W.: Histologie und Spermatogenese des Damhirschhodens außerhalb der Brunstzeit. Z. Mikroskop. Anatom. Forschung 16, 21–54, 1929.

WESKE, C.: Die Gestaltung des internationalen Handels mit Geflügel und Wild. Rother, Berlin-Neukölln 1934.

WETTSTEIN, O.: Versuch einer neuen Art von Wildmarkierung. Z. f. Jagdw. 1–2, 64–67, 1955/56.

WETZEL, R. und W. RIECK: Krankheiten des Wildes. Paul Parey, Berlin 1972.

WHITE, M., F. F. KNOWLTON and W. C. GLAZENER: Effects of damnewborn fawn behaviour on capture and mortality. J. Wildlife Managem. 36 (3), 897–906, 1972.

WHITEHEAD, G. K.: Deer and their management in the deer parks of Great Britain and Ireland. Kapitel X, Fallow Deer (Cervus dama). Country Life Limited, 151–168, London 1950.

– Deer of the World, London, Constable, 7–18, 1972.

WIENS, H.: Über Verhaltensweisen bei einem domestizierten Rottier. Z. f. Jagdwiss. V, 2, 41–51, 1958.

WIESNER, H.: Zur Neuroleptanalgesie bei Zootieren und Gatterwild unter Anwendung des Telinjekt-Systems. Kleintierpraxis 20, 18–24, 1975.

– Zur Immobilisation von Wild mit der 'Hellabrunner Mischung'. Vortrag 1977.

– Zur Narkosepraxis mit dem 'Blasrohrgewehr'. Kleintierpraxis 22, Nr. 8, 1978.

WILKINSON, P. F.: Current experimental domestication and its relevance to prehistory. In: Higgs, E. S. (ed.): Papers in economic prehistory. Cambridge Univ. Press, p. 107–118, 1972.

WILSON, B. and R. HARRINGTON: A case of bovine tuberculosis in fallow deer. Vet. Rec. 98 (4), 74, 1976.

WIRTHS, W.: Kleine Nährwerttabelle. Deutsche Gesellschaft f. Ernährung e.V., 27. Auflage, Umschau Verlag, Frankfurt 1977.

WÖLFEL, H.: Ranghöhe und Geweihbildung beim Rothirsch. Pirsch 32, 996–999, 1980.

– Zur Jugendentwicklung, Mutter-Kind-Bindung und Feindvermeidung beim Rothirsch (Cervus elaphus). Diss. Universität Wien, 1981.

WOLLSTÄDTER, H.: Wildfarmen in Neuseeland (1–7). Feld & Wald Nr. 32–44, 1980.

YEREX, D.: Deer farming in New Zealand. D. F. Jones Ltd., Wellington 1979.

– The farming of deer. World trends and modern techniques. Agricultural Promotion Ass. Ltd., 1982.

YOUNG, C. D.: The future of deer farming. BVA Congress, Univ. Aberdeen, 9.–14. Sept. 1979.

ZEUNER, R. E.: Geschichte der Haustiere. Bayrischer Landwirtschaftsverlag, München 1967.

ZWART, P. and F. G. POELMA: Pseudotuberculose bij een damhert. Tijdschr. Diergeneesk. 84, 945–946, 1959.

ZWIRNER, F.: Wildtiere in Menschenhand. VEB Dtsch. Landw. Verlag, Berlin 1972.

Statistics

Bundesministerium für Ernährung, Landwirtschaft und Forsten: Vorschätzung der Situation auf dem Milch- und Rindfleischsektor 1979 und 1982. Berichte der Organisation für wirtschaftliche Zusammenarbeit und Entwicklung. Bonn 1978.

– Statistisches Jahrbuch für Ernährung, Landwirtschaft und Forsten der Bundesrepublik Deutschland. Hamburg 1978–85.

EUROSTAT – Statistisches Amt der Europäischen Gemeinschaft: Bodennutzung und -erzeugung 1974–1976. Luxemburg 1978.

– Tiererzeugung 1968–1977. Luxemburg 1979.
Food and Agriculture Organization of the United Nations: FAO production yearbook 1977. FAO Statistics Series No. 15, Rom 1978.
– Projections of meat production, demand and trade to 1985. Rom 1979.
Statistisches Bundesamt: Aufwendungen privater Haushalte für Nahrungs- und Genuß-mittel, Mahlzeiten außer Haus. Fachserie M. Preise, Löhne, Wirtschaftsrechnungen Reihe 18. Stuttgart und Mainz 1976.
– Spezialhandel nach Waren und Ländern. Fachserie G Außenhandel. Reihe 2. Stuttgart 5 und Mainz 1971–1978.

Picture Credits

J. Coenen: Pl. 1.2, 1.3, 7.1, 7.2, 7.3, 7.4
H. Egger: Pl. 2.29
Finke: Pl. 11.7, 11.8
W. Hartfiel: Fig. 7.1, 7.2, 7.3, 7.4, 7.5, 7.9. 7.10, 7.11
E. Körner: Fig. 8.1, 8.2, 8.3, 8.4 Pl. 8.1, 8.2, 8.3, 8.4
R. Maier: Pl. 2.9
G. Reinken: Fig. 7.3 Pl. 1.1, 1.4, 2.1, 2.2, 2.3, 2.12, 2.13, 2.14, 2.19, 2.22, 2.23, 2.26, 2.28, 4.1, 4.2, 4.3, 4.4, 4.5, 4.6, 4.7, 4.8, 4.9, 4.10, 4.11, 4.12, 4.13, 4.14, 5.1, 5.2, 5.3, 5.4, 5.5, 5.7, 5.8, 5.9, 5.10, 5.11, 5.12, 5.14, 5.15, 5.17, 5.18, 5.19, 5.20, 8.5, 8.7, 8.8, 8.9, 8.10, 9.2, 11.1, 11.2, 11.3, 11.4, 11.5, 11.6, 11.10
Roebild (Enders): Pl. 2.21
W. Schiffer: Pl. 2.9, 2.10, 2.17, 2.18, 5.6, 5.13, 9.1, 11.9
Staatliches Museum für Naturkunde, Stuttgart: Pl. 2.5
Tierbilder Okapia: Pl. 2.24
A. v. Treuenfels: Pl. 2.4, 2.15, 2.16, 2.25, 2.27, 5.16
Westdeutsche Gerberschule Reutlingen: Pl. 11.11
I. Ziegler: Pl. 2.6, 2.7, 2.8

Zeichnungen (nach Vorlagen der Verfasser): H. Poeschel, Stuttgart.

Index

Farming Press Books

The following are samples from the wide range of agricultural and veterinary books published by Farming Press. For more information or for a free illustrated book list please contact:

Farming Press Books, 4 Friars Courtyard
30–32 Princes Street, Ipswich IP1 1RJ, United Kingdom
Telephone (0473) 241122

The Veterinary Book for Sheep Farmers
David Henderson

> A wide-ranging, detailed guide to the prevention of sheep ailments, increased lamb output and the diagnosis and treatment of disease.

The TV Vet Sheep Book
Eddie Straiton

> A pictorial guide to all the common sheep ailments. The concise text includes a major section on lambing.

The Modern Shepherd
Dave Brown and Sam Meadowcroft

> Links the technical advances of the past two decades to the best of traditional husbandry practices.

A Veterinary Book for Dairy Farmers
Roger Blowey

> Accepted as the classic guide to the management of the dairy herd for high health status.

Goat Farming
Alan Mowlem

> Includes housing and fencing, feed and nutrition, breeding, kid rearing, health and disease, milking and milk products, fibre production and goat meat.

Farming Press also publish four monthly magazines: *Livestock Farming, Arable Farming, Dairy Farmer* and *Pig Farming*. For a specimen copy of any of these magazines, please contact Farming Press at the address above.